SIGNS OF INFINITY
Keys to Awaken the Soul

PAULA DIANNE UPTON

Grail Cup Publishing

Any autobiographical statement herein is factual to the best of the author's recollection.

Signs of Infinity: Keys to Awaken the Soul

Published by Grail Cup Publishing

First Printing June 2016
First Edition June 2016

ISBN 978-0-9974460-0-5 (Paperback Edition)

Times New Roman, Vivaldi and Cambria fonts used with permission from Microsoft

Cover Design: Steven J. Catizone

*To the enlightened ones who have
opened the mystic temple
and claimed the grail cup of Divine Love,
thank you for showing The Way.*

Paula Deanne Upton

Contents

Prelude

Before I started writing this book I contemplated the gravity of that choice for three years. I felt an indeclinable demand had been placed upon my shoulders by majestic hands pressing me to bring teachings to the world, but I questioned which path the book should take, whether or not I could fulfill such a sonorous task, and if the time was right to reveal my insights.

Mostly, I wondered if Spirit would impart the jewels of knowledge I needed that could truly benefit others. And then something extraordinary happened to convince me to take a leap of faith and begin.

Close to 9:30 pm on April 15, 2011, my phone rang, and though I rarely respond to anonymous calls displaying as "Private," that time I answered.

"Are you the healer?" a man asked.

"Yes," I replied, struck by his thick accent. *India*, I guessed. I told him that for the past year, though, I'd been focused mainly on counseling.

"From the standpoint of the soul, I offer spiritual guidance to those on the path who want to awaken and better understand their lives."

"Right," he said, elongating the note in the vowel before swinging it down a full step. "How do you do the healing?"

"I work with consciousness," I said, watching him sway the conversation back to its inception.

"Right," he repeated, rolling his voice in the same dramatic cadence as before.

"Why are you calling me?" I politely asked.

"Your number came into my head and I *needed* to call."

My antennae went up.

"My number came to you?"

"Yes. It was given to me in meditation," he replied matter-of-factly. "I saw it, and I am calling you from India."

I asked for his name. He gave it to me and with an air of dignity he explained, "I am a spiritual teacher. You will help many, many people."

I sat straight up in my chair. Such a teacher and especially one from a distant land had never before sought out insignificant me. He said I was working with the kundalini energy, the light of Shakti, and that I needed to enlist its force. He spoke in a fast clip with a regal authority, reminding me of a Zen Master who raps his students awake with a stick when he catches them drifting off to sleep during meditation.

He stressed, *"If you master the kundalini, you can infuse the power of the white light with everything you do and everything you are."*

I let a few seconds pass.

"I know," I replied softly.

"You know?"

"Yes."

And then, *whoosh*—like a match set to napalm, he lit this bomb: "You will write a book."

My jaw dropped open on its hinges. I suddenly felt elated, like somewhere in the galaxy a wishbone fleshed with divine marrow had just snapped in my favor.

"How do you know about the book?" I said, my heart fluttering.

"I saw it. *I know.* Have you started writing it?"

"No, I haven't," I replied, growing intrigued by his acumen.

"Why not?"

"Well, is writing it now such a wise choice?" I offered. "And will people really want to read it? Will it help anyone? I don't need to write a book for the sake of my own ego," I confessed.

"Yes! Yes! You must write it!" he said emphatically.

Next, the bell of his voice rang out, peeling the air and for all I know, splitting atoms into quarks in the process.

"You must finish it because it will teach people a great number of things!"

"You think so?" I could almost feel my words lifting off the tip of my tongue like ascending, effervescent bubbles.

"Yes!" he insisted.

Then he changed course.

"Tell me, what were you thinking of today?"

I was engaged by this new tact and said to him, "Well, before you called I was thinking about infinity and how its symbol shows the rhythm of consciousness. The intersection where the two loops cross can be seen as a threshold, the juncture of human will and surrender, a place of suspension—a crossroads where soul returns to Spirit. Plus, if you twirl the sign again and again at its axis, it looks like a strand of DNA. The current of infinity can move in spirals... yes?"

I paused, curious to hear his thoughts.

"Right," he remarked, once again surfing his voice over the crest of the vowel. "You are working with *The White Light of Infinity.*"

I assumed he was referring to the mystic's white fire, the empowered divine light, and we began to speak in rapid fire back and forth about its action and purpose, even bringing up the winding cosmic river of the Milky Way.

Then, from out of nowhere, he threw a curveball.

"I am calling to offer you a blessing. What do you want?"

For several beats, I touched on the pulse of the atmosphere brewing between us. When an enigmatic stranger offers such a lofty gift, one should proceed with caution and respect, so I judiciously weighed the prospect of opening that door. I mean, here was a man ostensibly handing me a sempiternal rose, but what if he'd dipped its thorns in venom? Undoubtedly, he'd brought up truths and principles in the exact language I'd been contemplating as if they'd appeared in a scroll embossed with my name, stamped with a red seal of authenticity.

Somehow an inexplicable twist of providence had found me and now it was accelerating, building momentum and bearing me down. I felt caught in this open field with nowhere to hide, compelled to face the impact of an unpredictable cyclone, one spun by an unknown finger of fate and born from a black-gold pitch of smoldering myrrh, its rippling smoke unfurling into a towering funnel. I knew that all I could do was simply surrender to such a force, and so I accepted the rose.

I declared, "I want what I've always wanted. My destiny. My true identity. My ultimate self. I want to know that my soul is fused with God." I spoke purposefully, thinking there was probably nothing I needed that I didn't already possess, that there wasn't a realization this stranger could give me that God had not previously bestowed, and yet I was stirred to ask him if he could.

Moments passed, stretching into a long silence. When he spoke next, his voice had turned serious.

"All this would be very powerful to receive. What would you *do* with it?"

It was an epic question to examine the motive behind my desire to embody such a vast realization. While I explained my intentions he validated each one by repeating, "Right," punctuated in that grand, oceanic, rhythmic dip. Next, an urgent conviction arose in his voice as he shared his vision about the future course of my life's work. Finally, upon receiving my consent and enlisting my cooperation, he granted me the blessing.

In truth, all along we'd been testing one another by making deliberate inquiries and then responding in code, the way adepts from esoteric orders signal arcane hand gestures and surreptitiously cast out a cryptic net of language in order to catch verification of each other's tribe and rank before doorways are opened and secrets are exposed.

We haven't spoken since, but I want to thank him for reaching out to me from clear across the planet and beneath the glittering embers of stars to impart brilliant sparks of spiritual fire, and for encouraging me to believe in this book, which I began to write two weeks later, its path spontaneously unfolding. Coupled with his inspiring directive, the mystery of that night kindled in me the will to bring this teaching to fruition.

Although I must admit I was at first a bit wary of his true intention, by the next morning a firm sense of knowing replaced my last traces of doubt. For the blessing he had called to deliver unexpectedly manifested in the middle of the night, arriving as supercharged energy that swept and turned throughout me multiple times, sealing an inner realization of the White Light's breathtaking arc and proving he was no impostor but an emissary sent by The Divine to offer me grace.

May this story serve as a reminder to those afoot on the spiritual path—you must request, expect, recognize and ultimately be grateful for receiving divine signs. You must be daring enough to answer and heed particular calls and accept the terms of certain demands, despite their seemingly incredible, frightening, unfathomable, surreal or irrational facades.

In doing so, the purpose of every higher message extended to you is received and acknowledged. And, like a gilded arrow sprung from a celestial bow and bound for your soul, The Truth will soar through the ether and surely pierce the core of its miraculous destination, already stationed in the innermost chamber of your heart.

Overture

I am often asked how I came upon my spiritual understandings. Although I have had many significant mystical encounters, the following series of events irrefutably changed the trajectory of my life. I would like to share them with you before I begin the teachings, for had they not transpired, the keys of knowledge in this book would not have been elucidated to my mind.

It was a blustery Sunday morning in the spring of 1992, and I was getting ready to go mountain biking with the man I loved. That day began on a promising note, the brilliant azure sky as pristine as an open vault holding nothing but the sun's golden coin. Before we left my heart unexpectedly revved and then skipped ahead of itself, sending my hands trembling. I wasn't so alarmed because this curious trend had begun several weeks before, lasting but a few minutes before it disappeared. I said nothing about it as the car wound its way down Route 16 to Salmon River State Forest in East Hampton, Connecticut.

We had just finished a ride on the first path, and as we glided back to the main trail, it was then my heartbeat shifted into a dense pound and gathered speed. All at once I was seasick woozy, dizzy and faint, and then I was ditching my bike on the shoulder of the road. Sweat bubbled and streaked on my skin while I violently retched and defecated until it seemed I was wrung of every last drop of slush and liquid not pinned to my bones. My brain spun in ovals, my chest crumpled under a crippling pressure and then I hit the ground, landing face up on a patch of tall grass bent into a citrine dome by the wind.

All around me hemlocks and oaks were thrashing their limbs while sunbeams burst through their leaves and struck the earth in roving columns of light. Then the crows came, convening high in the quivering branches and screeching such shrill cries I could swear they smelled my terror. They lit off the boughs in one great wave and careened in chaotic loops above me for several minutes before they split apart and fled in several directions, weaving wild and fast through the sky as if they were being unleashed from a tight, black knot.

I fought to catch my breath and stay conscious while my heart punched again and again against my ribs. I rolled to my side and curled my spine to a nautilus, my clammy cheek pressed to the cool earth, my jaw rimmed by a surfaced tree root as smooth and fat as a boa constrictor.

I looked over at my boyfriend impatiently shuffling from foot to foot and crossing and uncrossing his arms. With the bloom decidedly sheared off the vine by those launched missiles of body fluid, he had strategically positioned himself a few yards downwind from the fallout.

"We need to leave—*now*," I said somberly.

He unwittingly huffed out an exasperated sigh, squinted and then squeezed his mouth to a queasy slit. I pushed to my feet and took a few steps before I stumbled sideways then slid to a slump like a scarecrow breaking free from its peg only to find its limbs stuffed with nothing but sticks and straw that couldn't bear its weight.

"I'm not kidding." My words wavered as I struggled to stand but with my muscles having turned to the substance of pudding, I collapsed.

Seeing this, his expression grew tense and his hazel eyes cast off a look of worry. Although he was plenty strong enough to carry me back to the car, we didn't want to abandon our bikes, so I decided to chance it and wait, all the while inwardly praying that my strength and equilibrium would soon return.

Thirty minutes passed. Finally, my brain stopped doing cartwheels and my heart rate re-stabilized. I regained my balance enough to lean on my bike like a walker, and then I feebly steered myself back to the parking lot. On the way home, the nausea began to lift and although I was still shaky and very weak, I reasoned that perhaps I'd experienced a touch of food poisoning. Denying those ominous alarms, I avoided going to the emergency room or even calling my doctor.

The weeks passed into fall and I failed to regain my strength. My heart palpitated erratically, and I noticed heavy bags had pooled under my eyes that wouldn't budge despite any amount of rest. My eyeballs grew dry and gritty as if sand had somehow gotten lodged within them. My hands shook and my pulse skyrocketed off and on. I was sweltering one moment and shivering the next, and then I began to rapidly lose weight.

By now it was October, and I was awakened one morning by an unfamiliar female voice speaking close to my ear, plainly saying, *"Check the thyroid gland..."* except when I opened my eyes, there was no woman in sight.

I got out of bed and immediately called my doctor. Days later in November, I was diagnosed with Graves' disease, an autoimmune condition of the thyroid gland that creates its hyperactivity and all the other symptoms I experienced, along with Thyroid Eye Disease, a related condition that affects the eyes and inflames their supporting tissues, causing internal scarring, eyeball protrusion, eyelid bags and other problems.

Connecting my dangerously-high thyroid levels with the episode in the woods, my doctor lowered her voice and told me, "You're lucky you didn't die out there. You were in Thyroid Storm, and it sounds like you probably had a heart attack that day."

She explained that Thyroid Storm is caused by a catastrophic cascade of metabolic reactions triggered by a massive release of thyroid hormone that leads to sudden collapse and can be fatal if not immediately treated.

By then I had lost fifteen pounds and the gland was enlarged to a visible goiter. I started on medications to regulate thyroid hormone production and another to slow and stabilize my heartbeat. Within months, like a tumbling string of dominoes, additional physical ailments befell me, triggering a tsunami of debilitating fatigue and emotional distress. Despite it all, I held an unshakable faith that I would someday, somehow be healed. It was at that time my relationship with my partner ended.

In an effort to deepen my connection with my soul essence, I increased my spiritual cultivation practices to several hours a day, particularly meditation, starting in November 1992. I was no stranger to methods, having begun the spiritual path in 1984. Since I am drawn to practices associated with sound and vibration, I recited and chanted devotional mantras, my favorite surrounding the mystical syllable "OM"—the seed and origin of all sound. To commune with God, I sang prayers while sounding overtones and harmonics, often using ancient Names of God that included the Tetragrammaton. I listened to Tibetan mantra overtones and Gregorian chants. I used the Tibetan bowl as a sacred instrument, used essential oils, took vibrational essences and committed to methods that incorporated color and light. I focused my intention on consciously aligning my heart and mind to God while asking for the influx of divine light and remaining open to receive an intervention in any way possible.

It was now early April 1994. I was in a dorm room in Montpelier, Vermont, having returned to school to finish my bachelor's degree at Vermont College of Norwich University. I rose for a day of classes and glanced out the window onto the campus green where wispy vapors of morning fog were levitating between the trees like wavy specters.

As I pulled on my shirt, I heard a different unknown voice in the room, one that came from just behind my right shoulder. A man was speaking, and his words were deep, firm and commanding.

"*You have suffered enough,*" he proclaimed.

Instantly, my legs buckled, I fell to the floor and then I began to weep. I was stunned to be brought down to my knees, to be so overwhelmed with emotion, and I wondered who had made this mystifying decree.

That week I began to hear all kinds of noises that I assumed were coming from campus or town, sounds resembling jingling bells, bird chirps, crashing cymbals, ringing chimes, toots and whistles, along with deep bass notes, hums and sibilant rushes of air similar to the shush a librarian makes when she places a finger to her lips to hush a noisy patron.

One morning while walking up a crowded stairwell with a friend, one blaring blast erupted, as if someone had pounded a low chord on a gigantic organ. I snapped my head left to right only to find that nobody else seemed at all concerned.

"Did you hear that sound?" I asked my companion, figuring that an alarm had probably gone off.

He lowered his head and dubiously frowned at me over his round glasses.

"No," he answered.

It was then I knew that these eerie noises were specific to me, that no one else was hearing them. Back home in Connecticut, when I closed my eyes at night, flashes of white light exploded against my mind's eye like fireworks, some shredding the blackness in jagged lines and swirls, while others burst into stars that widened, grew points and spit out a dazzling friction of sparks.

It was near 12:00 am on the night of April 24th, 1994, when I awakened from sleep to find a dense cloud of milky white light hovering several feet above the foot of my bed. I watched it silently billow and churn, the way a cumulus cloud sips moisture from the air and swells. I thought, *Am I dreaming? Am I being visited by something or someone from the spiritual realms?*

"Who are you?" I called out, blinking my eyes in incomprehension.

I sat up, transfixed by the expanding cloud that grew to about four feet wide. Within seconds, a single tendril of light emerged from its core and began to meander toward me, undulating up and down through the midnight air and lengthening like a tapered, iridescent arm of a squid reaching out to me from the murky sea.

"Don't think about coming into me," I said apprehensively.

I physically recoiled as the tendril drew near; the closer it got, the more I backed away, but I soon found my shoulders pressed against the headboard, the ribbon of light now wavering just inches from my chest and quickly advancing.

While I could have run from the room, I decided to allow the tendril to come very close, and in the next instant its tip lunged forward and speared my chest, piercing my heart. Like a sudden explosion, profound bliss erupted inside my heart and swiftly consumed its expanse.

I lay back down, my worry instantaneously quelled, my mind and body becoming increasingly galvanized by *an electrifying force of love* that began to stream from my heart. It seemed as if a steep dam had fractured inside of me, spilling a teeming flood of bliss, an ecstatic current of love. The love progressively spread throughout me like a torrent, rapidly coursing through my whole body, filling me with an overwhelming rush of exhilarating power.

Then all of my thoughts abruptly stopped, as if my reactions and the contents of my mind had been wiped clean, erased. I had no personal will whatsoever to speak or move or generate thoughts because *I was paralyzed with love*. Next, the impression of my body, along with the entire material world, dissolved, becoming non-existent. There was no sense of sight, touch, taste, smell or sound. Time itself evaporated. I don't remember if I was even breathing. From the moment my mind was emptied, none of these things occurred to me.

My consciousness was completely ablaze, however, charged with utter bliss that felt, well, *alive*. I was fully conscious, yet the singular impression that remained was one of being *seized by a vast and riveting love*, meaning there was *only* love, nothing *but* love, a stupendous and rapturous love *multiplied by infinity* within which every trace of my consciousness was suspended. My whole being had become one thing—*the sheer, unequivocal force of enlivened love.*

Although I was not aware of the passage of time, at some point past the influx of love, revelations began to arise, among them, *I am being loved. I am turning into love itself.*

I started to consciously revel in the *charge the love created*, perceiving its astounding essence jolting me, resonating throughout my being until slowly, one by one, more revelations spontaneously emerged.

I am being apprehended, held by a limitless, numinous power. I am a being of pure consciousness. I am one with The Divine Force. I am one with God.

I gradually became aware of frenetic energy that was surrounding my body like a matrix, infusing *non-physical parameters* of my being, executing its tingling force. Then new revelations arose. *My body is composed as physical form that embodies energetic presence. I am enjoined and instilled by love.*

More minutes must have advanced when I began to sense my material body as being somewhat more solid, but now every last cell was *pulsing, as if each one were singing love.*

Later, a single thought emerged.

"This must be what it is to ascend," I said aloud, wholly convinced that I was being raised up.

At the precise moment my mind acted to cause me to think, speak and be vaguely aware of the materiality of my body, the bliss initiated its exit. The love started to leave my toes first, and as it moved out of my feet and up my ankles I sensed their dense structure once again; I noticed they felt wooden, disappointingly dull and deadened, defining a stark contrast between the places within me where the love was surging and the parts where its infusion was absent.

Next, the love began to incrementally drain from my shins and knees. Immediately, an epiphany struck me. *The enlivened parts of me feel so much more real than the parts that are vacant of love.* Acutely aware of this blatant difference, I was sure of something more. *Under no circumstances do I want to be separated from this love.*

As the love withdrew from my thighs and hips, I felt powerless to stop its escape, causing a momentary upsurge of irrational panic mixed with an unfamiliar quality of sadness. Soon the love evacuated my fingers, followed by my hands, then wrists, then arms and shoulders.

I began to sense my surroundings and then felt the weight of my body pressed against the mattress. With the love now missing from my extremities, I became aware that it was being extracted from my head, starting at the crown and simultaneously draining down the back of my skull and front of my face before it trickled down and out of my neck.

The love began to leave my trunk next, and I then felt its enormity gravitating inward, migrating back to my heart. My sight began to function, and I could see again the simmering, opaque cloud stationed above me. I beheld the wavy bolt of light still attached inside my chest and bringing down the cloud's voltage, charging my heart with rapture. Then, each molecule of love that had been diffused throughout me culminated within my heart's chambers, where it concentrated and multiplied its massive sum to a staggering energetic crescendo, causing me to be absolutely thunderstruck by its effects.

The love stayed housed within my heart's walls for some time, the whole organ palpably vibrating as if it were a hive droning with hundreds of bees. Finally, the diameter of love narrowed bit by bit, its volume ultimately collecting to one central, sharpened heart-point. Then, the tendril extracted from the nucleus of my heart, causing a plucking sensation like a root being pulled from the ground. Feeling the great magnitude of love leave me, I was floored by a crushing swell of grief.

Finding myself back in command of my body, I sat up in bed. I was spellbound by the spectacle unfolding above me, for as if a cord were being reeled in by a mighty rod, the tendril's thread was reversing its path back inside the cloud. In a reflex, I rose to my knees and lunged several times to grab onto the tendril, frantic to catch hold and somehow bring the love back inside me, but the tail kept pulling away, staying just millimeters out of range until the last bit of it disappeared into its source.

Without fear or reservation, I felt a hasty impulse to remain engaged in this love forever, whatever the cost.

"Don't leave! Please don't leave! Take me with you!" I cried, my arm outstretched and reaching for the cloud, my hand spread wide and clutching the air.

It was then the cloud began to rapidly shrink, compressing to a flickering flame of light before it dissolved into tiny sprinkles that dispersed in the atmosphere and vanished. I lay back down, my heart still thrumming and thrumming, while an electromagnetic mix of vibrations and currents rumbled through and around my body.

I looked at the clock and it was close to 2 am. My mind and emotions were so stirred with awe and wonder that I couldn't sleep the rest of the night. It wasn't until dawn pressed its glare against the window shade that I became stilled by a permeating peace, as if some delicious, soothing potion had kicked in, and I fell into a kind of twilight sleep, my body composed in serenity but my mind somehow stunned and superbly awake.

I was living with my mother at the time, and that noon I joined her on the back porch while she solved the daily crossword puzzle and I drank a cup of coffee.

She looked up from the newspaper.

"Who were you talking to last night? I heard you speaking."

"I think it was Spirit. Something happened to me."

Motioning with my hands, I explained the cloud building upon itself, how a curving tendril of light struck my heart and turned me into love.

"I think I might be healed," I heard myself say, groping for words to describe a state of being for which I had no frame of reference.

"I hope you're right," she said, her aquamarine eyes alight with marvel.

Hours later, it grew impossible to concentrate on anything productive, for my thoughts would only be superseded by an excruciating emotion of yearning for the love to return. No sooner would my longing begin than my heart shuddered and started to thrum once again, causing a measure of burning love to re-erupt within it. My heart then poured forth a fiery magma of merciful passion that seemed to incinerate a path through every vein in my body, devouring me the way a ferocious flame consumes a blade of dry grass!

Of course, at the time I did not know that my illumination would completely transform my life, that my essential being really had been so remarkably altered. I knew unequivocally that something extraordinary had transpired—that I had been met by The Divine, but I had no presage just yet of the meaning and far-reaching impacts of such a state of union.

Days progressed, and like the aftershocks of an abiding earthquake, my heart continued to spontaneously hum and intermittently release divine love and its splendid bliss, causing my desire for The Divine to turn so irrepressible that I could not stop myself from desperately yearning for its closeness.

Day and night, the scene of the cloud revolved in my mind as if a film were being played on an automatic loop. It seemed love's revolution had been set into ceaseless motion and now it was incapable of halting. My thirst for bliss grew downright unquenchable, so that in its absence my being was left emaciated and starving, irrationally craving love's fix the way an addict feels withdrawal from the most exotic drug.

This realization made me hopelessly and irretrievably heartsick, as if The Beloved and I had fallen so deeply in love that I was broken and practically inconsolable without our mutual affection, for I so acutely needed The Beloved's fulfillment, and I so sorely missed love's supernatural provenance. The only way my wretched torment could be relieved was to relive the ecstasy of being so loved. It was then I simply knew it was *God's love* that was dominating my thoughts and overtaking my will to ravage my heart, body and soul on a daily basis.

One day I felt drawn to *will myself* to evoke love from within my heart rather than wait for it to emerge on its own; I found I could provoke its release by generating a sense of raw yearning for bliss while building and intensifying an inner desire to love and be loved by God. Thus, I learned to attune the goblet of my heart, enabling it to be reinstated with The Beloved's thrilling wine. Love's enchantment would soon spill its sublime passion within me and trigger adulation for The Beloved on scales I had never before approached. Once so thoroughly replenished, I'd forget myself for hours and be drunk on love's intoxicating nectar, causing a consequence of tears to drench my face.

So grievously did I need God to exalt me, so deplorably stricken did I become by love's ebb and so moved by love's seismic rush, that each and every night for many years I looked up from my bed in the darkness, weeping and entreating, *"God, please come back to me, come back to me, come back to me. God, please don't forget me,"* praying that the glorious cloud and shaft of light would reappear to illumine me once again.

After I discovered that God was love's sole provider it made me only more dependent on its *Source*. It became clear that no human being could ever come close to providing me with such an astounding quality of unconditional love. Please do not underestimate the profundity of being so similarly adored; do not dismiss the scope of such shared devotion, for compared to the immeasurable breadth of the ocean of divine love, human romantic love is but the width of an infinitesimal teardrop.

In short time I learned that if I tried to verbalize my condition or explain my encounters to anyone else, the whole affair became inexpressible, for my vocal cords would only tighten and close before tears would overcome me. To confess my inner station and try to narrow it into words meant that I would only compromise its blessedness, and so for many years afterward my enlightenment remained my most precious secret shared in the beginning with only a select few.

I hardly dared to believe that I had actually been *enlightened by divine love* and given what countless others have set out to seek, that the mystical cup hoped for upon the mythic quest for the Holy Grail would be found and filled to overflowing. Unquestionably, I had been touched by the grace of The Divine and gifted with the beatitude of its love. But me, become enlightened? And why in heaven's name would The Divine choose me?

During this time the material plane demanded my presence, but my brain could no longer focus its attention there. I was now like an astronaut, rocket-launched eons from Earth for the very first time and newly enthralled by the grandeur of novas, entranced by the sheer and endless majesty of starry space, made humbled by her small and insignificant relation to it.

Thus, the passage of time took on a surreal tone so that hours felt like minutes, and whole weeks passed in which I simply observed my perceptions, rather than feel a need to decipher them. I marveled at the most ordinary things—watching flecks of dust waltz through a sliver of sunlight would offer a long and tireless obsession. There were days in which material objects disappeared, bent and wavered or melted and reformed right before my eyes. There were many months in which my entire field of vision was tinted in one color, like violet, pink, blue, gold and others.

My hearing intensified to such a towering level that when lights were turned on, I could actually hear the bulbs emitting needling electrical frequencies that so harshly scraped on my nerves I thought my eardrums would bleed. To this day, I can perceive subtle, tinkling sounds called by mystics the "music of the spheres" that ceaselessly plays in the background of my mind.

The outside world looked extra-sharp and defined, meaning everything I observed was startlingly more *apparent*. Colors were saturated and vivid, as if a sooty windowpane that had once obscured my vision had been wiped shiny and clean to reveal the material realm's vibrant brilliance.

My vision so expanded that I could see marked gradations of light, shadow and color, as well as geometric and energetic structures enveloping and moving out from people, objects and living things. I began to witness the omnipresent workings of Spirit as being evident in breathtaking, luminous fields of light that not only emanated off my flesh and hands but shone through the air within delicate, glimmering webs.

The splendor of trees mesmerized me, their twigs gleaming in phosphorescent umber, their leaves glittering like bushels of emeralds ricocheting a million bits of light, their foliage radiating a hazy amber aura rippling gently against the sky. And yes, even the way one branch seemed to reach over to caress another would make me cry with joy and appreciation. The natural world itself proved to be a precious treasure, and incredulously, I began to hear messages that seemed to be coming from plants, flowers and trees.

My sense of smell transcended physical location, and in one instance I detected a friend's brand of cologne from a block away. Just inhaling the delectable scents of rose, honeysuckle or sandalwood evoked in me unanticipated, touching emotions like gratefulness and reverence.

At times my sense of equilibrium would tip my bearings sideways, making the ground appear so off-kilt it seemed I was walking on a slant. I felt buoyant and weightless and although my sight verified that my feet were on the floor, my mind said that I was hovering above it. On particular days it proved impossible to drive because my car felt as if it was lifting skyward from the road like an untethered zeppelin.

Any bit of intuitive ability that I had tried for years to cultivate was blown into oblivion and replaced by extraordinary healing and psychic powers and even episodes of telepathy, which began to scare others around me. Because my perception became so highly tuned, until the year 2002 I couldn't look someone directly in the eye for more than a few seconds before his or her attitude, emotions, character and intention rushed into my consciousness, and soon I would see corresponding expressions of light, color and texture emanating from his or her body. Running my hands above a person's skin, I easily sensed energetic substances where a physical imbalance was present, manifesting or healing. As I progressed, I found I could simply link with someone's consciousness and register it within my own, even hearing the names of specific herbs that could improve his or her health, whether or not I had even heard of the plant or its benefits beforehand.

There were many more ramifications of awakening that continued for years. I became, and remain, empathic to peoples' emotions and ailments, able to embody echoes of their pain, illness, suffering, joy and other imprints.

It was drawing near the month of June when I told my endocrinologist that I had received a forceful impression urging me to stop taking my primary Graves' disease medicine.

"No, you can't just go off it," he began.

I interrupted him and nearly crying, begged, "But I heard a voice. Something happened to me."

His brows stitched together.

"A voice? What did it say? What happened?"

I felt the vice in my voice box wind shut once again.

"I can't tell you," I managed to utter in a whisper.

We stared at one another for a few seconds.

"Okay," he acquiesced. "You can stop taking the medicine for two weeks. During that time, I want your blood to be tested—if your hormone levels are still abnormal, you'll need to go back on it."

After the reprieve, I was back on his exam table, its skin of white paper crinkling beneath me. He bumped my knees and inner elbows with a reflex hammer. So he could track my eye movement, I kept my head straight and watched his pen draw invisible lines in the air. I held out my arms zombie-style while he angled his palms against my fingertips to gauge for tremors. For a number of months he'd been watching the progress of several lumps that had developed in my thyroid gland, so I took a sip of water and drew back my head while he meticulously palpated the gland's edges and dimension.

He picked up my new test results and compared them against the previous ones. His gaze narrowed and then opened wide.

He turned to me with his face lighting up and said, "Your thyroid gland is back to normal size. The goiter is gone and so are the growths. And your lab findings—they're in the normal ranges. You're in spontaneous remission."

An insight flashed in my mind. *Spirit has granted me mercy.*

He leaned toward me and looked into my eyes.

"Paula, tell me," he said quietly. "What did the voice say?"

"It said I had suffered enough."

Surprisingly, my larynx had relaxed, and as I unraveled my story, wonder sparked in his eyes and a smile dawned across his face. I have since remained in remission—knock on wood—his only patient with a similar medical history to remain so for this many years.

Although Spirit has continually made its presence known to me since 1994, the magnificent cloud has yet to return. Inconceivably, as a beautiful reminder of the miraculous force of love, its pulsing thrum remained vibrant in my heart's mystical chamber for many years, dispensing bliss in increments. Whenever the rhythm of love rumbled within my chest, a semblance of its ardor played throughout me like a heartbreaking melody, until over time its notes gradually lessened to only an exquisite whisper of passion.

At the time of my awakening, it seemed unlikely that I would attain enlightenment because I imagined I was too flawed and unworthy of receiving such a tremendous realization. But then I dared to trust it was true, for it became glaringly explicit that my experiences and inner states are classic of the contemplative life of the awakened mystic.

I realized that the great blessing I received was not so much one of a cured illness, but rather that Spirit itself had descended into the matter of my heart to provide a remarkable mercy. As a result, I received an infinite grace, one in which Spirit illumined my being and enlightened my Soul, causing the attainment of unity with The Absolute and forever sealing its Eternal Presence within me.

My Orientation

I grew up primarily in New England and was raised in a middle-class American family. My parents came from a Christian background, and although my mother acknowledged her belief in

God, my immediate family did not attend church or practice religion. Discussions of faith were not a part of my childhood.

Growing up and into my mid-twenties, the topic of religion hardly surfaced in my circles and there were only a handful of visits to Christian churches, mostly for the purpose of funerals and weddings. Before my conversion by the light in my thirties, I had not read much of any theological scripture. It was evident, though, from my early childhood to adult experiences that I was an intuitive person who had many accurate premonitions, along with unexplained encounters with the unseen world, both pleasing and, honestly, terrifying. For as long as I can remember, the idea of God remained a viable one, yet The Supreme seemed an illusive, remote prospect, one whose power and presence remained located "out there" beyond my reach.

It took me many years to mature after enlightenment before my abilities, spiritual gifts and sense perceptions grew more subtle and refined. Over a period of more than twenty years, I devoted much time to be in a receptive state of mind, spending long periods in solitude and contemplation so that knowledge of my Self-realization could crystallize and ripen.

My mind, which had been made so expanded by the effects of awakening, eventually rebalanced over time to establish within me a better sense of stability. My personality, which had been made so conspicuously introverted by enlightenment, has grown somewhat more extroverted over the years, but it has never returned to its previous outgoing nature.

While many of my states and experiences were readily discernible and certain spiritual signs were made obvious to me, others required much reflection and inner inquiry, while still others needed years of investigative study to come within reach of their higher nature.

It was during my tireless search to unearth the secret mystical parameters of my life that knowledge and wisdom of my interior states were made implicit. I found the closest correlations to my life within the realm of classic mysticism, and I began my exploration into it by reading the personal accounts of saints and mystics. Within their experiences, I found so many astonishing similarities to mine it became obvious that I, too, was a mystic.

Bolstered and greatly impassioned by this discovery, I started a voracious comparative survey of mystical texts and scriptures. I delved into writings from a wide expanse of world traditions, including the *New and Old Testaments*, the epics *The Zohar* and *The Bhagavad Gita*, as well as the Vedic Sutras, teachings from Sufi and Buddhist mysticism and others. In addition, I explored writings of the *Pistis Sophia* and the Gnostic and Essene teachings of Jesus, including The Gospels, among others.

In my search, I found hundreds of mystical gems of knowledge to be evident within sacred texts and the teachings of saints, mystics and spiritual Masters. I saw that although the methods and doctrines of each tradition may differ, the underlying spiritual keys and signs they discuss are often linked and mutual and demonstrate that, although there are many alternate branches pointing skyward to the heavens, the mystical tree itself stems from a singular root—the path of the seeker.

This book is thus an assimilation of many important spiritual keys of knowledge and the accompanying signs of the process of spiritual awakening that are prevalent throughout various forms of mysticism, and it includes those set forth from my personal insights and Gnostic awareness.

Throughout the book, I reference God as being the originator of all that is in existence. I alternately use other names that honor different mystical traditions, including *The Source, The Divine, The Absolute, The Beloved, The Limitless Light, The Truth, Reality, The Infinite, The Eternal, The Creator, The Architect, Brahman, Narayana, The Supreme* and more. I feel that by acknowledging a Supreme higher power, you can begin to accept your personal mystic nature and divinity.

In ancient Gnostic mysticism, the direct apprehension of God is called "Gnosis." The word Gnosis comes from a Greek word meaning "to know" in the sense of "being acquainted." A Gnostic is one who receives direct perception of the greater divine Mystery and intimately perceives the substance of Spirit from which God works.

The Gnostic lives his life in accordance with The Supreme, drawing upon his unfolding knowledge to translate the true essence of his states and experiences. But can anyone claim to comprehend the complete amplitude of God?

By Its limitless nature, I concede that God is fathomless and therefore only minutely conceivable through the medium of the mystic's Soul. Gnosis, however, is marked by an unshakable, unmistakable *state of certainty* that one's perception is both Real and delivered by The Supreme. Therefore, I do not assert that I know the depth of that which is fathomless, but I will unequivocally confess that I don't merely believe, but rather *I am certain that God's presence is vital in my Soul*.

Structure and Process of the Teachings

There is knowledge available in this book for everyone, so that wherever you are in your evolution, the subject matter will make sense to you at your own level of understanding. One chapter and some sections are dedicated to select practices and means, but rather than focusing on spiritual methods, this book stresses keys, mystical gems and varied signs, many of which indicate specific levels and degrees of spiritual growth and their perfection.

While important signs and keys of knowledge are designated by a key symbol (☛), keep in mind that any knowledge contained in the book is also a key unto itself. Each chapter begins with a poetic mystical quote meant to appeal to your heart and stimulate consciousness that spurs the contemplative process.

You are encouraged to read the book numerous times to mine it for spiritual gems. This activity supports the intention of *seeking breadth* and *finding depth*. Gems are sprinkled in each section; this way of seeding consciousness is duplicated in every advanced and ancient spiritual text. These spiritual treasures are not truly buried but are made apparent to your consciousness based on your level of awakening. This means that if you are a beginner, certain gems may at first sound cryptic, but as you encounter your personal depth, then their essence, found beneath the surface of things, will be revealed to you. This will be excellent evidence of your progress—a sign that you are awakening because you have been given a key granting knowledge of sacred mysteries leading to spiritual wisdom.

Specific keys, signs and some gems are set forth in language that may appear quite paradoxical, but rest assured that anything you feel is aimed over your head will certainly be implanted within your heart. Some themes are reinforced in order to promote absorption. As you work over a period of months or years, reread passages and your notes and continue to write down your impressions. You will find that as you grow, the language in the book will begin to make perfect sense and even take on added dimension, and this will be a wonderful sign of progress. Wisdom is thus layered in degrees upon knowledge, and it is unveiled depending on your unique path of advancement.

The beginning chapters address more basic keys, with the mysticism growing deeper in some sections as the book advances, showing how the mystic's consciousness unfolds and expands in steps to intersect past time and space and transcend the concrete mind. The more established mystics will not find anything in this book out of reach—ideas will instead be near to their hearts and stand out to be relevant and accessible to their minds.

I often encourage you to acknowledge "signs" of awakening to reinforce their recognition. There are instances I urge you to "remember," which equates to recalling latent soul data so that you can reclaim knowledge of your true Origin.

For the sake of simplicity, when I refer to the "mystic," I use a masculine pronoun engendering "man" to represent the human race. When I capitalize the word "Soul," it implies *a sleeping soul that has been enlightened—awakened to its latent being-ness.* Alternately, I may also capitalize the word "Self" to describe *the conscious mind* of the awakened Soul, most especially one that has been recognized by its Origin.

There were many times I stumbled on the path and made grave mistakes, which delayed, derailed and hindered my progress because at certain impasses, The Way proved to be arduous and treacherous, and the opportunities to fall back asleep, lose ground, get distracted, go astray, become afraid and resistant or take a misguided turn were constant and numerous. I hope that my insights in this regard will help you avoid some obvious spiritual pitfalls, temptations and perils of which the spiritual Masters speak.

I have no doubt that awakening is not beyond belief and reason, but it is a birthright instilled in every human being. My hope is that I will transmit to you some of the mystical consciousness that has been imparted to me so that you may drink its distillation to the delight of your deepest thirst.

My wish is that you receive the teachings as blessings, ones that stir your heart and mind and lead you to become more loving and compassionate souls. My sweetest dream is that you realize the bliss of divine love waiting to be aroused within the secret membrane of your mystical heart.

ONE

Approach the Kingdom

When you bring your heart to the crossroads,
the path will appear. Ever before the soul,
The Beloved expects you at each and every gateway.

Nearing the Kingdom Gates

You're approaching the gateway that leads to the path of the inner kingdom and opens into the realm of the mystic. The Beloved is waiting for you. You see, because its force has called you to follow your heart to the crossroads, The Beloved is fully expecting your arrival at the threshold of the gate.

Suppose you worry you aren't quite ready. What if you think you ought to read a hundred books first to become versed in spiritual tenets so you wouldn't feel so unprepared? Maybe you think it would be better to get your head straight beforehand, so you'd feel more adept, balanced, peaceful and confident. But don't make excuses. Don't over-accumulate information to appease your ego. Don't convince yourself that unafflicted people are the only ones who get to awaken. Don't fantasize about some future time that may never come.

What if you think you're unworthy of spiritual favor? What if behind your facade of contentment and compassion you are burning with resentment or souring with bitterness from past misfortunes that have deeply wounded your heart? Suppose you feel eaten alive by shame and guilt. Maybe you think it would be best if you solved your self-loathing first, so you'd feel more deserving, more equipped. But all of those terrible things that happened, those big mistakes you've made and those unconscious acts you've committed before today will not prevent you from seeking. You can't afford to waste time chronically reliving a past that you could never change.

What if you think you're way too damaged to seek? What if you've been traumatized by another or have intentionally wounded yourself with addiction, bad choices, or compulsive actions? What if your body is consumed with illness or your mind is with preoccupied with misery or some mysterious malady? Maybe you think it would be best if you waited until you're more healed, until you can better concentrate, until you don't feel so negative about all your missed chances or feel so anxious about failing. Maybe later, at some point in the future, you'd be more capable. But don't obsess about things gone wrong. Don't procrastinate.

To begin to walk the path, you don't have to be a heck of a lot more virtuous than you are today because the mystic passage is not reserved for pious goody two shoes'. When you start the path, there's no ticket agent standing at the gateway to freedom waiting to judge your credentials for prior merit. You don't need to be an expert at theology, devotional prayer or anything too religious. At this juncture, there is nothing to be but *willing* and *trusting.* And what about those messy, so-called insufficiencies? Untidy things are always best for readiness because if you're too polished, perfect, settled and comfortable in your ways, your mind will want to resist change.

What if you think you already know the answers? Well, if you're sure that you already possess every key, your unawakened mind will protect its dogma and grand ideas and that will contribute to rigidity, locking out the chance for fluid, flexible movement and clouding your natural lucidity. Fixed, calcified minds are more difficult to pry open to a different way of being. The most oppressive thing stopping you from embracing the path is your mind, stuck in its tracks by the stubborn rust of resistance.

Thus, as you stand on the tarmac of the path, there is no task to complete, no one better to become, no where on Earth to go to get ready to enter the kingdom of the mystic. So come as you are to the gateway, because by being highly flawed and imperfect, you are in a perfect position to start. Being unready is definitely best. Insufficient, unhealed, not forgiven, misguided, unsettled, impure, unresolved is fine. Not knowing is perfect. Being a beginner is even better. Therefore, this very second is the optimal time to start or restart the path.

Why is *now* so relevant? The answer is simple. Within the expanse of enlightenment, there is room for only one thing—unity of your soul with The Divine—meaning nothing you were *before* will exist during the state of union. After enlightenment, the past loses its grasp on you because the future depends on transcending even the present moment. You will find that while you are in the midst of enlightenment, the past and future will coalesce and even the precious, present moment upon which you plan to build a future will be expanded beyond all sense of structured chronology, meaning all that remains afterward is your full, undivided, unchanging presence.

Therefore, you will not be allowed to drag your past history kicking and screaming into your enlightenment because that flawed, unworthy, unready person you identify yourself as being dissolves within the superior state of awakening. You will later see that your worn-out baggage was so stuffed with the past's souvenirs that you couldn't fit it through the gateway even if you tried. You see, to a mystic, there's no such thing as living the history of his life in reverse. There is no such choice as planning for a material future that is set in stone. Pristine consciousness is empty of history, be it awful, neutral, or pleasant.

Imagine an immortal state of being, where there are no memories, no clocks and calendars to live by. Ask yourself whether all along you've been projecting a probable future based on a limited past. *Don't be so predictable*. Don't be the mournful effect of a depressing cause. Don't let your complicated past, jam-packed with failures, mucked-up opportunities, horrible accidents and bad decisions dictate a miserable present. Stop collecting antiques of the past, for they will only take up valuable space that would be better filled with your presence. Don't buy into "then," lugging behind you the ball and chain of all your old trophies and triumphs, allowing them to outweigh your prospects of waking up. Avoid amassing the clutter of future plans that will only obsess your mind with desires that are based on your unawakened past. You see, if you want to embrace the eternal moment, you cannot retain a death grip on all the objects of your past or future, for they will naturally fall from your arms and drop into oblivion when your awareness finally dawns.

Paradoxically, enlightenment is not found within linear time, but the present moment does hold a secret to your awakening. You may have been told that by experiencing the temporal world as existing as *now*, then you may awaken within an actual moment of time. But moments are given to you so that your mind may one day *transcend time*.

Since time does not exist during the state of enlightenment, then how useful will it be for you to focus on moments? Well, the mystic knows that *this moment* is exquisitely, mysteriously alive with possibility, not dead with probable cause. It is by bringing your attention to the action of *staying present* that is the key to your future awakening, and you can be most present within one particular moment at a time. Thus, each singular moment is perhaps the most useful vehicle to tune your intention to staying awake. Later, if you become enlightened, you will find that you will willingly sacrifice even the precious bauble of the moment and toss it into the volcano of your heart for the chance to leap into the flaming Mysterium, the place that exposes the unknown timelessness of Eternity.

Since it is within the state of timelessness that the mystic is born, you will grow increasingly unconcerned about attaching to *any one moment*, whether it is based in the tense of the past, present, or future, for you will be seeking your *inception*, a state that exists *beyond the limitation of time*.

Because you are reading this book, it's obvious that you want more from this lifetime than you are presently receiving. You want out of your limited way of life so that you may gain entry into the expansive inner realms of the soul. You want to know yourself as someone who is more than a robot maneuvering through the same day, the same month, the same year, reinforcing rote and inanimate machinations. It's clear that you want to live, not merely survive.

It's time to heed your impulse to seek and be who you are meant to become. There are no excuses. You're ready. Get it? *You have suffered enough.*

Trust Yourself

Perhaps in the past you have flown thousands of miles to meet with shamans upon the windy plains of mountains, and while you may have reached an enhanced state of consciousness, in the long run you didn't feel so appreciably changed. Maybe you have been one out of a hundred seekers who were emotionally uplifted in a transformational workshop led by a famous sage, but within weeks of returning home, all the heightened energy you felt there fizzled.

You could have scaled the ruins of Chichen Itza in Mexico, sang Celtic hymns while standing in a circle at Stonehenge, meditated in front of the Great Pyramid, walked miles over scorching coals, tread barefoot upon brick labyrinths and sweat out pints in backyard lodges. Let's face it, in the name of advancement, you have probably paid all kinds of experts your hard-earned money to be ritualized, harmonized, hypnotized, Feng Shui'ed, smudged, accelerated, rebalanced, recalibrated, re-birthed, realigned, restructured and retrieved. Maybe you have been prayed over, drummed to, blown upon, sung and danced with and yet you still feel stuck, uninspired and mostly asleep.

Please don't think that all of your efforts have been a waste of time, because even if you have not felt profoundly changed, *your intention to wake up has served to draw you inward and build your receptivity to the light.*

Be confident that everything you have done thus far with a pure heart in the name of growth has not gone unnoticed. Be convinced that every second you spent sitting in meditation has not been a pointless endeavor. Be assured that every oblation and sacrifice you made to live by your highest ideals has not gone to waste.

Know that every time you chose to be kind instead of cruel, to forgive instead of punish, to give instead of withhold and to love instead of hate has aided your cause. Dare to believe that every sincere prayer you have whispered, every devoted OM you have sounded and every authentic word you have voiced has been heard.

Whether you know it or not, *your commitment to stay awake* has impacted your inner state. Little by little, you have forged a *willingness* to transform your life. Step-by-step you have demonstrated strength, perseverance and resolve to leave behind roadblocks imposed by yourself and others who would rather keep you detoured from the path. *Because you have stayed true to these tasks, you are more awake than you think.*

It takes a sense of single-pointed duty and inner courage to continue to stay present and seek your higher nature. It is clear that all of your tasks and experiences to date have coalesced to bring you to this exact inner crossroads at this precise time in history. Most likely you have spent many lifetimes on the spiritual path, which has served to lead you to the intersection. *If you had not made solid progress, you would not have reached the crossroads.* You have already set into motion enough spiritual consciousness to propel you to the threshold of the inner kingdom, meaning it is highly probable that you are ready to radically awaken.

At this time it is very likely that most of your outwardly-seeking pursuits have accomplished their purpose of helping you prepare your interior consciousness, and you have finally come to the realization that there are fewer and fewer *external doors* to knock upon. Maybe you don't realize it yet, but *the exterior doors need to close before the interior doors can be opened*—the ones waiting to form within you.

Please understand that you do not tread the path in hopes of finding a God that is outside of you. By virtue of seeking The Numinous, *you are in fact questing to realize your deepest inner nature*—your highest Self that resides within you. You see, one of the greatest keys you can hold is to understand that by seeking the answers that are already inside you, you can achieve Gnosis that leads to this awareness.

Now is the time to trust your soul and follow your inner self. When you trust yourself, you train your mind to keenly heed your heart. As you listen to your heart's guidance, you are in turn stimulating your *natural inner voice* to communicate. This voice will whisper through the ears of your intuition, it will register messages in your body, it will sing to you in dreams, it will translate signs from nature and the spiritual world, and it will advise you as you build the ark of the soul.

Understand that you are approaching the portal to your freedom. Be willing to surrender yourself, unencumbered, to your highest potential. Remind yourself that you were born with the heart of an explorer to sail to new worlds, to climb to new vistas. Vow to listen to your inner call and forge your path. Pledge to accept the mission of the mystical heart that ignites the life of the soul. Gather faith in yourself, trust that your soul is fully equipped for such a daunting expedition, and know that you are ready to awaken to divine love and your original Self. Dare to dare!

What is The Path?

The path is the way back to your own divinity. It is not a well-paved, frequently-walked, accessible and familiar road—it is a passageway through wilderness, indicating that only a few intrepid souls will muster the strength and bravery to tread its expanse. It is your task to enter the wilds within you to lay down a singular passageway. To accomplish this mission, you must be determined to sharpen the scythe of your mind and use it to cut through the thick reeds, thorny brush and tangled vines of your limitations in order to hone a footing through unexplored terrain.

The path is a solitary, inner journey that is designed to, over a number of years, change your body on a biological and subtle level, stimulate your awareness of the impulses of the ego, make you aware of the machinations of your mind and the intentions of your heart, show you the predilections of your personality and thereby help you to resuscitate your dormant soul.

Every ancient religion has a mystical branch that teaches scientific methods specific to its doctrines which leads the postulant toward Self-realization. Regardless of the many different mystical paths, each of them points in the same exact direction. Hence, there is only one path—that of the indweller leading to one's exquisite Origin. There is the seeker and the path, but in essence, *the aspirant becomes the path.* Thus, *you* are the path. *You are that which you seek, for divinity itself is within you.*

The path has manifold and varied avenues, each possessing its own challenges and empowerments. Every avenue is *interrelated* and built upon the *interpenetrating* energies of a preceding, existing and future stage of advancement, meaning as you walk individual boulevards, all of their energies coalesce. Some avenues stimulate formative energy, others activate energy, while still others balance and stabilize energy.

The path needs to be built, and the basic blueprint for its structure is already in place within you. By developing your spiritual self, you will be laying interior *energetic tracks*—inner pathways by which sparks of consciousness from the One Mind travel through the constellation of your spirit and body, meaning your consciousness *is designed to function so that it interacts with an internal blueprint designed and informed by the One Mind.*

The path is not an easy trek. In truth, it is your reluctance to commit to the path and devote your life to it, your natural aversion to sacrifice for it, that makes it the most demanding and difficult thing you will ever do. It is your lack of proof of soul and your lukewarm desire to know your infinite self that prohibits your advancement. It is your dismissal of the desire to need God. It is your sense of omnipotence, your fear of letting go of who you think you are, your resistance to forfeit material comforts and amusements you think your asleep self so desperately needs, which makes the path such an impossibly daunting prospect. Once you face your inner conflict regarding all of these factors, then the path eases—*it becomes straight and narrow.*

When the aspirant fearlessly seeks to know the mystery of his soul, the path will rise up before him and provide its own guiding forces. As you progress, the path gives way to expose a simpler route that is much less wrought with complications because easement of *the nature* of your suffering is one of the results of awakening the soul. It is not so much that anguish disappears when you wake up, but rather you will be eminently more equipped to cope with the side effects of life, and you will be less prone to overreact to each and every dramatic bump in the road. As you awaken, insight heightens and awareness sharpens to witness your condition, enabling you to bring clarity, patience, acceptance, poise and a soulful heart to life's most difficult circumstances.

During your crusade to find your way back Home, you'll cross sea, air, earth, mountain and ether. Aim to develop endurance because it will be a demanding journey. It can take many years—perhaps your whole life—to make your passage, confronting the attachments, fabrications and misconceptions of your mind and acknowledging the impulses of your ego before significant spiritual realization occurs.

Keep the following keys in the knapsack of your mind while walking the path:

🖙 Release your expectations, for you can neither dream up an exact image of awakening nor anticipate its full effects. You see, to the Soul, there is no future tense.

🖙 Don't plan to arrive at a destination; just be open to the trek. Since God is eternal, the path is endless. Since the soul is infinite and God is fathomless, your search only leads deeper and higher into the Self. There is no end point. There is only your immortal nature waiting to be uncovered, and once it is exposed, all of your potential to love and all of your possibilities to create and manifest will be made obvious.

🖙 Stay conscious, for once the Soul's illumination starts to infiltrate your being, your awareness will brighten, spread and cast its luminosity and progress will naturally follow. Once your awareness is cultivated, the heart can open, the mind can get out of the way and then you can understand more of who you truly are.

It is time to return to your Truth. Do not fear because you won't get hopelessly lost, for the flame built by your exquisite presence is already on duty, throwing its everlasting beacon against the lighthouse windowpane, guiding you through every darkened wasteland, drawing you back to the glowing hearth of your soul.

What you might not know is that you can start the path at the place where it will ultimately lead, *for the means is also the end.* Why not aim to stay awake, to be present enough to continually show up for yourself and others while maintaining an open heart and mind? For truthfully, after you are enlightened it is these simple things that remain.

Why not begin where the ending is and aim to embody the virtues of unconditional love, compassion and loving-kindness? Such beautiful forms of love *eventually lead back to their source,* meaning when your mystical heart awakens, it generates the very same beauty.

What is a Mystic?

A mystic is one who has established a relationship with The Divine. You could say that he perfects the art of receiving and listening to the Word of God. The word "mystic" is traced to the Greek word *mystikos*, signifying one who is initiated into the unseen mysteries, one who masters that which is secret, hidden and concealed. Versed in the secrets surrounding the wisdom of faith, the mystic is able to transcend mundane reality and access non-ordinary states of consciousness to commune with The Beloved and perceive spiritual Reality.

The mystic's foremost intention is to know his supreme nature. He seeks to be recognized by The One Source and to embody and radiate that Source. In doing so, he glorifies The Infinite. As he gains recognition of his true Self, he is privy to God's light, perceiving his own presence as being intimately enjoined with it. His life revolves around witnessing God within every condition and circumstance—seeing The Absolute as being present within all that is materially created (the manifest) and not created (the un-manifest).

His object is to gain direct knowledge of the interior realms of Reality and achieve mastery of consciousness. He achieves advanced awakened states and/or attains enlightenment. Depending on his tradition and belief in the nature of the human soul, the mystic may seek to awaken through its vehicle, for he knows that only by its stirring will he be directly linked with the Godhead. Such a mystic employs his human will to seek contact and union with The Divine, but ultimately he relinquishes personal volition to submit to God's will. He practices methods often associated with his tradition to further stimulate and awaken his spirit. His awakening techniques are quite numerous, some well-known and others kept classified. His methods include breathwork, prayer, mantra, contemplation, concentration and meditation, and those related to sound and movement. Practices are approached and adhered to from the basis of a mystical science with an aim to expand and elevate consciousness, initiate contact with The Supreme, rouse the soul and stir the devotion of mind and heart so that the inner life is transformed.

Many lesser awakenings may occur before reaching the ultimate state of enlightenment, and a great many mystics will never reach it. The advanced mystic garners the facility to reach transcendent states by merging his awakened, enlivened spirit with The Divine Light-Energy. Mystics like Jesus are considered fully-realized, supremely enlightened avatars—Masters who achieve unity and perfect the ability to perceive and work with forces of spiritual consciousness. Only a select few become avatars, and such a Master acquires the wisdom to apply a mixture of consciousness to govern inner conditions that can affect outer materiality, to "turn water into wine." Many spiritual Masters have come to the Earth to be teachers, leaders and miracle workers, and it is within their timeless writings and talks that indispensable keys and esoteric methods of soul development are found.

Mystics live in two worlds at the same time—the material world, and the spiritual one with its compound domains, described as being alternate realms, planes, spheres, or dimensions of consciousness. It is said that mystics are *in this world* but are not *of it*, because they can exist within and walk between principalities that are located beyond the confines of material reality. To a mystic, the material and spiritual worlds are not separate entities—the material realm is seen as a reflection of crystallized consciousness, while the spiritual realm remains pure and fluid.

Throughout the ages, each Master, prophet and teaching mystic has expressed a unique perspective regarding his interpretations of Reality. There is only one version of The Truth, but in comparing their writings you may wonder why each mystic holds a slightly alternate viewpoint of the nature of consciousness and the spiritual route to God.

As the mystic receives signs, keys of knowledge, wisdom and revelations from Creation and The Absolute, they are articulated through the filter of his personal consciousness and are colored by his particular culture, era and unique personality. Further, his views are based on the vision gleaned from the telescope of his own station, training, intellect and individual degree and level of elevation. Interestingly, regardless of differing perceptions and the language used to express the inexplicable, a harmonious consensus of Reality often surfaces within the mystic community.

There are those mystics who are not so strident in their efforts to seek. They would argue that in fact, no seeking of any such Absolute is required; that if one just fully entered the moment and then allowed the mind to open far enough past the notions of space and linear time, Eternity is immediately recognizable— right there where it has been all along, beyond material projections and identifications. These mystics don't focus so much on *doing* but on *being*, meaning there are two main styles of passage to enlightenment—the path of the doer and the path of the non-doer. Non-doers simply view Eternity as being demonstrable within all which is manifested and un-manifested, legitimately asking, *How could one seek what is already here—what is, has been, and always will be, present?*

The modern mystic is now infiltrated among you, sitting beside you on the bus, singing along with you in the choir and meeting you on the bend in the hiking trail. He is most often recognized by his open heart, deep humility, unflagging certainty of faith, sharpened perspicacity, keen wisdom, dedicated service to others and passion for The Infinite. Loyal to the spiritual path, his aim is to *seek and be found, to knock and be allowed entrance, to ask and be received.*

TWO

Sleep or Wake

Deepen the ground of your root and water the life of your bud.
Watch how the musky fern rises from a malachite blanket of moss.
Fiddleheads uncoil and fronds crave the rain. Blades reach out
and the wind spreads a balm of spice through the air. You see,
it is the desire to unfold that waits in the heart of one's fragrance.

Are You Asleep Or Awake?

To a mystic, being asleep means you live in a kind of trance state, making it impossible to recognize your true and vitalized self and leaving you to exist on the fringes of life instead of feeling alive at its center point. This action of sleeping keeps you in a perpetual state of blindness and disconnection from living your highest promise.

You don't see that this kind of separation causes you suffering. Without having been awakened, however, you cannot compare the difference between a sleepy, blurry world and the sharply alive realm of the awakened Soul. This is understandable. Since you haven't yet seen the Supernal Light, how would you realize you're in the dark?

The path requires that you make a choice. Do you want to be awake or remain asleep? Because you cannot have one half of your mind be pounding the concrete highway with steel-toe boots and doggedly clutching onto the trappings of your material life while, at the same time, the other half is unencumbered and shoeless, walking the intangible path of freedom and grace. You can't intend to snooze if you want to be alert. It is simply not possible because both conditions cannot simultaneously coexist. Thus, your full conscious presence is needed to accomplish the task of staying awake.

To the degree that you wake up to your ordinary unconscious tendencies is the same degree to which you will be afforded awakening. Awakening happens within the province of Reality, not within the illusory sleeping world. The difference between these two territories is so exceptionally striking that compared to the luminous realms of the spiritual world, nothing—no personal relationship, children, job, college degree, status, acclaim, success, money, possession—no *"thing"* in the mundane world holds so much as a candle to it.

Just as you believe that day is opposite to night, awakening amplifies and illumines the soul, while sleeping muffles and dampens the most vibrant parts of your life, keeping the highest part of you dormant and unaware of your inner potential.

Imagine that the sleeping soul is like an oblivious worm who is slumbering his days away staying tightly wound in a straight jacket of silk threads and safely tucked within the confines of his fuzzy cocoon. He does not presently know that hidden within his heart is a beauteous dream of being a lunar moth, that one day he will be completely transfigured, fly out of bondage and be drawn toward the light of the moon. Will you stay a lowly, entombed worm? Or will you dream the life of the soul and be transformed into a magnificent winged being that breaks free and soars to stellar heights?

What if mystics are telling the truth—that there is a fuller Reality beyond the confines of the concrete, temporal world? *The simple decision to remain open to such an idea begins a process to deconstruct old, worn-in programs that are holding you back from one day perceiving Reality.* The unawakened mind is fenced off to this perception *because it has been conditioned to do so.*

The mind functions to consider that which is entirely plausible, that which can be cogitated, figured out and concluded—*that which it has, based on its material projections, convinced itself to believe.* But awakening itself cannot be deducted because it is above the thinking mind's reach and unlike anything you have ever encountered in your thoughts. This is why it is not possible for the imagining mind to figure out and comprehend Reality.

Understand that you have a choice to awaken or not, but being awake relies on your quite deliberate action to do so. Until then, you will unknowingly sleepwalk through life until you decide to wake yourself. This is why the path is called *Self*-Realization, for *you* are one who holds the power to receive the key that opens the door to Reality.

If you would only set your heart to awaken, you will find that you already carry within you everything needed for that endeavor, for your body and mind are elementally designed *to embody and master the forces of nature.* You have the element of air in your breath, of water in your blood, sweat and tears, of earth in your bones, of fire in your belly, along with the cosmic force of etheric space that vibrates across the expanse of spirit and soul.

Because you are truly bent on awakening, there is an intrinsic memory inside you that periodically reminds you to wake up. Like an alarm clock ringing its bell, your inner quest for Truth will sound a base note of need to which The Divine will provide a complementary grace note in response to fulfill that need.

When you feel an overwhelming desire for anything authentically spiritual, remember to connect it to the *origin* of your need. *For it is The Divine that winds the alarm, it is The Absolute that trips the hammer to ring the bell and it is The Supreme that strikes the fuel to awaken such burning inner passion.*

Here are some keys to consider:

☙ Before you attain the soul of a mystic, you will first grow hungry to awaken. *You will yearn to be stirred and crave to know who you really are.* You will be insatiably thirsty for the wine of The Divine.

When you are thirsty to inquire, you will in turn become *willing* to be satiated in the answer. When you become driven by your desire to experience the truth of your existence, *you will then receive in your heart an urgency to seek.*

↝ In the same breath, in order to approach groundlessness *you will become more and more willing to face the unknown and be brave enough to forfeit your preconceived notions of that which you imagine is true.*

By being brazen enough to approach the unknown, by investing in your compulsion to realize the Real Truth, you are showing a willingness to be met by The Mystery within a receptive and open space wherein your awakening can ultimately transpire.

What is Consciousness?

Your personal spiritual consciousness can be kept asleep and left dormant as basic, ordinary consciousness, or it can become awakened into *spirit*—spiritualized, awakened consciousness.

Mystics across the ages have attempted to translate the word "consciousness" and its terms, but can it be defined? Since the word implies a quality of *spaciousness*, it cannot be restricted by definitions, but in the spirit of offering some explanations, the following section will help.

As a broad concept, consciousness is associated with *awareness* and *mind*, but it is mystically regarded as being the *Substance* and *Force of Reality* that, by its *presence*, influences the material and spiritual worlds.

Let's explore how consciousness relates to *awareness*:

Being Present - By *being present*, you engage in *mindfulness* to bring your conscious, aware, alert and awake mind to the picture of your life and your inner condition.

Being Conscious - By *being conscious*, you participate in *wakefulness* via your perception, senses and cognition. When you are *conscious*, you *engage your attention*, join the flow of the moment and bring your full *presence* to your circumstances and existence.

If you commit to remaining conscious your spirit can be roused. Without becoming a conscious person, awakening remains out of reach. Mystically speaking, when you inject conscious awareness into the moments of your life, you are actually *spiritualizing your natural mind*, inviting your presence to stay awake on an atomic level. Therefore, *your conscious and awake Self is the one that stimulates awakening,* while your unconscious (sleeping) self does not.

Presence - Your *presence* is your true self, a being of consciousness, who, by the action of bringing attention and alertness to all that arises internally and externally, engages with the One Mind.

Witnessing - *Witnessing* is an action that naturally arises out of the act of being completely conscious. It is only when you are awake and present that the process of witnessing happens; thus, when you are unconscious, the Witness does not emerge. It is a highly wakeful condition, one that is preceded by bringing your presence to the relationship of your condition in order to achieve awareness of it. The activity of witnessing bridges that which is unconscious to that which is born of awareness.

The Witness - When you are conscious you are able to birth a state of awareness that leads to revealing *the one who watches*, called *the Witness*. The Witness is the one who is *aware that he is aware.* The Witness is the aspect of your conscious mind that observes circumstances and conditions and remains wakeful to them. Thus, the Witness is the receiver of your awakened consciousness.

As you work to encourage the arrival of the Witness, *it spontaneously arises* during your normal waking hours and dream time. The Witness also appears as a result of bringing personal unconsciousness to light. As the mystic transcends his rational mind, he depends not so much on his perception, but rather, on his witnessing nature. Thus, the Witness does not rely on perception, but rather, a state of mind that emerges from clarity and silence.

Let's explore how consciousness and awareness relates to *mind:*

Personal Consciousness (Your Personal, Individual Mind) - Your mind's awareness of itself as it regards its experience and inner state.

Soul Consciousness (Your "Natural" Mind) - That part of the Self which watches the conditions of the soul. Associated with your individual spirit, Soul Consciousness is your spiritualized mind in its awakened state which creates an awareness of mystical perceptions.

Collective Consciousness (Collective Mind) - That to which the masses of humanity contribute, which in turn influences your natural mind. Collective consciousness is contributed to by each and every sentient being along with consciousness which accompanies all forms of life, including the entity of Earth itself.

Divine Consciousness (Primordial Consciousness) - That which remains eternal and changeless in its *principle;* Primordial Supreme consciousness that is God and Its active principle; Consciousness which is omnipresent, omnipotent and omniscient.

Eternal Consciousness (Absolute Mind) - The One Consciousness contributed to by God, The Eternal; the entire sum of all forms of consciousness amounting to One Mind.

Awareness - A state resulting from a mind that has become *aware of being conscious.* The *natural mind* is the part of you that witnesses awareness that exists beyond the boundary of your rational mind. *Awareness is a primary key to awakening, laying the platform for spiritual processes that transform and influence consciousness itself.*

Awareness as Consciousness - Awareness that is *mindless* and *formless,* existing as unfiltered consciousness that is beyond the witnessing identification of a personal "you." As the one who witnesses drops out of the reflection, the ego naturally falls away. What is left is pure awareness, pure essence, pure consciousness, undiluted mind—the Clear Light.

The Mystical Particle Wave

In terms of more advanced concepts, the substance of *mystical consciousness* is endowed with a spark—*a vibratory flash* that is traced to the basis of creation. The flash (or "Force") *originates from* pristine consciousness; at the same time Force is being *influenced by* the terms of consciousness.

This relationship is symbiotic, meaning the particle affects the wave and the wave affects the particle. All mystical change, action, stasis and motion points to one unchanging principle—the flashing Force.

Consciousness is never destroyed, but rather its substance is re-absorbed and drawn back behind the veils so as to return to its original pristine condition. Once withdrawn, it can revert to its undiluted, indestructible, immortal state, or, become transformed to manifest in accordance with a different creation.

The *substance* and enlivened *flash* of consciousness is capable of being:

- Pervasive and omnipresent
- Animated, kinetic and interactive
- Built upon, multiplied, angled and fractioned
- Bound, sustained and coagulated
- Unbound, subtracted, withdrawn and reversed

THREE

The Force of the Soul

The fabric of your soul is wreathed by love
and braided with gossamer yarn.
You are never far away from The Weaver,
for deep in the Heart of Its Heart
you and The Beloved are interlaced,
embossed by threads of light, unceasingly entwined.

Who Do You Think You Are?

You are not who you think you are. Your true, original nature is vaster than your mind can imagine. On the surface, you might believe yourself to be a combination of thoughts streaming from your mind, emotions percolating from your experience and the sum of your personality, all rolled into the flesh, bone, blood and breath of your physical body. And yet, if your daily thoughts disappeared, and your brain had no ideas at all, would your sense of self still exist?

If you abandoned certain parts of your personality, would your identity as you know it remain intact? Or if, because of trauma, the distinct appearance of your face and body became unrecognizable, who exactly is left? If all of the above transpired at once, would the person you think you are diminish or completely vanish?

You might be convinced that you are your thinking mind, but when you are fully conscious within the state of enlightenment, your thoughts and your capacity to think them temporarily cease, so you cannot solely be your thoughts.

You will see that when you were asleep your thoughts, beliefs and ideas about your identity were obstacles to spiritual achievement. When you choose to awaken, new impressions of knowledge and wisdom will spontaneously arise within your mind, compelling you to ask, "Who is the conscious being beyond the 'I' that is creating my thoughts?"

You might think the fiber of your physical body is your prime identity, but when you are in the midst of enlightenment there is a lapse of the sense of materiality, meaning no such "thing" as a body exists. In fact, your body was designed to be a spiritual vehicle, and if you develop it as such, you will experience multiple levels of growth.

In order to advance your physical form, it helps you to select spiritual cultivation methods like mantra, meditation, or other practices to purify, prepare, transform and maintain your body as a means to a spiritual end. You will find that when you diligently walk the path, both your body and mind will progressively adapt to perceive a new reality.

You might think yourself to be your personality or ego, but while you are being enlightened your distinct personality is veiled —it temporarily shatters to become the thing which shatters you. You will later see that all along you had been behaving as if you were exceptionally small. After enlightenment, smallness is no longer an option, for you will experience bigger desires that will enormously expand your life.

Right now, your consciousness seems small because your spirit, soul and body are not activated and aligned to the light. Your mind is too small because it is too dependent on revolving thoughts and future plans. Your brain is too small because it cannot receive revelations and direct Gnostic knowledge. Your body is too small because its senses can neither receive nor process perceptions or spiritual energy. As long as you remain so small, you cannot gain entry through the inner doorways to soul.

But the fact is you are not so insignificant. *You are more immense than you know.*

What if you let go of your presumptions? If you are not the total sum of your ideas, emotions, desires, personality and body, combined with your inherited genetic programming and entire life history, then acknowledge that perhaps you are a being of consciousness that is far beyond any calculation—one who is unaware of its own precious promise and infinite potential, one that has been sleeping every second of its life until the moment it decides to claim its greatness. Understand that you are a sleeping giant, *and the colossus is called Soul.*

Until you take steps to awaken and actually make some good progress, the smallness of your thoughts cannot yet conceive of the massive spark of the soul. Right now, the reality of soul seems so elusive that it feels like a distant, unreal, nondescript, fictitious notion, but if you could just get some tangible proof that it truly exists, you would surely not turn away but run toward it with outstretched arms. And along the way you would begin to discover who you really are and unravel the secret of why you are alive.

The essence of your Reality is not a notion. Awakening is not a lie. Somewhere inside you is the real you, and the most important thing you can do in this lifetime is seek your personal source of Truth.

What is the Soul, or Self?

You might think of yourself as a person with a soul, but soul is not a possession. You could think of soul strictly as being an identity, but you are not so restricted.

The fundamental pattern of the soul was designed specifically to be a joined force of consciousness, one made up of the eternal God spark consciousness and your personal soul consciousness. The awakened Soul is considered the progeny—the "son"—of The Creator. Soul is thereby an heir of God and thus, soul inherits *a limitless and immortal quality.*

The God spark part of soul is considered perfect. Being of God, the original spark itself cannot be improved upon, reduced, or defined. Just as the solar flare is not the sun, you are not God, but your consciousness could not be set ablaze were you not made in the same image and filled with the same elements that are capable of building such a tremendous fire. The Force of Spirit is purposely embedded within your personal soul force, and without this spiritualized connection you would not have an awareness of being conscious and alive. Neither would your body be vital without your soul, nor would your body or soul be animate without the infusion of Spirit and its light.

This intermingling, this *knitting of consciousness* demonstrates the creative binding (joining) principle that keeps you aware of time and space. Also, it keeps you physically and spiritually plugged into The Source, and it stimulates your desire for and remembrance of The Beloved.

Soul is like a lily bobbing on the surface of the stream of divine consciousness, its roots extracting life from the pond's muddy floor while simultaneously being enriched by sunlight from above. When soul is expressed, the bud expands and then unfurls, exhibiting its radiant petals. One would be inclined to think the lily's specie is identified by its flower, but remember that inside the shell of the seed, The Eternal provides not only the source of the lily's life, but also its compulsion to bloom.

A constant relationship is being actively maintained between the God Spark and your personal soul consciousness, for Spirit provides the soul's inherent impulse to develop and change. Thus, soul can inhabit both the urge and expression of consciousness.

You are a soul of the One Soul, a spark of The Divine, and the Great Spirit within you is kin to your spirit. Just as petal by petal the lily unfolds to express its creation, Spirit reciprocates by casting its fragrance to the winds. Just as Spirit takes action to exude its own subtle influence upon all things, soul consciousness embodies Spirit's *emission*, encased as the vibratory *movement* of God. Although Soul and Self are often used as interchangeable terms, you can think of *"Soul"* as being *your awakened presence* and regard *"the Self"* as being *your eternal consciousness*. Thus, the Self is associated with the developing, crystallized and realized Soul.

Here are two fairly advanced tenets to consider:

➴ *Soul is always able to reflect its causation because it is not separate from it.* Soul is neither cause nor effect—it is a union, a fusion, of the extremes of Alpha (above), Omega (below), and that which exists between and beyond Alpha Omega.

➴ The primordial *activity* of the soul is due to its being the *effect of God*, although awakened Soul can also initiate causation. Soul can *initiate action* or *be acted upon,* meaning Soul can bind *to* and be bound *by* energized consciousness. Soul can *unbind* energized consciousness and be *unbound by it.* Soul can *become stabilized* by energized consciousness as well as *be made* stabilized by it.

What is my "spirit"?

Your spirit is considered your Soul self's *higher mind*—the intelligence of your awakened Soul. Think of it as being your *awakened personal consciousness—the perceiving mind of your Soul.* Your awakened spirit is thus the *spiritualized consciousness of your natural mind*, and it functions as a kind of intermediary brain that processes impulses that travel between the material world and the non-ordinary one. If soul is your true presence, then your spirit is your true mind, your higher self. If you are asleep, then so is your *spirit,* so it stands to reason that a hibernating spirit inhabits a sleeping soul.

Ordinary sleeping mind buys into the mundane, while the awakened spirit is vested in the extraordinary. The unawakened "base mind" primarily identifies with third-dimensional ordinary reality—the body, the material world, time, space and objects. Your base mind is calibrated to react to ordinary reality, one that is intimately tied to experiencing the world through your five senses. Until you wake up, your spirit does not even realize that there is such a thing as the non-ordinary world because your base mind needs to depend on your senses. Your *natural mind*, though, is *clear and free from any conditioned reality* that so strictly identifies with the senses and the 3-D world.

The goal is to release your base mind from the ties that confine it to the material world, for when soul is circumscribed to react to the senses, it will be ignorant of its own spirit, and it will be prone to be apathetic to The Divine and its workings. The mission is to unravel the knot that keeps your spirit entangled in sensory desire that conditions you to restrict your identity to the body, concrete mind, time, space and the material world.

When your spirit begins to be engaged by spirituality, it means that your soul is being re-ordered by the God Force to perceive and respond to The Light originating from those realms that are not limited to the third dimension. *As you are being influenced by The Light, keep in mind that it is Spirit itself that enlivens, stirs and awakens your personal spirit.*

Once your spirit is sufficiently roused, its force can grow strong enough to expand and break its own chains, for only a soul that has responded so thoroughly to its inner calling will seek such extraordinary freedom. It is the liberated Self, *awake to its own mind and heart* that propels the seeker to sever the heavy link that binds him and holds his natural mind hostage beneath the surface of his true identity. Once unbound from materialistic confines, the true Self will rise up and become *re-linked with the intangible*, causing it to be polished anew, made sparkling with the shininess of The Absolute's pure light.

For a time after you are newly awakened, you will be positioned far away from your mind's reliance upon the dense material realm. Thus, your former mind structure is *purposely displaced so that the intimately close spiritual dimensions of The Beloved can no longer be rejected.* Instead, you will be mightily influenced by the subtlety of the spiritual light realms and *your spirit will be directed inward*—drawn to its home within the glowing, secret sanctuary of the mystical heart. As a result of your enlivened, awakened state, ego desires, the mind and the body become *newly arrayed* in order to respond to the influx of spiritual light garnered by the awakened Soul.

The Soul as Quantum Force

You are used to thinking of soul as being an idea or a thing, but soul is neither a lowly, lifeless object nor an invisible abstraction. At the end of your life, if an autopsy is performed on your remains, no substantial evidence of your soul as a solid, compact entity will be found. This would lead you to think of soul as being something other than a substance, or an object made of condensed matter.

What if soul is quantum in nature, one whose sphere is subject to the laws of electromagnetic energy, one able to reflect the qualities of both *a particle and a wave?* What if deep down your consciousness is able to influence the emission and pattern of scalar waves? What if the sphere's reflection whirls and spins in angular momentum?

These questions suggest that soul consciousness can act like an atomic particle, as if it seems to temporarily hold form like a substance, but soul is not exclusively a form. Soul can behave like a wave, but it is not strictly a magnitude of speed. In theory, if soul is quantum in nature, its wave would not undulate, save for its substance, and its substance would be lifeless without the potentiality of its wave. *But the reality is that a wave and its corresponding particle are only polar expressions emanating from a common Point of Origin, polarities that proceed from the totality of the sphere's incidental perception.*

Your each and every perception *influences*, and is *influenced by*, light waves of frequencies created by consciousness. What if divine forces are able to put forth specific *conditions* that influence waves, particles, energy and substance? What if your personal consciousness is exposed to those conditions?

For example, let's revisit the life of the lily. Each second that it expands in size, it owes its growth to sunlight, nutrients and water. As it grows it makes movements, sending out ripples on the water's surface, echoing evidence of an inner shift that creates a corresponding wavelength. But its wavelength is also dependent on the shift of the lily's body, the medium of water and other forces of nature. Just as the lily responds to factors such as wind, heat, rain and sun, so too does soul symbiotically respond to higher consciousness forces within itself, Spirit and the collective consciousness. Indeed, deep down you are a *force of nature* whose life depends upon and perfectly coexists within the natural, cosmic and divine realms.

This means that although awakened Soul creates independent actions, it is interdependent with Reality. The force of the soul is specifically designed to exist, act and react according to terms of consciousness set forth by ancient spiritual laws written by The Creator. In addition, these laws of consciousness *act in tandem* according to terms set forth by forces initiated by the soul and God.

Remember: You are a soul, a force to be reckoned—one that has the chance to shift, develop and advance. Understand that the sphere of the soul is stationed deep inside you, tucked within the bud that holds the promise of the seed, and your mystical heart is the secret kernel housing the soul's divine love spark.

You see, you are not merely the stem and the bud and the bloom—*you channel the force of the root that lives the mystery of the inner life of the seed holding the promise of its perfume.* The root is the vine by which you are entwined to God, and as your fragrance emits its sweetness from the heart of the bloom, your essence will be carried by the winds, and you will draw unto you damselflies, bees, butterflies and other winged creatures that will land upon your petals and spread your pollen far and wide. And you would not exist save for the cosmic elements by which you are deliberately held.

FOUR

The Whirl of Spirit

Pull a blazing white sun through a singular gaze.
Taste the nectar of honey melting on the tip of your tongue.
Draw the elements north through the foaming fountainhead crown.
From Zion to the Earth and back, perceive a whirling dance.
Ah, The Beloved is turning, its wide embrace enfolding!

What is Spirit (*with a capital "S"*)?

Spirit is God's creative impulse and activity, for The Supreme is not separate from its causative action. Spirit carries God's effulgent coruscation, reflecting God's brilliant particle of light that demonstrates the activity of shining. If God is the existence of spiritual fire, then Spirit reflects Its shimmer, combustion, flame, smoke, heat and ever-glinting flicker.

In one aspect, Spirit is seen as the identity of God—the *Is-Ness* of its totality. In another, Spirit is said to be *The Beloved,* the consort, the complementing feminine force delivering the expression of The Creator. Lover and beloved are destined to be together as one, just as a flame would be motionless without its glimmer and dynamic energy. If Ultimate Reality were to exist as the original quantum particle, then Spirit is its accompanying endless wave, eternally returning to its Source.

Divine Intelligence expresses itself as Spirit through the medium of the cosmic consciousness force. If you are awakened, expect Spirit to flow through the vessel of your body and manifest through the instrument of your personal consciousness. Spirit is the prime component of the original "mixture" of divine consciousness that is made available to your soul and all creation. You will discover that you cannot govern the full and unbridled power of Spirit, for its primordial action is subject to God's provision and dispensation. You can only hope to influence and master your portion of the mixture.

Spirit's emanation is found throughout mysticism, culture and religion, and it is referred to in a great number of ways. Among its names, in Christianity it is called *The Holy Spirit*, the *Wisdom of God* and *Christ Consciousness*, and in Hinduism, the *Adi Shakti*. Similar terms are *Jnana* (Sanskrit) and *al-Rūḥ al-Quddus* (Arabic). Native Americans refer to it as *The Great Spirit Mother*, associated with *Mother Earth*, while ancient Celtic religion calls it *Goddess*.

In the New Testament, *Spirit* is regarded as *Pneuma*. Among its Hebrew names, *God The Spirit* is called *Ruach Ha-Kodesh*, with the single word *Spirit* translating as "Ha-Ruach," meaning breath, wind and soul. Distinct from the Ruach, Judaism recognizes *Earth* as being a divine representative of God, and the word's Semitic roots means *to settle, inhabit* or *dwell*. In the Talmud, the Earth is seen as a source of prophecy linked with the transformational spirit of God.

Spirit has been classically acknowledged as *The Divine Feminine* and *The Divine Mother*. She is Creation/the creative principle, the universal power and the active force of God. She is the vibratory manifestation, the *Word, the calling*, the *audible voice* of The Divine. She can visually manifest as a moving white cloud or a mist.

In Gnosticism, the varied aspects of female divinity are identified with *Sophia*. Sophia's reach includes being identified with The Holy Spirit and feminine wisdom, but she also encompasses the range of feminine consciousness—the Universal Mother, Virgin, Womb, Holy Dove and female counterpart to the male logos.

In Sufism, The Holy Spirit is associated with the angel Gabriel, who is depicted blowing his horn (expressing an audible vibration through his instrument). Gabriel is the Archangel who delivered the annunciation to the Virgin Mary by way of The

Divine Breath. In scripture, The Breath emitted from the Horn of Gabriel represents the force of God sounding the Word as Gabriel delivers Gnosis of the Godseed and Mary's conception. In the Holy Qur'an, this blasting vibration is seen as a warning sign of the last judgment and resurrection, and it signals the vitalization of certain souls. Here, the blasting Truth is heard in a Great Announcement and violent vibration, and for the ones who experience the blast, a *Cool Breeze* results, called the *Wind of the Resurrection,* perceived as energy flowing from the hands, head and other parts of the body.

While the horn of Gabriel foretells a groundbreaking movement—a seeding within the soul, the Trumpet of Archangel Michael augurs a profound instillation of Spirit, enlivening the sleeping soul by injecting it with vitalized spiritual consciousness. Exploding in a thunderous sound, Michael's trumpet rains down the vibratory influence of Spirit so that the soul receives a quaking blow. Having been struck by Spirit itself, the aspirant is instilled with the will to create from this supernatural force.

Spirit acts as *the agent* for The Infinite, being both Revealer and Enlightener. If you are given wisdom, *then understand that it is unveiled* through the agency of the Spirit of God. If you are enlightened, Spirit itself mercifully acts on God's behalf to illumine your soul with grace. Enlightenment thus serves as *the activation of Spirit within your soul.*

Being The Manifest *in motion,* the light-sound emission/emanation is thus *a projection* of The One Source consciousness that is carried and delivered by the medium of Spirit. *Those who have ears to hear* are given the ability to perceive a mystical sound that articulates both the soul's and Spirit's vibratory expression. This audible emanation has been called *Naam, The Shabd, The Living Waters, The Word, The Holy Ghost* and *The Living Stream of Jesus.*

Keep in mind that there is a polarity of subtle consciousness, a *soundless sound*—a *non-sound* which is Un-Manifested, nondifferentiated, pristine and all-pervading—and it is *the unabridged Silence* that exists within *everything, everywhere—now, then and always.*

The Vibration of Spirit

Everything of material substance manifest in the universe is either moving or in the stages of being influenced by force. Anything moving vibrates, and that which vibrates creates wavelengths of frequency. Even inert matter, at its most minute level, is involved in a process that is being influenced by force. An object that appears static wobbles because *its integrity is being actively maintained and held by balancing and opposing forces of electromagnetism.*

For example, suppose you used a high-power microscope to greatly magnify a ruby. You would see chemicals of aluminum oxide and chromium behaving like particles while being suspended within large expanses of emptiness. Such expanses of space are not truly empty, *but rather they are electromagnetic fields.*

Electromagnetic forces keep the ruby's particles close enough together to maintain an octahedron composite—otherwise, its form would simply collapse and dissolve. At first glance through the microscope lens, some of the stone's components would appear to be in motion, traveling in waves or spirals or behaving erratically, some crashing into one another, bouncing or jumping, fragmenting, *or oscillating between being a particle and a wave,* while others would appear to be suspended in space. *But if you looked at the entire picture, you would see all the particles pulsing as a whole and creating energy.*

If you had a device that could amplify sound loud enough, you would be able to hear the ruby's signature. The signature is composed of tiny, individual musical notes being sung by each separate particle's vibration that builds into symphonic frequencies, *for each and every note affects the other as it rolls to collect into a giant wave.*

Just because you do not yet have the ears to hear such seemingly inaudible frequencies does not mean a vibration isn't present. Just because you do not yet have the eyes to see atomic particles and elements in motion doesn't suggest they are static and inert. Everything being manifested in the universe is alive with motion and momentum due to the forces of elements, the life force itself and the emissions of Divine Consciousness.

But there is something else.

Just by gazing through the lens, *by bringing your attention* to the gem, you are influencing its presence, meaning *it is being affected by that which watches.*

There is a reciprocal agreement in place that causes particles of light to coexist with their pulsation, establishing that they can appear to oscillate between being particle or wave. Hints of this capacity are found in the scriptural words, "And God *said*, let there *be light.*" The Creator sets into motion light, a vibratory force—the force of The Holy Spirit—and simultaneously its emission sends waves that emanate light, making consciousness visible. The light transmits and radiates the cosmic life force and its various manifestations of force, motion and vibration. These forces intrinsically influence your subtle and physical body, your personal consciousness and all of consciousness itself.

Each and every cell in your body emits and is influenced by frequencies. As your own cells are sparked by the life force, they create sound. You are making distinctive waves that contribute to the collective force. Since you radiate a personal field of light that emits frequencies, you are sounding a signature soul note that is being heard by God and all of Creation. *You are a manifestation of Spirit in motion.*

You are part of the grand wave, the cosmic chime, the celestial symphonic music! Decide for yourself which kind of conductor your consciousness will become—will it produce a movement that makes disharmonic, cacophonic noise, or will it create a sweeping, orchestral masterpiece?

The mystic listens for Spirit's approach within himself, and he hears, sees and perceives its accompanying flash in various forms. Shown to him as signs, such forms include cascading streams of energy and serpentine coils of electrical fire, as helix rings, rippling waves and rumbling volts, as sizzling sparks and platinum dust, as indigo smoke and a filmy mist, as dense, opaque light and more.

What Are Signs?

Signs are heralds, messages, impressions and harbingers that announce the calling of Spirit to your soul, showing you Spirit's presence and offering you divine energy, sustenance and guidance.

Signs are given to be pondered and reflected upon, to be richly explored for meaning, rather than be ignored, dismissed, or passed off as coincidence or happenstance. He who develops the capacity to observe signs and arrive at their correct interpretation is one whose perception has been made finely honed by Spirit to do so. And he who turns his gaze away from divine guidance will not gain much spiritual insight, for he makes his own eyes dulled to the light.

Thus, it is a mistake to reject or ignore a sign, for by disregarding its presence and significance, you are seen as one who similarly neglects Spirit and rejects the grace of God. Instead, if you live your life noticing, accepting and appreciating signs, you embed within your consciousness their accompanying mercy, shoring up divine favor within your soul. The volume of favor you earn will be matched with mercy in times of your greatest need.

The Divine's communications are often *spiritual in nature*, rather than literal, meaning *their action is intended to spiritualize your consciousness*, and if this spiritualization also results in a literal message or indicator, that is like receiving icing on a cake.

Spiritualization prepares the soul, it cooks your consciousness based on an alchemical recipe, and although a message may be written on the frosting, don't forget the importance of the cake's aroma, its particular spices, texture and taste that completes the entire creation!

Signs are indicators summoning your soul to stay awake, showing you that the cause of Reality is purposely influencing your consciousness, its foremost reason to *seal your faith*. You receive signs as solid proof that the spiritual world is communing with your soul. Signs offer you assurance that you are not alone, showing you that Spirit is interacting with you and providing evidence that you are never too far out of range to receive the grace of divine signals.

Signs manifest in many different ways and shapes, spontaneously arising to draw your attention to the synchronicity of the present moment and so that you may attend to their indications. Signs can also portend future events, warn you of present or oncoming circumstances or alert you of situations.

Although The Supreme sends signs in the form of *actions* that are carried out by Spirit, you also receive them by way of personal sensory and intuitive perceptions, as well as via your dreams. Signs may arrive via angelic, celestial and spirit messengers, as well as through nature, animals, insects, humans and other emissaries.

The messages you receive can often be spoken in language that is not always easy to understand, but many times Spirit will incorporate familiar words, literal and non-literal images, sounds and vibrations to express its voice and convey meaning. Alternately, you may receive signs in foreign or ancient words, phrases, symbols and sigils.

If you look for signs, they will be found. If you expect and request them, they will manifest. If you heed them, they will continue to speak to you. If you ponder and understand them, their meaning will sharpen your instincts. If you acknowledge signs, they will multiply to recognize you and honor you with their infinite power.

Very specific signs are given as indicators that select spiritual processes are taking place within your personal consciousness. *Supreme signs* are those that are inordinately powerful in their manifestation and irrefutable effects, and their purpose is to provide Gnosis, create knowledge and reinforce the consciousness of faith and confidence in The Supreme.

Speaking of faith, *its substance is the foundation from which Spirit conducts the actions of God.* For example, if you wanted to bake a loaf of bread based on ingredients you can provide, then faith would be considered as a basic staple, like flour. In other words, with the addition of faith, Spirit will have enough usable substance to create what you need. Without such a staple, no confection is possible, so you must continually stock your inner pantry with faith. Hence, should you feel you lack or have lost faith then ask Spirit to restore it. Whenever faith wanes, we must go to its Source for replenishment. When you continually build and fortify faith, growth can then naturally follow.

Here are two important keys:

☛ *You must ask for signs, and just as importantly, you must request that you not only recognize them as such but also comprehend their meaning.*

☛ When you watch for signs and then receive them, you will soon realize that *your mind is being wakeful to itself.*

Active Signs of Spirit

If Spirit speaks to you personally, here are some of the ways you will encounter its presence and active principles:

☛ As an audible voice, speaking or calling out your name, seeming to come from the material world and not your mind.

Expect you may hear the call at various times in your life, and it may be spoken in several different voices.

Hearing your name being called by Spirit is a very auspicious sign, one that not only augurs awakening but would also indicate that *your will is being tuned to be receptive*. Such a herald confirms that *Spirit knows you personally and is moving within you, inspiring an inner calling.*

Listen for the *tone* of the messenger's call—is your name being spoken in an urgent manner or a calm one? Remember that you may be called only a select number of times. When Spirit speaks, do not reject the message; with all your heart simply answer, *"Yes, I accept the call,"* and in turn, you will be seen as one who is willing to keep receiving Spirit's guidance.

⟿ As inner words, phrases and expressions deposited directly into your mind or seeming to come from outside you in the material world.

⟿ As symbols and sigils presented in visions, dreams and waking states.

⟿ As inner sounds heard in your head that resemble ring tones, bells, cymbals, animal or insect-like noises, buzzing, beeps, conch shell sounds and others. You may even hear your personal internal vibrations.

Your soul receives vibratory perceptions that are being channeled through auditory pathways and processed by the brain. If the sound is forceful enough to cause a gross vibration, it may be felt through kinesthesia. Cosmic sounds can also be perceived overall as white noise, but if you listen more closely you will hear a compilation of various and multiple sound frequencies that often appear to be interpenetrated.

⟿ As noises, tones, or a cacophony of sounds seeming to arise from the material world.

⟿ As the literal sound/vibration of *OM* iterating its unmistakable syllable while simultaneously creating a gross physical vibration. The OM seems to come from the atmosphere, and its dramatic vibration is felt in the head and physical body.

☞ As *The Naam – The Shabd – HU – The Living Stream – The Word – Christ Consciousness –* its manifestation felt as vibration and tingles and interiorly perceived as subtle sound frequencies. You could say subtle sound is the operative vibration of consciousness itself.

☞ As the *Horn of Gabriel* or *Trumpet of Michael*, experienced as a thunderously loud blast or screeching noise seeming to come from the atmosphere, often resulting in your physical body being grossly shaken.

As a sign of massive awakening and calling, God fiercely stirs your soul through the emissary of an archangel so that you are resurrected and reborn, and by evidence of shaking, it shows you are being *vastly moved.* If a horn or trumpet sounds, it means that in the very least you are receiving a *wake-up call.* The startling tone of Gabriel's Horn is also considered to be a warning, announcing a mass shift of consciousness.

☞ As fine or coarse oscillations, waves or spiral forms of vibration felt within and around your body.

☞ As vibrations perceived in the form of scalar rings or flattened saucer shapes moving in a vertical (or other) direction through the body's energetic centers. Spirals may spin around and through your body in a left or right direction.

☞ As visible spheres, sparkling stars, or other shapes displayed in colors and light seen in the atmosphere with *open eyes in broad daylight.* As inner "lights," flames, or sparkling stars seen interiorly within your mind's eye with *closed eyes.*

☞ As manifestations of *clear* light.

☞ As a cloud or a mist of animated *living* light.

☞ As a dense, opaque mass of *black light* or black web-like matter.

Signs from Creation

You are more likely to notice signs coming from Creation when you place yourself in a quiet, pristine and beautiful outdoor setting and cultivate a receptive state of mind. It is then that you are prone to receive a sign from nature that you will be able to decode.

Perhaps you will be shown a sign in the form of a cirrus cloud morphing to a wispy heart shape, or feel a puff of wind caressing your cheek as if an angel were tracing a letter in Braille. Perchance a willow tree branch weighed down by a child on a swing will joyously creak, or ten hawks will start to pirouette clockwise over a wounded dove. Maybe rivulets of water will skate across your windowpane and converge into one slick stream, or a scorpion will uncoil its tail on a broken and dried cactus spine. All of it will draw your attention and stimulate wonderment and unknowingness—what could it all mean?

You see, it is not so much that *you* are seeing signs all by your industrious little self, but rather, it is that *nature itself is drawing your attention to show them to you.*

Nature has its own voice and it is willing to express it, for *Creation is also an emissary*, a medium for Spirit. When you begin to regularly receive signs from nature, you will see that *nature responds to your attention. When you ask for a sign and nature provides it, it means God has told Creation to answer your inquiry.*

All forms of creativity can spring from a source outside the confines of the personal mind. Artists, writers, actors, poets, dancers, singers and musicians are particularly attuned to receiving higher inspiration and are used to spending hours in solitude steeped in the creative process, where a sense of timelessness emerges.

You might consider beginning a creative endeavor, like writing, sculpting, composing, dancing, painting, cooking, decorating, gardening, or any other medium that serves to imitate creative fire. To take it deeper, the act of creating *devotional* (honoring The Beloved) art, poetry and music *emulates the Creative principle* and easily magnetizes you toward your natural mind, where you can surrender yourself to incoming inspiration. The mystics Hafiz and Rumi, for instance, became known for their beautiful ecstatic and devotional writings.

Spend time in outdoor settings, witnessing the effortless action of Creation contained in the elements of earth, air, fire, water and space. See these elements as agents of stability, movement, dissolution, creativity, potential, expansion and spaciousness. Grow curious about the natural world and all of its creatures, and engage the animals, insects and other living things you encounter that seem to be speaking to you. The more familiar, friendly, intimate and aligned you become with nature, the more its dynamic attributes and conditions will resonate clearly within your consciousness, honing your perception of nature's language and participation in your life.

Deciphering Spirit's Messages

Engage in wonder and be introspective about signs and messages, but do not rush to understand their meaning. Sometimes you will receive a literal sign whose meaning is quite obvious, *but not all signs and messages are intended for such a literal purpose.*

Unless the exact meaning is placed directly into your mind, don't hurry to translate a sign or message. If you analyze everything too soon and randomly assign a quick interpretation, you will find that you are liable to contradict your understanding in the future because the underlying significance will most often surface later in time. You may inwardly inquire about the encounter, but then watch your impulse to get hooked on instant gratification, on getting quick, superficial answers by way of your mind's logic.

While you may watch for signs and listen for messages, leave it up to The Divine to communicate their true symbolic depth. You will not always know in the immediate moment what exactly is transpiring, but it is important *to achieve comprehension of being seen by Spirit, and this is the point of such enigmatic signs.*

Although you may concede that you will not always be 100% certain of the height and breadth of every message you receive, you must recognize that *Spirit is working to influence you.* Thus, when you make this acknowledgment, *your realization that Spirit is actively working to spiritualize your consciousness will provide more than enough understanding.*

Here are some keys:

↪ Each time you receive a sign, become grateful for its presence and acknowledge and give due thanks to its Source.

↪ Before you rush to analyze signs, allow them to percolate within your consciousness for days, months, years or forever. If you do not immediately gain full understanding of the sign's meaning, you will find that in time The Creator may reveal its essence.

↪ Do not assign an immediate *material* reason for a *spiritual* event, for you will be missing the sign's *spiritual target*, and the point is that you will never, with your logical mind, figure out the full nature of God's fathomless spiritual actions. Think about it; if The Immeasurable cannot be tangibly gauged, how would you expect to sum up its intangible measures?

↪ Watch your tendency to invent your own "reasons" for signs and their messages, which creates narrow grounds for The Numinous. It is not up to you to authorize or substantiate the drawings of The Architect.

↪ Make no demands. By repeated demanding signs and grasping for their reasons, it means you are demanding proof of Reality. The energy of such actions places a roadblock to progress because a mystic does not make similar demands. He may make an appeal, he may humbly ask for understanding and he may inquire in the form of petition, but he does not demand.

There is a difference between humbly asking and arrogantly demanding. Persistent demands will only be read as acts of disrespect and hubris, as being immature, and grace is not gained in this way. What more proof do you need but signs of your own progress, signs that you are being seen? Do you not see that nature itself is proof of Creation? Can you not accept that Creation invented the figure of your body, the corpus of Earth and its creatures, and every celestial body in space?

What is Divine Revelation?

Revelations are divinely-inspired literal and non-literal signs, messages and impressions that spontaneously arise outside of your own reason, logic or cognitive thinking function. Thus, you do not think up revelations, they are given to you. Related to Gnosis, revelations arrive via perceptions that are directly transmitted from Creation/The Creator. Since these messages are not generated by you, you do not deduct from them—they arrive *intact and whole* in the language of The Divine to be disclosed to your wakeful mind and are translated through your perceptive faculty. Although revelations often include divinatory prophesies, they are not limited to that category.

Throughout history, awakened individuals have recorded their revelations, prophetic perceptions and visions, and many can be found in scripture and mystical treatises. For instance, the Kabbalist book *The Zohar,* whose author is assumed to be Rav Shimon bar Yochai, is a mystical tool founded on divine inspiration. The *Holy Qur'an* is based on the Prophet Muhammad's revelations that were instilled within him over a period of twenty-two years. The Bible's New Testament includes *The Revelation of Jesus Christ,* which is thought to be based on the Apostle John's revelation foretelling apocalypse on Earth, elucidated in symbolic language that spells out a startling series of signs. Without advanced mystics gaining revelation and wisdom, important teachings would not have been brought to the planet, and these writings contain secrets, symbols, signs, keys, passwords and codes.

A contemplative is a person who can make his mind a *tabula rasa*—a blank slate, a clear and open arena to receive revelation. The contemplative mystic thereby knocks on the door of consciousness to be allowed entry into stillness of The Mysterium. Such a mystic patiently waits in silence, tuning every fiber of his awareness to increase his receptivity so that he may not only receive revelation but also the answers to his questions. He listens, watches, asks and then he receives a blessing, placing no terms or conditions on that which is imparted by The Supreme.

Through the medium of his consciousness, the mystic manifests the un-manifest, and because of his non-knowing stature, he embraces The Mystery, which in turn embraces him. He understands that it is The Mystery that already knows; it is The Mystery itself that provides forthcoming knowledge and wisdom. The mystic, then, does not claim to fully know The Truth; he only seeks to be met by its essence.

The contemplative is always expecting an eventual answer to his inquiries, and he is ever prepared to receive revelation. To encourage revelation, *begin to foster a sense of inner inquiry and wonder in your contemplation.* For example, you may prepare for revelation by actively wondering about a sign, a passage from scripture, or anything else, but then release your thought process in order to simply bring your full receptivity to the moment. Within a space of time, wonder transforms itself into deeper insight as knowledge suddenly bubbles up from your interior, or a sign is given to provide a clear explanation, all of it stemming from a receptive stance of non-thinking, not-knowing.

Here are some tenets:

☞ Spend time in solitude. Start a meditative practice and develop the capacity to sit in silence. As you disentangle your mind from making plans and thinking, you approach silence. As you create internal space for silence, you become a receptive vessel, an open field that is ready to be seeded.

☞ Take contemplative walks and make inquiries both inwardly and aloud. *Ask in the form of a question* and the answers will be given to you. For example, "Spirit, how will you guide me in this travail? Spirit, will you show me a sign? Spirit, will you help me to understand?"

☞ Next, surrender your thoughts and *simply become the question*. Expect that *you are already receiving an answer.* The response may come immediately or in the days or months to come, whether in the form of a dream, a sudden insight, an obvious sign, an inner picture, or more.

☞ Accept that you will never be able to know everything. Spirit deliberately veils certain aspects of your life and hides things from your understanding. This "not-knowing" stature of humility deconditions the mind from grasping at control and comfort and running from the unknown. *Knowing that you do not know* is a powerful mindset that helps you trust not only The Mystery but your own soul as well.

FIVE

Rouse the Soul

You will see the ornaments twinkling like heavenly stars.
You will be the spectrum, bending like a rainbow
through a perfect prism of crystallized light.

What is Enlightenment?

If you are enlightened, it means you have received an unparalleled awakening resulting from being in a realized state of oneness with The Divine. This state is distinguished by receiving an irrefutable, direct Gnosis of the supreme force of The One Source, leaving the revelation of unity forever embedded in your consciousness. Within this *state of recognition*, your soul remembers its Self as being fused with The Divine, your essential nature is revealed, and the processes of *perfection and crystallization of the Self* are initiated. Enlightenment transpires when the Soul *ascends*, creating terms for The Eternal Light of Spirit to descend and meet the Self.

Not an "experience," enlightenment is the attainment of a profound *state of consciousness* due to being in *conscious union* with The Absolute. It is as if the Soul's memory of God is reinstated after having been subject to its own amnesia for eons. Your former conception of having been distant from God is dissolved and later replaced by a perception of permanent mutual *inseparability*, one in which the Self remains *indistinguishable* from Supreme Consciousness. You realize that your Soul has housed The Light of Spirit all along.

This "real-ization" of non-differentiation galvanizes forces that transform your mind and transfigure your body at the cellular level, creating inner spiritual dimension. As a result, *the Self is seated in faith*, and this action alone instills *knowing*, removing all prior disbelief in The Infinite omnipresence.

The hallmarks of the state of enlightenment include the suspension and sacrifice of human will, a temporary lapse of thought and personal identity, cessation of the operation of the five senses, a perception of being in Cardinal union, and, for the "charismatic" type mystic, an actualization of divine love that consummates within the mystical heart chamber. Enlightenment, by its perfect design, begins to further disassemble your former base mind structure by dissolving that which limits access to the Self's higher consciousness while initiating the refinement of ego impulses.

Often, miraculous powers are bestowed and miracles of spontaneous healing accompany enlightenment, most especially those diseases and illnesses that have been contributed to and maintained by the unawakened mind. When spontaneous healing occurs, it is because enlightenment spurs a wave of perfection within the soul that ripples through the physical body, as if flaws of mineralization were being extracted from the core of a precious jewel, making it newly priceless.

Enlightenment draws an impregnable line in the sand of the mystic's life, dividing it into *before and after.* As testament to its life-altering power, no matter how much time passes, the shiny one will never forget the terms of his ultimate illumined state. His account of it remains durable, having been indelibly etched within his soul as the preeminent event of his life.

Although there are many different paths to realize Supreme Consciousness, mystics from different traditions most typically explain their most powerful moments of awakening in two primary ways. The first describes the state of realization as being *a communion with The Creator from the foundation of divine love.* To the love-filled mystic, God chooses the aspirant, who is realized as God reveals Itself within his heart and mind. This seeker's language reflects bliss, ecstasy, adoration and rapture, expressing a bond that is unmatched in intimacy. He might feel directly linked with God, a Supreme Being, or Spirit. He speaks of mutual recognition akin to a long-awaited reunion along with a sense *of being seized by and delivered into The Numinous*, in whose Presence his own divinity is recognized.

The second way of describing enlightenment illustrates a less intimate but equally powerful *realization of All That Is,* the unification with the sum of existence or nature that results in Self-realization. (Still others describe a state associated with depersonalization.) These mystics report their Gnosis of a vast and empty expansiveness. The word "empty" here suggests an ultimate state of receptivity, a non-dual state of consciousness temporarily devoid of separation and egoic sense of mind. When asked to describe this state, is it any wonder there are few words to describe "nothingness"? The Buddha reached this superior state, which he said led to his liberation from suffering.

Some mystics attribute degrees of enlightenment to having experienced the Void, its state associated with having traveled through something akin to a suction-like cosmic wormhole. Some describe entering into an Abyss, while still others recount being apprehended by a blinding blackness, wherein the initiate's objective impression is blanked, erased *and made nothing but Spirit itself* by being absorbed into the divine, primordial un-manifest light.

Regardless of the mystic's subjective description of his personal vs. non-personal vs. de-personal initiation, this exalted state becomes forever engraved in his spirit, shifting like a landslide the former proportions of his mind, heart and purpose.

In the Bhagavad Gita, "personal" realization is related to *the path of devotion to God* in which multiple forms of devotion are the means of unity, and the state is *distinguished by the awakening of divine love and bliss within the mystical heart.* "Non-personal" states of transcendence relate to *the path of knowledge and the perception of the truth of God,* where no substantial intimate heart connection by way of divine love is realized. (This is not to say that devotion does not play a part in this path.) Non-personal mystical states lead to achieving a state of poise of the Self, and some are associated with the Void and the Abyss.

I have experienced both personal and non-personal states of realization. My initial enlightenment to divine love by way of the mystical heart, however, was anything but an empty nothing. Enlightenment provides a state of being in which you are made receptive to *everything* Divine, and then you become this divinity.

In bliss-engaged enlightenment, if there is an explanation for "nothingness," then it means that the extreme state of receptivity creates a dramatic *inversion* akin to an evacuation of the vessel of individualized consciousness. A thoroughly empty vessel may then be wholly replenished with "purity," for only such a vessel which is truly inverted and made *so empty of everything that makes it impure* may be equally righted—converted and equivalently filled with pristine blankness. Once so blanked, your entirety then funnels the eternal reservoir of perfect love and bliss into itself, leaving behind a memory of fulfillment you will always treasure and never wish to forget.

If I were to scale my states, I would only wish to convey my sincerest prayer that you encounter the incomparable blessing of awakening to the intimacy of divine love, that you overcome the fear of being exposed to the very force that would open your heart to your deepest potential. Being privy to the breadth of divine love, I know that once it is roused within the mystical heart, it will intonate The Beloved's voice, help you hear its divine utterance and make you feel so deeply cherished. The Soul will then articulate Spirit's boundless inflection so that love is amplified to everyone.

Void and Abyss

Although the following concepts are quite advanced and complex, it helps you to have a basic understanding of the mystical underpinnings of Void and Abyss. These states are considered non-personal in nature. You may think they sound terribly abstract; however, to the mystic these states are very real. If you are serious about the path, they are important passages to be aware of.

The Void

My states due to the Void allowed me to attain previously unmatched realizations and understanding. Initially, when you are drawn to enter the Void you feel a massive acceleration similar to being magnetized by a Herculean gravitational force that causes a sense of being sucked by a turbulent vacuum. This perception is accompanied by the sense of being hurtled through space at supersonic speed through a lightless tunnel, as if you were traveling through a black hole in space.

In the Void, the Self is intercepted by a tremendous compressive force. Your mind's objective faculty is then interrupted and thwarted, so that everything you suppose the universe holds is disengaged and discarded, so that anything dependent upon your objectification drops into a well of *non-association*. Here, *Spirit intentionally strips the soul of its will and its prior realizations,* completely withdraws the Self's associative state and temporarily negates its natural tendency to relate its being to the viewed world of experience. The sole factor that remains intact is *the will and energy of God,* wildly circulating within the core of the Self.

By first severing the link, by removing everything upon which the Self assumes it depends, by temporarily uncoupling the soul's inner and outer associations, the Self is forced to see itself as *being a ratio of motion.* Thus, in order to gain the requisite locomotion to break through seals and shatter former identifications, the soul must be subjected to a forceful and violent *quickening.* The Void perhaps distributes a *new state of relativity within the Self, symmetrically apportioning it to a far greater Force.*

Even unitive states will briefly reverse and drop away to create a dramatic split from everything the mind believes. Through a blackened Void the soul plummets past its associative mind state to be shown its omnipotent state, one infused with human will to not only *manifest and create*, but also bravely descend to *withdraw itself*. Finally equipped with acumen, the Self can willingly descend into a state of Void to recognize its self-contained, pure I-Self.

Once such recognition is formalized, then from out of the Void the Self valiantly ascends to be led back to wholeness and so that its inseparability as Soul/Spirit is reconfirmed and firmly established; afterward the Self will live its knowledge of having been made equalized in a state of non-differentiation.

From my perspective, the Void is not an experience, but rather *it is a state of transition and exchange.* The Void serves three purposes:

1. To further purify the ego.

2. To strip and shed *personal consciousness* so that it may be reinstated with *higher consciousness which in turn bestows eventual knowledge.*

3. To serve as *a portal* through which the Free Will of The Divine intervenes to *re-distribute and refine the Self.*

The Abyss

Still further into my process, I encountered the Abyss (to the uninitiated, a perplexing and mysterious indoctrination into the realms of the unmanifest), and due to my ignorance and fear, I failed many times before I finally understood its intricacies enough to transit the passage. When I did, I allowed its authority to alter and instruct me.

Not such a *forceful* vacuum state, the initiation begins with a palpable perception of motion similar to a cool, fluid stream of airy energy powerfully flowing out of your crown. At first, you think you might faint if you let go and merge into that stream.

Initially it's scary and weird. You think you should resist the process because it's clear that your sense of control is being greatly threatened. You might want to shut down the process. However, if you are destined to awaken, *the Abyss will continue to present itself in the future several more times*, and it becomes obvious that you could be brave and jump into the stream. Instinctively, you know you must simply surrender and join the flow of energy.

You must be *all in*. And once you are all in, once you decide to fall, within moments you are rushed into *blankness*. Upon the fall, you don't know where it will lead or what could possibly happen next. Just merge with the flow and it will take you into nothingness, into a *clearing*; it is as if a black hole in space had collapsed upon itself, leaving behind a *blank hole*, an endless portal, *a white space devoid of matter*, into which you are magnetically drawn, pulled into a bardo, *a conscious state of formlessness* wherein you may feel as if you are being suspended between life and death.

In this state, you must gain the presence of mind to understand that you won't get stuck there, but rather realize that *your consciousness is being exposed to formlessness; it is being arrayed to know and accommodate its boundless and limitless spaciousness.*

In a way, this initial passage is a test, and once the state completes itself, you will be drawn back from the bardo to ordinary consciousness. Most importantly, once this bardo has been formed within your consciousness, once you have passed through its threshold, then later in time you will be afforded the chance to exercise your will and master quantum leaps in personal consciousness to actively join with the enlivened stream of energized divine consciousness coursing through your nadi system.

The living stream that leads to the Abyss gives a palpable realization that Tantric energy—enlivened kundalini—is indeed engaged and flowing within you. Keep in mind that *there are higher realizations beyond the Abyss to be had in other dimensions, so that one by one bardos can emerge as the soul is being refined.* One can see how a spiritual teacher or guru would be helpful to instruct how to navigate such states.

Some mystics ascribe their encounters with the Abyss to tumbling into the Void chasm of the heart. Since the chance to penetrate this chasm is offered a number of times, it is considered to be part and parcel to particular degrees of awakening and perfection.

After the Abyss presents itself, two prime choices to act are made obvious to the progressing soul—to make a courageous, masterful *leap of faith* across its expanse or to free fall within it. *Within the leap, you actually exercise will. Within the fall, you surrender to the Unknown.*

When the Abyss initially presents itself, *the personality* is confronted with its emotional barricades, personal fears and doubts, and things the heart must resolve. Later, it becomes clear that the initial blank state of Abyss leads to the opportunity that your *awakened mind* be trained to master inner states and meet subsequent bardos.

Repeated ventures into the Abyss exposes your consciousness to exceptional inner conditions that make you finally get that *the entire created world is manifested by The Un-Manifest. That space is created by Formlessness. That time proceeds from The Timeless.*

Void and Abyss serve to seal one's realization of the purpose of the coin and its two sides—the chance to see that *particles and waves are opposites posed by the unitive sphere of consciousness. That both emergence and manifestation of motion are relative to their withdrawal. That The Un-Manifest is the source of unification from which one's immortal life proceeds from the spectrum of death.*

Until you understand that these processes intend to broaden you, it is only reasonable that you would be worried about their effects and consequences. However, in order to evolve, you must learn to disavow doubt and trust yourself enough to submit to the terms of these spiritual forces. For all intents, it means you must learn to *willingly separate from your body.* If you cannot rouse enough nerve to take the risky leap to submit to such critical conditions, you will thwart your chances to evolve.

Before you grow confident enough to trust these higher dimensional states, expect to feel a natural aversion to entering into them. You may even experience a genuine panic and be terrified of that prospect because the base mind will tell you that you are in grave danger, that you'll never get out alive should you find yourself in such unsafe conditions, because rather than the unawakened mind recognizing Void and Abyss to be *inner dimensions*, it convinces you that circumstances are originating from an outside, unfamiliar source. In part, this symptom arises because Void and Abyss seek to *confront the Self* by urging it through unidentifiable wormholes or submerging it into foreign, dark territory with no guarantee of return. In a way, your impulse is correct, because when you reemerge from Void and Abyss you are not entirely the same, for you will have gained passage through the portals of your own inner dimensions.

To surrender in the face of the unknown is a tremendous accomplishment of courage and faith because humans and all creatures are innately ingrained with a mechanism that enforces a primal instinct for bodily survival, that, in no unclear terms, instructs one to stay alive no matter what, to avoid anything that might cause the body's demise. But it is only out of lack of knowledge of these states that you would mistakenly reject Void and Abyss. Equipped with this key of understanding, you will come to trust that these states do not intend to kill your body, but instead greatly transform your consciousness and offer you the chance to gain amazing realizations and spiritual acumen.

Both Void and Abyss feel imbued with particular intentions—to sublimate personal will and former ego consciousness, to sever ties of distinction between the personal I-Self and Thou, and to *expose the underpinnings of the energetic operations of consciousness*. Both Void and Abyss signal a kind of expansion of inner dimension, *an unbinding and re-coupling of consciousness*, as if deep space and dark matter were being precisely placed within and around the substance that reforms and re-informs your own particle wave consciousness.

Due to the intense quality of energy the soul encounters while transiting the Void and Abyss, a greater capacity is enabled within the Self that creates options to further shed hindrances, pursue fuller realization and self-manage energetic processes. Both internal conditions serve as grand initiations into super-conscious dimensions of the All-Pervading consciousness, helping to refresh the ground of personal consciousness and reboot it to new system of mastery.

Enlightenment is Ascension

In the mystical traditions of Buddhism the Buddha is said to have handed down, there are *degrees* of enlightenment and particular stages of perfection, meaning that in this tradition every enlightenment state is not necessarily seen as being equal. Buddhist mystics expound the virtues of "supreme enlightenment" as being the superior illumination, an initiation into spiritual Reality that results in attaining buddhahood and ultimate union with All That Is. Therefore, supreme enlightenment, the highest degree reached by the Buddha and the Buddhist Master, is regarded as most rare, one that Buddhist sages say may have taken one thousand or even a million lifetimes to attain. Based on this belief, it is not out of the question that a mystic would attain more than one degree of enlightenment, each positioned at a different angle than the next. It is certainly possible then that if you do not reach supreme enlightenment in this lifetime, you may reach other significant levels of attainment.

Enlightenment is not an end point, but rather it is *a commencement, an initiation,* one that finalizes and dissolves a way of life and launches a wholly different kind of existence. One is thus *reborn anew and resurrected into the life of the Soul.*

Enlightenment is ascension. "To ascend" means you are engaged in the process of gaining elevation. But one does not truly ascend unless a transpersonal descent is first made that creates the death of your limited mind, one that serves to deconstruct previous ego states along with hindrances that would prevent your climb. Such descents include Void, Abyss and the dark night of the spirit. Former mindsets perish along with ego desires that create suffering and false or less meaningful ways of life. "To transcend" means you are raised beyond one level to reach another; thus, as you transcend normal reality, you ascend beyond the mundane world and its impediments.

Rather than being a standalone event, enlightenment *initiates and sets up an interconnected series of spiritual processes.* The state itself produces immediate effects, but also sets into motion *additional processes that are intended to develop, emerge and play out over periods of time in the future*—suggesting that consciousness evolution is encapsulated in measured levels, degrees and phases. Because of this function, by the time you become enlightened you will have likely worked for years and many lifetimes to lay the groundwork to make it possible. Although many processes unfold on their own, advanced states must be fostered so that greater realizations can be made possible in the years that follow.

During enlightenment, you might say the moon of the soul eclipses the Sun of God, passing unimpeded before the blazing face of The Divine. By virtue of being so near to the Sun's expression, the moon is saturated with the Sun's glorious gaze. During this transit, the earth of your mind-obsessed self, the one limited by sense, dissolves in the moon's shadow. With the obstacle of the mind temporarily darkened and eradicated, the light of the soul is directly observed by God, meaning nothing earthly obscures a vision of the Self. Thus, you must bring your Moon self in the closest proximity to the Sun. Could this lifetime be the one you have been waiting eons to live so that your soul is similarly witnessed by the light of The Divine?

Enlightenment is a revolutionary awakening. The state is so monumental, if you are not left immensely impacted, then you may have experienced a lesser awakening rather than enlightenment itself. Although awakening reveals aspects of Reality that have heretofore been hidden, enlightenment is meant to change you from a sleeping person to a Soul who is awakened to his universal essence, one who has gained *conscious* union with The Divine, meaning *you will know you have achieved unity.* One symptom of having achieved unity is that enlightenment instates irreversible, unwaning compassion within the heart.

Significant awakenings produce interior effects that will either stimulate a spiritual process or echo its effects. Awakenings don't guarantee you enlightenment, but they often precede it. You may experience many awakenings that, over time, pave the road to possible enlightenment. Therefore, as you employ means to awaken, you take the first steps toward enlightenment.

Although enlightenment is regarded as a pinnacle awakening, lesser rudimentary awakenings can trigger inner spiritual processes and transcendent states. These awakenings produce ramifications and signs in the form of visions, dreams, revelations, voices, sounds, vibrations and other physical and mental effects. Awakenings can also be empty of any of these phenomena.

∞

What is Kundalini?

Kundalini is a force that is said to lay dormant beneath the base of the spine until it is infused with consciousness and energized. Also called *serpent energy*, in Sanskrit the word is associated with being "coiled, like a snake." Kundalini is a form of *Shakti.* Vitalized Shakti is your *animated* feminine spiritual energy *and its active, dynamic principle*. Thus, the White Light of Infinity is the white liquid fire of the awakened, empowered kundalini—Tantric consciousness which has been set ablaze.

Kundalini awakening is a tremendously complex process. In one essence, *feminine consciousness* is being internally facilitated to fuse with *the masculine, unifying them to work in concert*, thus resolving duality and allowing for the subsequent descent and re-ascent of energized consciousness.

The first stage of kundalini awakening can be considered a *gross awakening* because it is powerfully *sensed.* Once the *gross* is experienced you can progress to perceive and work with *subtle* energy, called Tantric energy (energized consciousness). *Therefore, the gross is typically sensed, and the subtle is perceived.* Without the gross having first been animated, you cannot perceive Tantric energy.

Several months prior to enlightenment, I experienced kundalini awakening during a bija (seed syllable) mantra session of the seven chakras. It began with heat building in my base chakra in the lower spine. Soon, that area grew extremely hot and a kind of detonation occurred within it which sparked a burning sensation. The burn intensified and then set off a cascade of explosive electric-like shocks that jumped up my spine through each chakra, one after another, reaching my heart and then shooting up to the top of my head. Prior to each chakra being lit, the heat in the one below it grew to a searing burn before the next one ignited and began to accumulate heat. Soon, my entire spine was conducting an uncomfortable, needle-like prickling spiritual fire whose intensity peaked and remained alive for a number of minutes.

Finally, the burning sensation resolved to a gentler temperature before eventually fading to tingles.

Significant spiritual advancement may not take place without the chakras having first gone through a similarly powerful purification, which can be gained through the practices of Kundalini Yoga. As kundalini transfigures the physical and psychic bodies, its transforming effects range from being quite dramatic to more subdued, often resulting in perceptions of light and sound that leave the senses and inner awareness expanded.

Although this book focuses much attention on the enlightenment of your mind and mystical heart, *just as important is the preparation, purification and enlightenment of the body* that kundalini awakening accomplishes. Thus, proper awakening of Shakti/Kundalini serves each one of these functions and helps to transfigure the body's physical and subtle gateways to begin to conduct spiritualized consciousness.

Here is how you may experience the process of kundalini:

↦ As energy sensations felt in the body that include spasms, contractions, prickling, crawling or creeping, jumping, throbbing, shaking, tremors, swaying, pressure, tingles, paralysis, numbness, rigidity, jerks, heat, cold, electrical sparks, or chills.

If the fire element is dominant in you, for example, it will feel as if heated serpent energy is bursting through blockages to travel up or parallel to the spine and to the top of the head and beyond the crown.

↦ As energy perceived as fine frequencies of vibration or inner visions of light in the heart; as energy similar to a cool breeze, tingling, or a flowing sensation felt in the spine, heart, crown of the head and palms; as weightlessness or a feeling of lightness, buoyancy or floating.

↦ As emotional registers in the form of ecstasy, bliss, tranquility, compassion, giddiness, euphoria, calmness, or tenderness. You may be magnetized toward the spiritual and feel a sincere longing for cosmic Truth.

↜ As a rush of movement, perceived as energy traveling upward and then out through the top of your skull; as tingling energy that is centered in the sixth chakra (called in Sanskrit the *Ajna, Agnya,* or *brow chakra*) located in the third eye set a bit north between the eyebrows and behind the brow bone, and/or in the *Soma* chakra just above the third eye chakra.

↜ As energy perceived as being centered in the heart or to your lower right of it.

↜ As a nectar-like sweet taste in the back of the throat or tongue.

SIX

The Divine Process of Enlightenment

You are created with Love and by Love,
and by its immortal cause you are brought back to life.
You are roused from sleep in order to Love,
to be loved and to become Love, forever and ever.

The mystic may search his mind for words to describe enlightenment, but he cannot fully explain it. Attempts to report the state present a sore compromise, so he resorts to words like "incomprehensible" and "ineffable" because its totality is not relatable. Additionally, its revelatory substance is difficult to encapsulate. Even the mystic himself may not realize the stunning implications of the state until later in time.

Historically, descriptions of enlightenment have been brought to light through the language of the mystic's spiritual tradition, and its process is colored by his knowledge, degree of awakening and scale of perceptive faculty. I will attempt to translate my state of enlightenment by way of divine love to you, framing it with my current (2015) comprehension of some of the mystical underpinnings of the process.

It is assumed that the state is whole unto itself, that there are no phases or steps to its process. Another conclusion is that the state initiates a continuum, that each part of the process weaves throughout the other, so that there is simply a beginning and an end—a before and after.

Although it appears from my description that there are steps to the process, I have broken it down this way only to introduce its *mystical parameters* from my point of view. Although it looks like one phase neatly follows the next, this is not necessarily the case.

Keep in mind that the description itself is not as narrow or all-inclusive as it appears, meaning additional implications are also present, but I have selected out particularly powerful aspects.

The mystical stages themselves are described *in italics.* Following the italic description, I offer keys that relate my understanding of *mystical implications, seeds, effects and ramifications.* Keep aware that the keys of knowledge I share when describing the *active state of unity* do *not* imply that my thoughts were engaged during the state of *union.*

It has been said that at some point in time, every mystic will contradict some of his earlier understandings, because as his perception elevates and he receives further Gnosis, he will be led to even greater insight. Since I have waited over twenty years to discuss my understanding of the underpinnings of this state, my hope is that I do not overly contradict myself in the future.

Mystical Elements of Enlightenment (by way of awakening the mystical heart)

Become still, invite divine love into your heart, and imagine that enlightenment is taking place as you read the following passages.

Immediacy: *You receive the calling of Spirit and you sense its immediacy. The veils are unraveling. An aspect of Reality is revealed to you as God announces Itself through the agency of Spirit.*

By briefly linking the material to the non-material, Spirit descends and makes its approach, causing an action and facet of Reality to be exquisitely apparent. You consciously sense the presence and affiliation of The Numinous. You do not anticipate Spirit's spontaneous and unexpected arrival, and presently you do not understand its enormity.

The veils of the mind disintegrate as Spirit dissolves the material in order to bind with the non-material Soul. The rock-hard foundation of your inner conditioning crumbles. Everything in your mind and heart that stands in the way of Truth is suddenly destroyed, annihilated.

Surrender: *You find yourself in renunciation, relinquishing your will to answer to Spirit's call. You do not resist but obey.*
You do not succumb to fear. You do not run away, refuse or ignore the approach of The Beloved. You accept the call. You let go of the present moment. You acquiesce to the mystery of the unknown. You sacrifice control and surrender personal will to submit to the will of The Divine.

Engagement and Union: *You are met and engaged by a limitless force. You are apprehended, seized by The Beloved. You are recognized. You become aware that you are being immersed in the vast, omniscient, Supreme Consciousness. You perceive an immeasurable power accompanied by the astounding quality of love. You have been returned to God, brought into a state of non-differentiation. The Soul is reunited with the Source of its light.*
The Self is seen and actuated as The Divine realizes the image of itself being reflected in your Soul. While you are fused with The Beloved, you do not exist as separate from it, for your ability to objectively differentiate between yourself and The Beloved has been withdrawn.
You do not become God, for God cannot be so contained. The Beloved does not merge into you, for the spiritual light radiates rather than envelops. If anything, you are ushered into this state and are fully absorbed into God. You and Reality have been made undivided, inseparable.

Love: *You are filled to overflowing with the fluid solution of Amrita, the fervent elixir of love. Spirit is delivering mercy. You are being loved while at the same time becoming love itself; you are the love and the love is you. The soul is treated and* *consecrated. You are being ordained. You are in an exalted state of grace.*

Your heart is becoming tempered as a perfect vessel because it is being immersed in the tincture of love—the mystic soma. The spirit of compassion is being vested within you. As decreed by The Supreme command and authority and in accordance with spiritual law, you are being initiated into a sacred and divine order, into a destiny set forth by the sovereign will of The Beloved. You are being invested and established anew with holy functions.

Suspension: *Once the immersion gains momentum, you can do nothing, for you have no volition, no control whatsoever. Because your being is surrendered into The Supreme Force, the will of The Beloved supersedes your personal will. There is no fear, no sense of threat or worry. There is only love.*

When you are apprehended by The Beloved, you are literally paralyzed with love, rendered incapable of thinking, reasoning, or sensing in the normal ways because those functions are temporarily suspended. As the state fully engages, your own free will and volition is automatically made nonfunctional, for your will has been sublimated by The Beloved. Even if you wished to remove yourself from this condition, you cannot, for the Greater Will is now in control.

You are being held by the force of The Beloved. That which is suspended is being sustained and balanced on the scale of above and below, within and without, and your consciousness is being positioned on the crux within the zero point of Infinity, coming to rest between being (presence) and action before encapsulating both.

Emptiness and Receptivity: *While you are suspended and in union, you cannot think or reason. With no personal will, you cannot initiate or process ideas. You cannot see, taste, touch,* *hear or smell, meaning you do not receive sensory impulses from your body or the material world. You see, at this point there is no separate "you" who can observe or react to anything because there is no material world to regard or sense. The objective world temporarily dissolves and disappears, and since it is non-existent, you have no sense of it.*

A kind of blackness or white-out prevails, for with no material world to observe, there is no *thing* to see, taste, touch, feel, smell, or think about.

The material world and even your body become temporarily "nonexistent," for the material world and all it holds has been withdrawn and dematerialized. At this point, with no material world to sense, you have no body. With no body, there is no brain to initiate thought. With no brain, there is no sensory information to receive and process.

A grand operation negates your sense of a corporeal, individual self. The way you encounter ordinary reality has been inverted, brought to stasis. You are ushered into in a state of emptiness, a kind of ultimate purification. Thus, due to the activity of purgation, you are *being emptied*, and once empty, the vessel of your consciousness enters into an open state of pure receptivity. Only a receptive vessel may be so thoroughly filled, meaning emptiness is associated with openness.

The knots in the side channels of the Sushumna (the central subtle energy channel) have been undone, and a rush of light-infused consciousness fills the central channel.

Collapse of Time and Space: *Becoming one with The Infinite, you experience sheer spaciousness of being and you enter into timeless, immortal eternity.*

The mind's framework of time and space dissolves to make way for expansion. Instead of being confined to third dimension structures, you are temporarily liberated from them. Since eternity is timeless and infinity is limitless, you experience boundlessness —your original nature.

Because you have been emptied of cognition, there is no clock time to assess, so time itself evaporates. Hence, there is no present moment upon which to focus. There is no corresponding space structured around form by which you or the material is defined or contained. You have been released from strictly identifying with the confines of physical form. Thus, enlightenment expands the mind past its imagined finite terms, allowing the Soul to encounter its timeless, infinite being-ness.

Gnosis: *You realize you are being engaged by the Force of The Beloved by which you achieve Gnosis of The One Source and the Self. You consciously attain "knowing" that love is being imparted by none other than Spirit/God/The Beloved Divine.*

A higher intelligence supersedes yours, and the grace of Gnosis is delivered to you intact and complete. Thus, Gnosis is a mystical understanding, one in which knowing is being transmitted and received without any requirement that you process word, thought, sight, sound, or sensation.

Since you are empty of personal will, you are unable to exercise volition. With no personal thoughts to ponder, there are no mental images or messages to decipher. There is nothing for you to examine, nothing to scrutinize, fathom, or query. There is no concrete data or abstract idea to ponder or decide upon, so you neither determine nor consider anything.

With no ears to use, you will listen to and hear nothing. Thus, in the midst of pristine silence, Gnosis flows unimpeded directly into your conscious awareness, dissolving all traces of your former ambivalence and skepticism in God and revealing knowing and its result—faith. It is through the action of knowing that *the knower,* or the *Gnostic*, emerges.

The Dawning of Awareness: *Having been freed of the obscuration of the mind's clouds, the immaculate, skyless sky dawns, and the luminous nature of subtle mind reflects clear transparency upon itself. Out of emptiness an acute awareness dawns that your consciousness, your non-material essence, is enjoined with God and stands in equipoise with All That Is. While becoming more conscious still, you perceive yourself as a being of "spirit." The threshold from body into spirit has been formally formed and crossed.*

Will is still reversed, having been inverted while it was sublimated by the Higher Will. The soul is being driven inward by a force of extreme introversion. Within this state, your awareness is being greatly increased and intensified as it is being directed to the spiritual Self.

As the external dimension of matter shrinks, the inner immaterial dimension dramatically expands. As the objectified mind dissolves, the immaterial looms. With objectivity having been fully withdrawn, your undivided attention is drawn toward All That Is, left standing in an immaculate field like a sole, central pillar.

It is due to the state of hollowness that you can be replenished, filled with The Beloved's light. Thus, consciousness is being synthesized to increase an internal condition, that of harmony and symmetry—equalization—as The Beloved weighs, measures and metes the Self's lightness of "being" with the complementing force of "becoming."

Emergence of Realization: *Out of Gnosis revelations emerge, and you realize the following Truths: You are fused with The Supreme Source. The foundation of your union is divine love. You are being loved by The Supreme Source. The Supreme Source is making you into love. You are becoming love itself. The Supreme is the source of this love. You are a being of consciousness. The Supreme Source's power is limitless.*

The Truth is shown as direct perceptions arise in the form of realizations (revelations) that circumvent the senses and thinking mind. Truths are not restricted to the above list, for the mystic may receive many more. Revelations are not limited to this one window of time, but they often emerge before separation.

Transfiguration: *You are being transfigured, literally rewired to be newly equipped for transcendent states of being. The mystical heart chamber is unlocked and is being purified by spiritual fire. The knots of the heart channels are being untied; the pulsing current of bliss is released, flooding every ounce of your being with the chemistry of love.*

Essences meet in the mystical heart chamber, triggering a release of the mixture of love. The chakras and nadis in the subtle body are treated and activated by the mixture, cultivating their petals and vines, charging and enabling them to accommodate currents of spiritual consciousness that are distributed to your mind/body/spirit.

You are being adapted to respond to energy and spiritualized consciousness so that your body may produce, receive and release single and combination neurotransmitters and neuromodulators, chemicals, enzymes, peptides, hormones and other biochemical items necessary for particular states of consciousness. A profound shift, the transmuting effects of transfiguration continues long after enlightenment, especially if you work to deepen your realization.

Resurrection: *You have been appropriated by the insurmountable power and authority of The Beloved. You are led out of the wilderness and are delivered into the Supreme Totality. The Soul is being awakened and enlivened, resurrected, redeemed and recalled. The Soul is being converted, reinstated to its original state and returned to its Source. The Divine realizes the image of itself reflected in your Soul.*

The Self which was formerly devitalized, made unconscious and put to sleep is resuscitated, brought back to life, saved, refreshed, empowered and regenerated into an expanded and heightened level of existence. The Soul is brought back to its inception and is restored to its pristine original state.

Inner Illumination: *The state of love endures as you continue to revel in ecstasy that has no Earthly comparison. You become conscious of being the medium for receiving love's radiating force. At the same time, you are conscious of being the activity of love, thereby radiating its shimmering effects and means. The Soul is naked, transparent—there is no covering concealing the Self from its brightness, no veil preventing the Self from seeing and savoring the knowledge of its true nature and foundation. You know who you are—you recognize your Self. As Gnosis births the knower, you are made conscious that you are conscious; you remember that you remember. You birth the Witness.*

You feel The Beloved present and active within your Soul. The force of Spirit charges you in its vital current as you relish in its almighty power. Astoundingly intense, the quality of love is marked by its incomparability, but in this state you do not mentally compare ordinary human love to divine love.

As you revel in ecstasy and the blessing it conveys, you simply know divine love in its immaculate form; thus, you perceive its unparalleled substance (for you are its Witness), and you receive its active force into your being (for you are its activity and the action is you). The action of love infuses your being with its unconditioned qualities (for you are a fusion of both "object" and "subject").

Emergence of Discernment: *Illumination continues as you discern that you are being extremely affected by the electrifying force of love. You perceive that love infiltrates you on the* *physical, emotional and subtle consciousness level. You now know The Real.*

With such discernment, your senses restart and become operational, and the ability to perceive energized consciousness has been integrated within them.

With The Divine essence deeply resonating within the Soul's subtle body framework, you consciously know that love's substance and action has penetrated every last recess of your physical being. Your mind gains a conceptual realization that you are being altered by The Beloved's stupendous force.

Separation: *As thoughts trickle through your mind, discernment swiftly steers into "separation" so your ability to reason is reactivated. As the intensity of love gradually diminishes, oneness is being withdrawn by degrees. You witness that in your present state you are part active energy, part awareness, part material substance. You acknowledge the company and movement of The Divine within you, for you are now a being of energized consciousness—one of presence and its exhilarating activity. Love revolves back to the heart chamber, returning to its inception point. Over time, Spirit finally disengages from the foundation of the heart to ascend back to its Cause, leaving the heart trembling in the echo of Spirit's retreat. The veils, though thinner, are being closed back down to calibrated degrees. Your eyes are forever opened.*

The grace of union is concluding, and the tidal wave of divine love that drenched the heart is being reabsorbed to its Source as it ebbs to its oceanic horizon. You are crossing back through the threshold of Infinity to be seated more firmly into the matter of your body and the material world, only now the Force of your Soul has been set into motion.

The state of transcendence is dissipating. The dimensions of time and space are reforming and reemerging, so the Soul is no longer in an extreme state of union. Since you can form thoughts and use them to reason, your will is being restored. With your senses filtering perceptions, they can now receive and transmit impulses from the subtle energy system.

Since you can sense love energetically coursing within your physical body, your consciousness now exists as being *relative to* The Divine's, rather than one with it. As you become conscious of the Self's approximation to its Cause rather than being in a state of union with it, you become aware of object and subject, so that the highest grace instantaneously passes into a state of lesser grace—that of discrimination—for union and separation cannot and do not coexist.

The state of unity causes a cessation of rational thought; therefore, when you can sense thought or logic arising in your perceptions, then separation is underway. As separation concludes, you gradually return to normal waking consciousness.

The Evolving Process

Rather than reducing the state of enlightenment to a one-time, self-limiting event, *Spirit continues to dispense and intensify its power within your internal condition for years to come* to make deep Self-recognition and crystallization possible. Yes, when you reach enlightenment a certain level of realization is attained, but it is in the time period *following the advent of illumination* that the Self may be *crystallized* to know itself as a divine encapsulation of the light, meaning you will be afforded the opportunity to become perfected, to become *fully* or *supremely recognized.*

Elements of subsequent evolution:
Rebirth: *As you emerge from the state of grace and reenter waking consciousness, you remain irrevocably reformed. Because of Gnosis you acknowledge The Supreme's astounding power, to which you owe your deepest reverence and awe. You have seen Ultimate Reality with opened eyes. You have been blessed. The*

Clear Light has dawned—revealing the innermost subtle mind that is the source of consciousness itself.

As the hours and days pass, it is obvious that your former way of being is ending, initiating a new path within you. You know you have been reborn, having been changed back to your original nature.

Since for a time period after enlightenment your consciousness is still quite expanded beyond ordinary space/time, the visual representation of the material world appears drastically different. The veils have not been fully resealed, and they remain open to varying degrees, closing and parting according to your inner state of consciousness or waking state. With the passage of time, your mind and entire sensory system starts to reconcile, balancing the material against the spiritual, meaning you perceive Reality as being mixed with the corporeal world.

You are being converted from a sensing human to one who perceives its Self as a being of consciousness. The five senses have been integrated to function with your mind, emotions and intuition, and you are able to perceive the material world in heightened, extraordinary ways. Your sensory system's capacity to manage energy increases as it refines and adapts to spiritual Reality. Although via enlightenment some spiritual processes have been switched on, in time many more activations will follow.

Due to the transitions listed above, you will be in the most vulnerable state of mind immediately after enlightenment. It is easy for you to slip into transcendent states and experience visions and auditions, making it difficult (if not impossible) to function normally, for until reconciliation occurs, trying to force your expanded mind to squeeze back to the narrow material world may prove fruitless. (If you are an artist, poet, dancer, writer, musician or the like, then you will find creativity enhances this process.)

This is a transitory stage in which your mind submits to the spiritual and it lasts from weeks to many months or more before it naturally begins to temper. It is now that a sanctuary is useful to keep you safe and to facilitate your expansion, so you can see why gurus and enlightened teachers are often needed during this stage, along with a serene atmosphere, such as those found in nature, ashrams, spiritual retreat centers and monasteries.

You intuitively know things, for the sixth sense of intuition is enabled, and additional spiritual gifts begin to organically emerge. Your personality begins to be reframed, sometimes taking years for it to fully sync with its perfecting states.

Crystallization of the Heart-Point: *The force of Spirit, having been forever tucked as a promise within the membranes of the heart, draws the Soul back to itself within the magnetic, mystical chamber. Thus, the chalice of the heart is submerged in a cauldron of spiritual fire to be perfected into a thing of beauty— the ruby and diamond-embellished cup of the Holy Grail.*

For a time period after enlightenment, your will is superseded as Spirit draws you repeatedly back into the heart to multiply love and fuse your consciousness with The Beloved's. Spirit imposes an extreme sense of longing within your breast to keep your mind and heart focused on the splendid effects of love and its Cause. Thus, Spirit keeps you in close vicinity while it strengthens and seals your faith by turning a once viscous plane of love into a more solid foundation, as the now-sticky *mortar of tapped Rasa,* the fortifying resinous pitch of *mature Amrita,* binds the Soul to God.

In this stage, you are offered a chance to form and keep an imperishable bond with The Beloved by coming alive with love within the pulse of the heart, to relive love's power, to be loved again and again. Do not waste this chance to remember and perfect the Self, an impulse that spans within a specific window of time.

Following the original descent of Spirit, the Self becomes thoroughly compelled to climb upwards, to willfully reenact its own ascent, orbiting inwards to seek its highest vantage point as it transcends the material realm to return itself to God. This is the nature of *self-resurrection*—you may now employ the effects of Gnosis to co-create with Spirit, to climb the inner ladder where you surrender personal will to resubmit to God, the Void, the Abyss and various transcendent states.

True crystallization results in the Self's transparency and hence there is no obscuration of the light. In this stage, Self-recognition increases. In the years of practice it takes to navigate to the summit of its ascent, the Self seeks to become an *adept*, honing its climbing skills, overcoming its stumbling on the path to plant the flag at the mountain's peak. Internal power is to be actualized so that one's supreme inner recognition is won. Thus, the knower finds, "*I am one with the expansive cosmos, inseparable from The Eternal cosmic consciousness.*"

Just as wine takes the shape of its goblet, you crystallize to become a vessel that hold's Spirit's elixir so that the contour of your receptive form receives an equivalent consciousness of love and compassion.

True liberation, the victory of freedom, can at last be acquired, and the bejeweled grail cup can only be held by a Self whose inner dimensions have been polished to perfection. Only such a tremendous emancipation qualifies you as a knower of The Real. Only as a knower can you transmit the power of your enlightenment to help others approach their highest potential of Self-recognition.

Conversion: *As the Self is fully recognized, and, as the stage of perfection crystallizes the Soul, you are adorned with a garment of light from which the polished Shield of Protection manifests. The Divine Fire and the Light of Infinite Grace are yours. You see the inner and outer luminosities of pure subtle consciousness sparkling in all their glory. Your countenance shows that the* *wisdom of faith has transmuted you, and you live as never before —as unmistakable proof of one who is bearing The Light recovered from above. Having discerned The Real, you can distinguish it from the unreal, for discernment is born from knowing.*

In the months and years to come, Self-recognition ripens and converts your entire being. As you descend from the mountain peak, cradling in yours arms the Laws of God, your presence reflects a stunning maturity.

Because you have reached Reality, you have become a human torch, an *en*-lightened one, a wise luminary who is *in*-flamed with Supernal Light. As light shines forth from the point of the Self, beams project through the fabric of your garment—demonstrating that *the veils of Reality are literally being pierced.*

From within yourself you shall bring forth the light of God, and it shall be drawn to a pinpoint and spark the particle of the Self. You shall throw off waves of light as holy evidence of Self-recognition and hence the luminous ornaments are yours, forever and ever. Hence, *those who see-eth your radiance will see-eth The One that sent you back into the world.*

The towering obelisk of I-consciousness, the station of the ultimate Self, is fully formed, erected and concentrated within the central column; you have been in-stated as none other than the master of the Central Pillar.

The state of the Self has been permanently established as the pure I-consciousness of Reality, having gained Gnosis that the entire cosmos is contained within the Self's exalted state of being. When brought into this realization, the Self is made synonymous and identical with All That Is.

It is only by virtue of having attained pure I-consciousness that light may perpetually shine from your interior consciousness to be projected outward. As light emerges from its compressed point of nothingness—from the deepest recess of the Self—it flashes in splendor before it resolves to the void, only to spontaneously emerge and shine again and again. Hence, it is Self-consciousness of Reality that exhibits the trifold nature of the universal light, displayed in the ceaseless motion of *emergence, manifestation* and *withdrawal.*

The spontaneous appearance of light and color is the visible result of the activated bliss illumination of the Self. Colors and lights are signs that the oceanic nature of Spirit is one with your awareness.

Multiple luminosities in the form of "unconcealed and concealed lights" are generated along with their fields, and you see them interiorly in your mind's eye, exteriorly in broad daylight and in darkness with open eyes. Those deemed unconcealed include the white, effulgent light of enlightenment and the multicolored rainbow lights of the covenant. Also included are the clear, non-shining, non-glowing lights and the primordial, unhidden black lights, both of which appear before your open eyes.

Concealed inner lights are those expressions of light that arise within your mind's eye while your closed eyes are positioned or rolled, such as the golden light, the violet light, the indigo blue field generated by the third eye with an aperture emerging from its center point, and the sparkling star-like lights, along with a myriad of concealed phenomena that indicate inner states and processes. Since sound is considered a manifestation of light its frequencies are heard internally.

The Mystic's Perception

As you tune the dial of your heart to The Musician,
the music of the spheres plays through the lyre of your mind.
Listen closely. Advance your song to a sonorous rhythm,
an ascending arpeggio of notes that one day lifts you into Silence.

What is Perception?

Perception is an advanced faculty that enables you to sense and experience the manifested world in enhanced ways. When the Soul wakes up, the senses correspondingly awaken to dispense perceptive elements. For instance, due to perception, that which was previously unseen is now regarded as image and pattern, the unheard is detected as sound, and the unfelt is touched as texture, vibration and physical sensation. That which has not been tasted is sampled as flavor and that which has not been smelled is inhaled as aroma. In terms of intuition, that which was formerly hidden from your understanding is disclosed to the faculties of your mind.

From a subtle standpoint, perception allows your mind to receive impressions and revelations directly from the One Mind. Awakening redefines the former mind and reforms your consciousness to adapt to non-ordinary Reality. This process tempers you into an elegant vessel into which The Architect pours its molten Truth and makes refinements and adjustments to your material and energetic substance. The more perceptive you become, the more internal proof is produced that your consciousness is being progressively hammered and then polished to perfection.

When perception of the material world is engaged, your consciousness acts to filter and experience an *objectification of consciousness*, becoming the medium through which an object passes through your field of awareness. Advanced perception allows you to sense that the God Force itself is manifesting something to perceive. When you are enlightened, your perception allows you to go deeper and see *past the filters of objectification* so that consciousness is experienced in its pure, primordial essence.

The primary products of perception filter through the senses, *but perceptions are not always the direct or sole result of sensory organ stimulation. By simply applying your personal consciousness,* subtle and gross *energetic effects* take place that lend to perception as well. It is possible that the mystic *sees with new eyes* because, on a physical level, the rods and cones in his eye structure have been upgraded so that he can literally detect gradations of light and distinguish degrees of shadow and color. He *hears with new ears* because his auditory nerves have been tuned, and he *kinesthetically senses differently* because his sensory system has been retooled and upgraded. Another explanation might be that the mystic's subtle body is so developed that it allows his mind to sense *the effects* that consciousness inflicts on the concrete world.

In the unawakened state, your senses *go directionally outward* as they follow impulses the mind passively receives. From mind, impulses pass through the faculties of the sensory system to be processed by the brain and nervous system. For example, if you hold a clear crystal in the palm of your hand, by the sense of touch you will feel its cool temperature and, based on observation, your mind will judge its identity as being a mineral. The image then registers as "quartz." In this example, you do not exercise perception; instead, you use your mind to sense and deduct based on the product of touch, sight, memory and cognition.

A mystic might hold onto the same mineral, but in addition to sensing its temperature and observing a quartz stone, *he turns his senses inward* to then perceive additional things, like seeing subtle light or color emanating from the crystal's surface or hearing fine frequencies being emitted. Based on intuition, he might understand the stone's properties while they register impressions or sensations.

Why can't you detect those additional things? *Because until you are more awakened, your senses are not yet divinized, heightened perception is not yet installed and/or inwardly-directed perception is not yet sufficiently mastered.* This suggests that the way the unawakened person relies on his senses to see, hear, taste, smell and touch is hugely different from the way the mystic intuits the world. Therefore, among the awakened, *he who has eyes to see will see, and he who has ears to hear will hear* what the unawakened person cannot.

How is it possible that the mystic can see with new eyes and hear with new ears? *It is your heightened receptivity to Spirit and your direct exposure to the consciousness of Reality itself which radically reforms your inner state.*

Big awakenings and especially enlightenment *hyper-sensitizes the nervous system and senses, changes the subtle body, sharpens perception and energizes the consciousness of your personal spirit.* Before his soul is awakened, the seeker associates his mind with objects, but when he rouses he can literally observe and experience the workings of *subtle consciousness itself. He is now able to en-vision an illumined, interior world.* Because his mind and subtle body have been reformed and his senses have been restructured, he sees, hears, tastes, touches, smells and intuits on a level well beyond the ordinary.

Perception is most expanded, heightened and sharp in the periods of time *directly following awakenings.* It is as if the volume on those faculties is turned to maximum, and a *shift akin to a landslide in the representation of mundane reality occurs* because the newly elevated senses interpret and process sensory stimulus through purified and invigorated channels. Thus, the world may at first appear as a dream as your mind is exposed to its new terms. Sometimes the visual image of what the mind sees flickers off and on like a movie being projected on a screen.

If your perception is suddenly greatly amplified due to enlightenment, kundalini awakening, or other significant expansion, expect to undergo a tremendous inner adjustment period because overnight your entire notion and view of the corporeal world will have been readjusted. The time periods following awakenings can be mind-blowing, inspiring, disorienting, frightening or confusing because you will encounter the world from an altered state. As a classic sign of the awakening process, you may experience a sensation of weightlessness. Don't be surprised if your eyes or other senses seem to be playing tricks on you. The mind is simply processing subtle levels of consciousness through an *expanded mind.* As a complicating factor, the newly-awakened personal spirit can also create its own internal effects.

If you are engaged in your first big awakening, you will have no former frame of reference for your new perceptions. You may feel as if your body is in motion due to the rhythmic wave of Spirit's pulse traversing within and around you. You may observe objects in the material world dissolving, reforming, growing in dimension, animating, changing shape, warping, or emanating colors, sounds or fragrance—behaving like elements of nature (earth, water, fire, wind and space). As the tower of your concrete world is struck by the shocking thunderbolt of awareness, it will *dematerialize*—dismantle and crumble before your very eyes while *your mind and senses undergo thorough deconditioning.*

When objects warp and then dissolve, it suggests you are experiencing the alchemy of *dissolution*, a dramatic expression of dematerialization. Elemental behavior mimics and mirrors dynamic processes of inner and outer subtle consciousness and gives you hints into specific and transient inner processes that typically transpire. During purification of the earth element, for instance, you may experience heaviness, a crushing compression, or a sinking feeling whereby even the ground on which you stand seems to behave like quicksand. Dissolution followed by reformation mimics the creative principle of The Supreme.

Don't assume that this is a comfortable stage. Although during these altered states your mind may be fascinated by what it witnesses, this stage has dire consequences, for everything in your life and inner world will be shifting and irreversibly changing. *Enlightenment sparks a stage of thorough destruction because your former mindsets are blatantly fractured to make room for the all-expansive Truth.* As you inwardly shift, then the outward manifestation of your life often becomes destabilized and conflicted, playing out in challenges and changes in your health, job, relationships, purpose and mission. *This means that deep inner shifts correspond to significant outer ones.*

Perceptions are not intended to be a Disneyland for your entertainment, so don't grow enamored by their reverberations. The point is to *avoid becoming dazzled by your own process.* Do not dissipate and waste the energy which arises from this process, but simply watch your impressions and turn them inward. It is a delicate situation, for sensations will at first feel as if they are flowing outward, and you will be prone to let your mind pursue that outward flow with much analyzing and thinking, but perception itself is to be directed *inward* in a loop back to the natural receptive mind.

You may at first feel inclined to think that every new perception is revealing the multidimensional quality of the material world, and there is a kernel of truth in this, but the main point is that the quintessential quality of the subtle nature of mind itself is being revealed, *and it is being reflected within the boundless sphere of your consciousness.* The challenge is that you can become so infatuated with your perceptions you will tie yourself to the manifested world as a result; once so tied, you will overlook their *un-manifest* Origin.

You see, from out of the highest subtle dimensions proceed the lower ones of the manifested world. While you are being deeply purified (and especially during the states of Abyss, Void and particularly enlightenment), sensory perception temporarily suspends and becomes non-functional. Once you leap into the blank dimension of the Abyss, for instance, you will discover there is absolutely nothing material within it to perceive, for you will have transcended the third dimension that reflects such perceptions and makes them possible. The mystic's goal is to realize the impossible while at the same time appreciate all that is made possible and manifested by The Creator, both material and subtle. In fact, your physical form is a manifested creation designed by The Creator, one that serves to ground realizations into the earth of your body.

Over time, increased perception balances against and integrates with your senses, and uncomfortable side effects will naturally dial down and gradually lessen in frequency. You will begin to feel more mentally stable and "normal," indicating that you are starting to master perception, adjust to heightened levels of consciousness, and ground your realizations. This stabilization also indicates that the veils are closing and somewhat limiting your perception, allowing you to function better in the concrete realm.

The Mystic's Faculty

The mystic's perception proceeds from his conscious awareness to be reflected back to his natural mind. A skilled mystic can scale down perception at will to encounter ordinary reality and increase it to attend to the non-ordinary. Thus, the mystic is enabled to *attenuate*—to deftly maneuver, accelerate, decelerate and walk within and between the ordinary and non-ordinary worlds.

When a mystic says that the material world is not "real," it suggests he perceives the corporeal differently than you can presently sense, for he encounters a more total existence—one beyond mere physicality. The material and spiritual worlds are not necessarily regarded as being two distinct entities but are only opposite surfaces of the same mirror.

The shiny material world visually displays the gross, dense, crystallized side of the spectrum of matter that the mind reflects against time and space—the manifested world of finite objects, creatures and form. The spiritual world exists on the mirror's reverse side and reveals the un-manifest, unseen, infinite, incorporeal, subtle realms of formlessness being reflected outside the dimension that enforces time and space.

It is not so much that a mystic sees with mystical eyes, but rather, *he is being shown Reality by something far greater than his thinking mind could present.* By virtue of being awakened, when the mystic perceives, he is simultaneously *being perceived.* Each time the seer opens his perception to see, he is, in effect *being seen.* When the knower exercises his faculty to know, he is *being known. When the mystic acts, he is being acted upon.* Therefore, when you earnestly ask something of God, *you shall be answered.* Each time you fervently knock on the inner doors, *the ones within you shall be opened.*

The main point is that true perception takes place above the thought process. In this regard, the mystic is a conductive medium who is able to *become Witness to perceptions* that filter through him. He also acquires the faculty of *active perception* by which he can flex his perception at will to richly broaden it.

The faculty of perception is given to the mystic for elevated reasons:

᠊ To consciously perceive his being culminating in union with The Limitless One.

᠊ To consciously perceive that his true Self is not separate from the cosmos.

᠊ To realize that his pure consciousness is eternal; that it is neither created nor destroyed.

☞ To engage and become the Witness, whereby object and observer dissolve to pure consciousness—the Consciousness that watches itself.

If the mystic gains enough awakening, he will observe *fields of light* and their animated particulates—emanations of pervasive consciousness injected with life force—that surround his own body as well as those that permeate everything. With his naked eye he will encounter dark fields of blackness that appear as dark matter.

A mystic can perceive fine sound frequencies, including those emitted by his own form and those that emanate from Spirit, the collective and the spiritual and elemental worlds. Most classically, he is able to perceive the "Naam"—a mixture of sound that exudes from cosmic consciousness and perhaps the soul of the multi-verse. Imagine being privy to hear the rush of the cosmic wellspring, the flow of living waters issuing from the crevice in the bedrock of divine consciousness!

A good time of day to tune into these delicate sounds is during the mystic time of the elixir—a window that opens between the early morning hours after midnight and continues to close to dawn. It is during these hours that the pineal gland is most active and sounds are readily perceptible. In order to hear subtle pitches, just quiet your mind and cultivate silence so that they can surface.

As the mystic attunes himself to the cosmic sound vibration, his vision naturally begins to perceive various gradations of light. He sees the display of color, light and sound as being interrelated aspects of the mind's luminous and natural radiance. The enlightened mystic both actively and passively projects from his physical being degrees of light that other people can visibly witness in broad daylight.

Lit from within by the spark of The Absolute, the mystic shines the rays of the Soul against the matrix of divine creation. The exterior light seen shining from his being is material proof of the inner light of attainment—his *en*-lightenment—and it foretells of his secret ability to make light conscious, to channel The Holy Spirit, to bear the spontaneous light of Creation and thereby reveal the source of its clarity. If you see the mystic's body emitting light, then understand that *you are being shown the light.*

To be able to beam the colorful prism lights, the mystic arrays his body and soul to become *interiorly designed as a spectrum.* Indeed, if the fire in the mystical Heart-Point fully combusts its flame will burst into sparks of various colors like blue, red and gold, and the hues can be seen inwardly and in the exterior atmosphere. The color gold arises when the coppery heart link is pierced by the mercury arrow of Spirit that turns the heart into curling yellow flames. It has been said that the less restriction that is present within the mystic's inner state, the less colored and clearer will be his field of vision and personal light field.

If you become Self-realized, you will observe the crystalline sheen of cosmic light shimmering against the milieu of the material world like an aurora borealis. You will notice globes and particulates of light infused with the life force sparkling in the atmosphere. Both spectacles are stunning sights to witness, and you will thus observe The Divine's illustrious propensity for luminosity.

You will understand that the rich play of light and color and even subtle sound *displays the clear and radiant nature of mind.* The Tibetan Buddhists refer to the lustrous, clear and transparent light as the "Ground Luminosity." The awakened mind's luminous nature reveals itself only when its obscurations are dissolved, when one becomes free from the darkness of unknowing.

SEVEN

The Wake of Illumination

Apprehended by the agency of Spirit,
the heart of the sleeping soul is resurrected
by the startling current of The Mixture.
Suddenly recognized as God-stuff, you receive
the staggering consequence of being known,
the radiant effect of being loved.

How Does Enlightenment Impact the Personality?

Immediately after enlightenment, there is a marked shift of identification, a fundamental alteration in your is-ness because you now intimately associate with Spirit. Those who have attained this state see it as being the defining point of their existence. Enlightenment secures the yoke between the Soul and The Absolute, a bond that becomes a constant, crucial connection. You will realize that you have been *changed back* to your original Self, and as time progresses, you will continue to be changed to adapt to a wholly different Reality.

You will never regret that you were actualized. Regardless of your occupation, role in your family, community or work organization, despite friendships and partnerships, enlightenment becomes your primary reason for being.

In terms of awakening the mystical heart, its effects are extreme, instantaneous and long-lasting, making the expression of your personality noticeably transformed in the eyes of others. No longer will you need to project your former unawakened persona, for it drops away and is replaced by your natural Self. In addition, Gnosis itself refines personality, serving to fortify faith, so that instead of merely floating on the surface of belief, your mind will be immersed, baptized and converted in the Gnostic font.

Similar to your fingerprint, the strong traits that make you familiar to others will remain intact, but old friends may not understand your new demeanor. Especially early on after enlightenment, you may appear eccentric, *for the soul has been fused to the personality and now it dominates it.* Others that knew you before your enlightenment might be puzzled, scared, worried, angered, or confused by the new you or what you speak about and represent.

Since such radical change impacts your relationships, your partner, family and friends might suffer grief and loss as you walk away from outmoded forms of relating. Realistically, expect that it may take years for some people to believe that you truly were enlightened. Such is part of the consequence of radical conversion, but nevertheless, every mystic will say that the personal costs are ultimately worth the risks.

Understandably, at first you will not be accustomed to presenting your reformed, more authentic way of being. This is where the work of "perfection" initializes because personality is going to shift as old patterns are released, resolved and discarded. Unhealthy predilections are replaced by impulses that are much more constructive.

If you become enlightened, you will not disappear on yourself. The only things about you that are bound to evaporate are those that are false and unreal. When the real truth is exposed, *your higher nature becomes apparent.* Expect to feel exhilarated, for you will have *dis-covered* your Self, and you will see who you really are! The soul that was once shrouded by the smoldering crust of an untrue persona will finally rise from the soot and the phoenix of your authentic Self will take wing! Your distinct voice will ring above the ashes of your old façade, and you will be drawn to live your life in accordance with truth, compassion, simplicity, integrity, maturity and humility.

You may be tempted to think that by virtue of awakening you should have been made instantaneously content and automatically freed of troubling emotions, but it is a misconception to think that enlightenment causes you to be alleviated of every inner conflict, flaw and personal problem. Instead, you will find that *enlightenment does not so much dissolve suffering as uncover sticking points and barriers to freedom, joy and satisfaction, such as previous mindsets that prevent inner peace.* You see, enlightenment is not designed to guarantee you comfort and happiness; it has a wholly different function—to destroy anything that stands in the way of wakefulness.

What is "Perfection" and "Crystallization"?

"Perfection" means that a developmental stage is culminating and that aspects of the soul are being *finished, tempered and polished to a high state of refinement.* When the vessel of the soul nears impeccable finish, then degrees of "crystallization" form in which wisdom takes shape due to having attained advanced stages of spiritual realization. The truly crystallized state of mystical being indicates that knowledge, wisdom and love are permanently fused, their aspects placed in perfect balance to embody the presence and action of divine love, light and wisdom.

Imagine the rose. Even as the root sends leaves from the stems to form a bud, you will see that the rose evolves in a superbly organized fashion. Even as the hip produces the secret fruit, even as the first petal peeks through the coarse outer drape of its bud, you will find a faultless order to the rose's life. The perfection of the root is found in the flower that emerges from the hip's embryonic chamber. Each velvet petal embraces the other, unfolding from a center point to unveil a glowing, central sun. The sweet aromatic bloom culminates the glory of the root's sempiternal crystallization. Sharp barbs guarantee serious protection, a means to preserve such faultless beauty.

If crystallization is achieved, then the ego has perfected itself. In mystical terms, this brand of perfection suggests one has acquired complete clarity regarding egoic tendencies, in that the voice of the Soul becomes fluent and heard by the mind, guiding the personality to more effortlessly and freely reflect the Self's identity. Crystallization corresponds to the inspired work of *spiritual maturation*, in that the crude, dense corpus of the unshaped soul is organically sculpted into a precise body of beauty and then polished to a lustrous marble finish to accomplish the flawless degree of its design.

Perfection is seen as being the natural outcome of having been *worked on.* It arises as the process of purification completes itself, resulting in a type of "sweetness," wherein the course of the personality swerves to embrace one's untainted, unadulterated and deconditioned nature. Perfection allows the mind of the Witness to not only perceive Reality but also its gesticulations.

Crystallization depends on the activities of perfection, and your wakefulness contributes to these actions. *The perfection stages are extremely important* because it is within them that dimensions of wisdom, maturity and mastery are offered. If you do not attend to your perfection, you will risk stagnation, and you may remain ensnared in the visionary effects of mystical states, get lost in delusion, or become enamored by the paranormal and more, which means your advancement will not ground in the material realm and you will miss the chance to evolve into an advanced soul.

Don't expect to emerge from the state of enlightenment as having been remade into a perfect human being. As a matter of fact, *it is your imperfections and impurities that are born to your awareness and made perfectly clear as a result of awakening.* This means that even after enlightenment, you will still make mistakes and feel disquieting emotions. Part of you might want to feel "normal" again from time to time. It is very perplexing at first because you will have attained an extraordinary, unparalleled elevation; you will have breathed molecules of cosmic oxygen and yet you will be forced to come back down to Earth afterward to inhale ordinary air and confront personal traits, characteristics and impulses that need to be finely tuned by your heightened awareness. Hence, *enlightenment demands intense inner work*, offering you many years of adjustments.

During the perfection stage, the processes of *purification and purgation* take place to break down and dissolve the deepest entrapments blocking the super-conscious mind. The granthis, or psychic and psychological knots preventing spiritual freedom, are untied. Although on a physical level the body is purified and purged when you reach particular levels of development, emotional triggers also need to be uprooted and purged.

The nature of resurrection first requires a descent, a sacrifice and a death. Your former life, rife with misconception and illusion, must first bottom out and perish before the Self can be lifted from darkness and be reborn by the hands of light. Remember, nothing in your life will be removed that the soul wouldn't *willingly* surrender.

Although it could be many, many years after enlightenment before you encounter the most important emotional challenges presented in this stage, they are especially difficult on the personality. Here, the personality may well struggle with having made the decision to surrender its will to the soul. Hence, stubbornly embedded slivers of grief, loss and unrealized dreams will rise to the surface for examination, but unless they are handled correctly they will threaten to remain sticking points that prevent you from reaching subsequent initiations.

It is perfectly normal to grieve former ways of life, but don't let the personality get caught in the quagmire of supposed loss during this time. If, years after enlightenment, you begin to dwell on the past or uncharacteristically whine for your former sleeping life and the persona that lived it, you are at a critical impasse. Stay the course and remain seated in your realization that you are a spiritual being who is choosing to express your personality through the vehicle of the enlightened Soul this lifetime.

Here are some keys to keep in mind:

☙ Personality does not so much become changed by enlightenment, but rather *the false persona disintegrates to reveal the Self you have always been.* Your original soul nature is disclosed, and as it is exposed, personality is impacted to reveal a mindset that is ideally suited to equanimity—the ability to remain poised, calm and mindful.

☙ *Expect that your inner and outer life will adjust for a number of years.* Over time, your new alignment to God-stuff is reconciled with the personality. In a sense, the foundation of your former life crumbles because it is being refurbished and continually reformed. Do not panic when the trappings of your exterior life begin to shift and fall away, for this is actually a good sign that dramatic inner transformation is taking place.

At some point in the future the personality stabilizes and gels, but early on after enlightenment do not count on quickly establishing any fixed ideas about your life. In this stage of transition *you are living an impermanent life,* one in which you intimately understand the transient nature of being. As time progresses, you will become further purified, recalibrated and refined in very striking and particular ways so that you continue to evolve.

EIGHT

Ego and Desire

When you feed the insatiable mongrel of the unreal,
you only treat its hunger with savory treats that can never
satisfy its belly ~ you tighten the leash of cause and effect.
Perhaps you don't know it yet, but there is a pure breed of desire
that has nothing to do with trying to placate beasts.

What is the Ego?

Your ego can be seen as a mechanism, an instinctive operating system that drives your desires and impulses. In the mundane world, you need a functioning ego because it offers a structure for your emotions to relate to your intelligence, placing before your mind desires to act upon and fulfill. Therefore, a healthy ego is a good thing because it instigates daily cause and effect.

For instance, your craving for crunchy orange vegetables at dinner creates the "cause" of desire that leads to the "effect" of selecting and eating raw carrots, manifesting the desired result. In the unawakened, the ego puts forth primarily lower, *material desires* (desires for "things" like material objects) and *sense or sensory desires* (desires for "sensations" that stimulate emotions and the sensory nervous system). However, as you grow more awake, the ego will naturally begin to generate higher *spiritual desires* that lead you to seek out *immaterial* sustenance.

The ego does not differentiate between spiritual desires and material ones. *All the ego knows is what it wants.* The more locked in you are to the rewards the material realm offers, the more your ego keeps pushing its agenda to convince you to buy whatever sensory-driven impulses the material world is selling. When you crave the fix of the unreal, you are only reacting to pangs of worldly hunger. Because the unawakened mind supports

91

a limited identity living in a mundane world, it is not the ego's fault that it promotes such materialistic demands.

At this juncture, *your ego won't promote strong spiritual desire because it does not know its cravings are based on sleeping.* How would it know? You have neither experienced awakening, nor have you encountered Reality. So you keep indulging non-spiritual, lower desires, thinking you can satisfy an irrepressible material urge *that has zero capacity to be satiated.* It's like trying to keep a cracked china cup filled with tea; the cup will always be forlorn and leaking, complaining it's constantly parched, repeatedly demanding *more tea, more tea!*

Whenever you are raging in impatience and stomping your foot to grab what you want rather than calmly reaching for what you need, you can bet a materialistic ego is rearing its head. Whenever you can't ride through a temporary state of not knowing, unable to tolerate the gray areas of life rather than appreciate that a greater mystery is at work in the shadows, ego is pumping its muscles. Whenever you rush to self-medicate your uneasiness rather than enter soulfully into ambiguity and discomfort, ego is whining for an escape, a sensory fix. Each time you assert you know it all rather than humbly acknowledge you know nothing whatsoever, ego is clouding your judgment.

Being unconscious contributes to a boundary that prevents spiritual light from acting to *recondition the ego to desire the non-material and non-sensory.* Although you are never completely fenced off from the light, starting in childhood an interior boundary begins to build and harden around you like a rock wall. Early in life the wall was thin and porous and delicately etched, allowing in through its apertures spiritual light attuned to the soul's higher consciousness. But over time, the wall concretizes, thickens and dulls, screening out much of the light and separating you from your awareness that you are intimately affiliated with Spirit.

How does this confine develop? Even before you were born, you were being influenced by a combination of potentials and factors that contribute to the expression of your personality, temperament and traits, such as karmic imprints from your past lives and your inherited DNA. At birth, you are as close to your natal, solar-centered self as you can be, but over time you become greatly impacted by patterns formed by your thoughts, values and beliefs derived from your culture and environment, messages you receive via impressions placed by your upbringing, your subjective experiences and view of yourself and your genetic and activated epigenetic markers—all of these factors combine to inform the contents of your mind.

Just by virtue of being born, a veil is drawn between this lifetime and previous ones in order to prevent memories from your past lifetimes from seeping through into this one to overwhelm and confuse you and interfere with your present reality (although there are many souls now coming to the Earth whose past lifetime memories may remain intact). Each one of these boundaries reinforces the *lower personality and base mind* and contributes to the structures impinging on the soul's ability to receive great amounts of spiritual light.

The more driven you are by negative conditioning and unhealthy ego desires, the more you identify with false programming, drifting you farther away from your true self. The longer you buy into erroneous conditioning, the longer you remain separated from your real identity.

Can I Remove My Ego?

No, you cannot willfully remove your ego. You cannot exterminate this natural mechanism because ego is integral to the function that informs desire. This means you cannot exercise your ego to overthrow and unseat its own reign, for the ego will never relinquish its throne by way of threat from the mind, no matter how innocent or spiritual such threats may be. People think they can use meditation to "allow the ego to drop away." But you do not "allow" your ego to do anything because you cannot directly change your ego by way of such methods. If you think you are removing your ego drives by exerting force, it is simply your ego convincing you that you are accomplishing this impossible task. When you awaken, the ego does not get destroyed, but rather *only certain structures of consciousness dissolve*, those that impart ignorance, darkness and separation from the light.

Desire is the motivational force provided by the ego that influences your intention to behave, act and think. Desires are normal—they precede your impulses and help you to exercise your will to take an action. Just as you cannot control your ego, you cannot effectively restrain and dominate your desires. Such a manipulative exercise is like trying to herd cats; you can coral them for a time, but they will eventually wriggle out of the pack. The best thing to do is *watch your desires* as they go slinking in various directions, *notice how they impact your feelings and thoughts*, and determine whether or not they lead you to your goals or detour you away from them.

Disciplining your actions and behavior in an effort to restrict your impulses will not progress the soul, meaning *modifying behavior by itself will not temper the ego.* Yes, enforcing strict rules and applying discipline works for a period of time— impulses will be diverted and managed, you might pride yourself on your accomplishment, but you will not govern your original desires, *you will only control your reaction to them.*

Think about it—if you exert your ego to control itself, then you will tend to push down beneath your awareness the very impulses you wish to refine. You will only become a ticking time bomb, stuffing your most insistent desires down into contraction until one day they explode from built-up pressure. However, if you use measured and consistent discipline to weigh your options before you act, this can definitely help you progress, *but only if this action is complemented by your conscious awareness.*

It is illogical to think you should first kill off your ego so that you can awaken. What do you think led you to seek? It was desire! If you set out to remove your ego by suppressing all of your programming, you will be treating the symptom rather than the cause of the disease. The disease is your slumbering! The illness is your unconsciousness! The symptom of the sickness is the false personality that is clueless it's addicted to a never-ending supply of materialistic and sensory rewards. Would it not make sense to treat the disease, to remain consistently present and awake so that your symptoms organically heal?

Direct Means of Refinement

If you cannot forcefully control your ego, how then is it spiritually tempered and refined? Ego refinement can be internally influenced by *direct* and *indirect* means and measures.

To directly promote ego refinement, a prime method involves bringing your *psychological awareness* to your inner life, for with good insight into your emotions, progress can only be enhanced. *Psychological insight is integral to waking up*, but it is not the sole factor determining your awakening. It is by taking consistent action to *willingly engage in a wakeful state that sustains awareness which naturally leads you to awaken*. Therefore, the more you unearth the root of your emotional patterns and their themes, the more you will bring to the surface *the cause* of your underlying behavior and thoughts. Then you will uncover the hidden issues and compulsions that drive your ego desires. Hence, you do not focus on the object of your desire, but its *objective*.

To begin this practice, bring your attention to the nature of desires you most frequently encounter. You will see that some are *material in character, appealing to the sensorial world,* while others might lean toward *the province of the spiritual*. Lower consciousness manifests *material and sensorial desires*, while higher consciousness manifests *desires leading to spiritual pursuits*.

As a simple means to measure progress and gauge how often you are being influenced by lower consciousness, *keep a continual eye on the nature of your desires. Notice the overall percentage* of spiritual desires compared to material ones that are being generated. When you experience spiritual desires, they will be evident because you will feel the need for prayer, meditation, contemplation, time in nature, worship, etc.

If you have little to no spiritual desire, then the scale of balance is tipped to the side of the material, and you will crave material objects, amusements and emotional and sensory stimulation. By watching the nature of your desires, you can gauge whether or not you are growing, falling back to sleep or maintaining a healthy balance between spiritual and material impulses. As you progress, you can begin to watch lower emotional desires that urge you to be critical, judgmental, intolerant, impatient, resentful, etc., rather than higher desires that lead you to their opposites.

While certain desires are basic, practical and necessary, like needing enough money, food, water, clothing, shelter, love and companionship, others can grow to pathological proportions, pulling you deeper into unconsciousness, making waking up even more difficult to achieve. Certain impulses can spiral out of control and lead to excessive, obsessive/compulsive actions, unhealthy and dangerous behaviors and addictions that impact well-being.

Should you develop a vice, it is important to know that any addiction provides a means to stay asleep. If you have no idea why you need the vice, *it means you are unconscious to its terms*, showing you that you are still asleep. Trying to discipline yourself against acting on a well-worn pattern doesn't make for lasting progress, for unless you are conscious of the underlying impulse that created such desire for escapism, you are prone to unconsciously trade one addiction for another.

Rather than *primarily focusing on trying to suppress and control unhealthy sensory and materialistic desires, stay present to your impulses and intentions*, and then from the standpoint of your wakeful observation align your highest ideals with different behaviors that are conducive to well-being and spirituality.

Indirect Means of Refinement

Awareness gained as a result of meditation or a similar cultivation method is one prime *indirect* way in which ego desire is impacted. A refined ego is the consequence of your awakened presence, meaning *refinement is the by-product of being consistently present to the self.* As awareness increases, its opposite correspondingly decreases. Simply by continually applying *awareness*, the number of your unconscious tendencies will begin to somehow miraculously reduce.

Meditation generates presence, leading to the development of equanimity, tolerance and tranquility; just by staying here and now, just by showing up to yourself minute after minute and dedicating your intention to simply stay awake, *the awareness that develops will refine the ego and develop those same qualities.*

One way that you can judge whether or not the ego has been greatly refined by meditation is to watch your reaction when you don't get what you think you want. If you are still overreacting, flipping out and freaking out all the time, just keep meditating.

Here is a simple means to promote indirect refinement:

1. When circumstances prompt a desire, *just note that a desire has emerged.*

2. *Stay present* to the desire itself. The only requirement is to watch it and observe what it does to your mind, emotions and senses and to notice if you are being triggered.

3. *Do not analyze the root of your desire or circumstance.* Do not trace it back to its inception, but only stay present. Do not dissect the moment to connect patterns or question yourself to fill in the blanks. Do not be critical of your reactions. Do not look for

themes, causes, or reasons underlying the desire. The only actions you need to take are to become *watchful* and *just notice* the effects that are percolating inside you.

4. Next, become aware that regardless of internal or external conditions, *you are staying present. Watch yourself remain present to the moment.* Notice that you are awake.

5. Free your mind, and *let the moment and the circumstances it holds temporarily drop away.* Do nothing, think nothing. Exist in the expansiveness of nothingness. Experience this limitlessness state of being. You are now free to choose a healthy response and behavior.

Whether you apply direct or indirect methods, the ego will be *automatically impacted by your wakefulness. Thus, gaining the means to stay present is the prime key to your awakening.* As you bring your presence to the conditions of your life, good, challenging or neutral, you will begin to allow in the light, and where there is so much brightness, it is difficult to fall asleep. It is then that desires will organically migrate toward the spiritual without you needing to direct or control anything.

When ego desire points toward the spiritual, it proves that the light has chiseled through the ego's shell of unconsciousness, creating apertures by which lower material obsessions come to be seen. As the light of your conscious presence pierces the veil of illusion, the self will naturally crave its illumination.

Unhealthy Ego Desires
The mystic does not need to forcefully control his ego impulses. He is at ease in the world—watching, always observing his perceptions and desires. He notices everything, even his reactions and judgments along with each *impulse, attitude, emotion and behavior*.

Here is a key: Until you are awakened, *your dormant soul will follow the will of the ego.* This means that the more asleep you are, the more you are subjected to the whim of your lower-level desires. Remaining unconscious to unhealthy desires poses a risk to your development; the more deeply entrenched you remain in perpetuating unhealthiness, the more you build the lower life of the ego and contribute to your slumber. Asleep, you will be unaware that soul could even have a say-so in your life. Thus, if an overwhelming urge presses you to gamble away every cent of your life savings, shop until you drop, kick the family dog, or abuse substances, then a dormant soul is more prone to buckle under the pressure of fulfilling such unfortunate motivations.

You see, *a soul still asleep at the wheel cannot be a driver—it cannot influence the ego*. With the soul so asleep, the ego can urge you to maneuver the car how and wherever it wants, hoping to persuade you to commit any detriments it desires because the ego of a sleeping person erroneously figures, *nobody is looking, nobody is keeping tabs and nobody is going to find out anyway.* Although your conscience and good judgment may prevent you from acting in harmful ways, *only an awakened Soul can exert authority over the destructive workings of the ego.*

Look for this sign of progress: The more awake you become, the more you can objectively *preview the consequences* of lower desires, and your improved judgment will prevail to advise you against promoting lower attitudes that encourage harmful and unconscious behaviors.

How Does Awakening Impact My Ego?

When you are awakened *your Soul will begin to follow the will of your spirit.* You will then possess the ability to oversee every personal impulse. Unconscious forces will be rousted from the driver's seat of your life, and Soul will begin to steer the course, urging you to shun former tendencies that cause you to crash from destructive and unconscious deeds.

Soul will want to spur your human will to seek its supreme nature, so you will quite naturally want to take the high road in all your dealings with others. You will have an objective view into yourself and be privy to the themes, motivations and intentions behind your desires so that nothing about your inner life will be hidden from your vision.

Newly awakened and following the will of your spirit, the voice of the Soul will start making urgent statements meant to collapse an empire built on prefabricated falsehood, pretense, resentment, ignorance, fear and unconsciousness. Soul will exclaim, *"Resign from that soul-corrupting job, run from those soul-crushing relationships, move away from this uninspiring place, let go of your obsession with the superficial, the addictive, the harmful and unfulfilling!"* It will cry out, *"Live your passion and bliss—be free to be who you are meant to be!"*

Newly immersed in Reality, you should expect that after awakening the old ego will not function exactly like it did in the past because that creaky old cog will not fit into the brand new wheel. Because you will be disenfranchised from former desires that were driven by unconsciousness, many of your previous worldly desires will be replaced by spiritual ones. Although you may think the ego is dying, it is really ignorance and misconception that is perishing. Ego-wise, you are only experiencing a death of former impulses as they become radically refashioned by desires of the Soul, and this is seen as outstanding progress.

Most likely, by the time you become greatly awakened your ego will have already begun to refine itself. You will find yourself exploring old beliefs based on falsehood. You will show changes in your values that reflect divine attributes like unconditional love and tolerance, and you will shun negative ones like selfishness, greed and criticalness.

If you believe you have been enlightened, but your former materialistic and sensory ego desires are still firmly intact, then perhaps you have experienced some level of awakening but not enlightenment, because a *classic hallmark of the effect of enlightenment is the conversion of material and sense desire to the side of the spiritual.* Thus, as the byproduct of awakening, ego desires will be lifted above those confined to the material world.

During this stage, you will be prone to abandon the material to embrace the spiritual, and since you will be focused on fulfilling the needs of the Soul, even your hold on familiar obsessions and possessions will be released without too much concern.

When material desire begins to impose on spiritual desire by urging you to again crave sensory satisfaction, it is a sign that the awakening process is winding down to various degrees, signaling that a balancing effect is underway. This effect isn't a negative one because it helps you to function in the material world. However, it is during this stage *that the Soul is mightily tested,* for desires and temptations that you thought were previously quelled might resurface, offering you a choice to stay aligned with your ideals or buckle under the demands of the old personality. *It is at this time you will not want to fall back to sleep due to any form of unconsciousness.*

Here are two things to consider:

❧ The *base* ego is refined by *higher* consciousness. Refinement is a mutual endeavor done in cooperation with Spirit interacting with your higher self.

❧ Owe your gratitude, reverence, honor and awe to The Numinous whenever you feel strong spiritual desire, for it is responsible for feeding that desire. By acknowledging the Source you multiply the blessings it provides, and you create an open door policy for spiritual impulses to enter your heart. When material and sensory desires organically elevate to the level of spiritual ones with little effort on your part, you will know for certain you have made progress.

Watch for this sign: The soul who has attained All That Is desires nothing whatsoever from the material world because a soul so quenched by spiritual waters finds no thirst in material objects. *When all sensory desire is quelled within the soul*, then you will know you have truly gained fulfillment, *for you will have attained everything you need.* Once so completely satisfied, you will feel no sense of lack in your life, so what more could you ask for or need?

What is Spiritual Grief?

If you are fortunate enough to be enlightened by way of divine love, it is entirely possible that afterward you would greatly hunger for love's restoring balm, grieve for the loss of God's close and complete companionship, pine for the soothing touch of The Comforter, gasp for the charged air of angelic heights and reminisce your glory days dutifully kneeling at the feet of The Throne. Thus, spiritual grief is *an extreme consequence of desire* that arises after vast awakenings and intimate encounters with The Beloved.

This effect lasts for varied periods of time and is felt as *anguished distress mixed with intense and often desperate longing* for three factors: *The Beloved's company, its recognition and its love for you.*

Spiritual grief is differentiated from ordinary spiritual desire in two ways:

1. The initiate's extremely intense and single-minded focus on the above three factors *results in the exclusion of all other desires.*

2. The initiate's grief is not generated by him. This particular state of grief *is imposed on the soul by The Beloved, emerging outside of human will.* Thus, the longing that spontaneously erupts within the breast of the initiate is *due to Spirit's accord.*

As spiritual longing emerges, so does an unquestionable awareness that *the only one who can quell your desire is God.* Not only does the flame of love consume the Soul, but in addition the Self *realizes it is being loved.* Having no human object of affection that can fulfill this need, the sole outlet of desire relies on The Beloved.

So exclusive are the terms of this relationship, you feel *there is nothing in the universe except the Soul and God*, as the memory of every single thing that once thrilled your heart is muted, leaving behind only exquisite echoes of the Soul's subjective experience of being so thoroughly loved by The Beloved and of loving it in return.

Oh, if I could only explain the depth of the Soul's vulnerability and its wont to be filled with God's light during this time. There is no single word for the emotion that emerges because it is a perturbing combination of so many things. As you ache for The Everlasting Embrace, your tears flow—not out of a blackened pit of abject bitterness, but rather from a wondrous well mixed with multiple drops of distress, yearning, impatience and anguish combined with adoration, gratitude and contentment. As God takes mercy on your Soul to alleviate your suffering, you are overcome by the holy beauty of your own condition seeping and bleeding out from the innermost folds of the heart's abyss. Thus, as you weep, you are not so bereft from lack of God, but your heart's swollen artery is only breaking open to send forth *a rush of love-soaked blood to every cell in your body*. Soon love's sweetness and tactile force begets tears of joy and pain that cause you to swoon in devotion, as once again you feel so tenderly adored by The Beloved.

Feeling such towering grief, the Soul can grow desolate, for it is powerless to provide its own consolation, having no recourse to quell its longing with anything other than The Beloved's touch. Be not dismayed, for The Beloved sees your tears and intimately feels your condition, and because it loves you so, it will provide a torrent of living water to soothe and comfort your spirit, to nourish and refresh you and offer you solace and inspiration.

Over time, the momentum of spiritual expansion will slow and your mind will start to stabilize. Correspondingly, the volume of love produced by Spirit will incrementally decrease, causing the gradual withdrawal of bliss. As the volume of bliss reduces, you might at first feel distant from God, as if you were somehow lost and shipwrecked, lonely and bewildered. This is only a temporary effect, for Spirit will soon seek to reassure you and soothe your distress with its affectionate touch, reminding you that in relation to The Admiral, the vessel of your heart is never far away from the home port of its voyage, never invisible to that which captains it to shore. As the intensity of spiritual grief subsides, you will accept your alteration and more willingly re-enter the material world.

It is clear to the love-awakened mystic that enlightenment deliberately imprints the heart, leaving behind a magnetic attraction within its core, for The Bridegroom continues to greatly beckon its betrothed to the boudoir, drawing the Soul back to its center point to reenact the nuptial of oneness. Thus, enticed by an undeniable promise of love's redemption, the seduced Soul excitedly runs to the mystical chamber and entwines with its lover to strengthen and deepen the marital ring and ensure that the bond develops, matures and bears fruit. Thus, the masculine principle of God invokes Its presence within the Soul, and the feminine Goddess principle is evoked within the open heart so that the Holy Womb of the Divine Goddess is presented and filled with seminal, fluid light.

While during enlightenment the Soul is unified with its Cause to exist in the state of love, it is later, after enlightenment, that you fully feel the prolonged and rapturous taste of love's blissful effect on your emotions and physical being. Due to the rewards of this effect, the Soul is fervently impelled to cloister itself again and again within the mystical heart so that it can be pulled near to The Beloved. At this juncture, there may be times when God *unexpectedly commands your free will and sequesters the Soul* within the heart's cell walls. During these states it is not unusual that you would be found in trance, your mind made incapacitated and your body immobilized, all due to Spirit's overwhelming provocation and dispensation of rapturous grace.

This stage is neither a comfortable nor peaceful one, because the Soul so feverishly and impatiently demands the Beloved's wondrous touch, meaning *it wants nothing more than to be wanted by God*. No human connection suffices to quell the Soul's distress and fill its insatiable need, for *The Beloved has separated the Soul from desiring anything other than the love of God*, stripping it of every need save for the pursuit of communion—the Soul's single and primary objective.

Here are some reminders:

⊶ By undergoing the experience of spiritual grief, it will help you realize that the ego's propensity for worldly desire *has been duly converted* to the side of the spiritual. At this stage *the ego needs to become dominated by spiritual desire*—the type of desire not driven by a sleeping person's ego that needs to push worldly impulses.

⊶ Debilitating grief increases in intensity because the soul's subjective state is compressed to *exclude everything except itself and God*. Over time, the painful, burning quality of distress finally tempers and lessens in degrees to become more tepid. Yearning reduces to become less arduous and sore as well, transforming grief into "ordinary" spiritual desire.

⊶ Spirit's action of *gradually lessening bliss* is the safest, most humane means of reduction. Should bliss be removed suddenly and all at once, such abandonment would only leave the seeker in a state of incontrovertible sadness and utter dismay from which he may feel he would not recover. Thus, out of adoration and care for the aspirant, Spirit withdraws its volume from the seeker's heart in manageable, incremental amounts.

⊶ It is natural that you would yield to your passion to stimulate the flow of love from your heart to fulfill your ongoing desire and draw near to The Beloved. If there were no such reward of love, *no exquisite recompense that stimulates and establishes permanent intimacy between you and The Adored*, then complete conversion of the mystical heart would stall. Such amorous levels of passion create an unconquerable zeal for love to be re-stimulated within the heart chamber *so that you become the lover.* And as you become the lover, the elixir of ecstasy is released to cascade throughout your being, *causing the effects of bliss to further transfigure your heart center and subtle and physical bodies.*

ᵊ⁻ It is not unusual that certain degrees of longing would remain alive and active in the heart for years, and, for some mystics, would last forever, especially as The Beloved takes possession of the Soul and sequesters it from the temporal world and its creatures.

ᵊ⁻ Should you begin to re-experience aching grief long after enlightenment, it is a sign that you are being drawn back to The Beloved's chamber for several reasons: Your faith is being refreshed; you are being prepared to be brought into another stage of growth; Spirit simply wishes to bless its disciple with grace.

TEN

The Mystical, Magical World

After the cosmic storm the raging river will veer to a fork.
Instead of the maelstrom, choose the tranquil stream.
There you will find the diamond light sparking the atmosphere,
gleaming in the fountain of Creation. You will feel the glory
of The Infinite crowning your life and reigning over everything.

Encountering Mystical Phenomena

If you have significant awakenings and especially if you attain enlightenment, a plethora of mystical phenomena spontaneously emerges within your perception and continues for extended periods of time. Phenomena arise both interiorly (*non-corporeal* - experienced within your own mind and intelligence) and exteriorly (*corporeal* - experienced "outside" of you, literally manifesting in the material world).

Phenomena have several purposes, so it is wise to be alert to their source and indications. One purpose is to inform you that a process or stage is initiating, underway or perfecting; others are given as heralds to presage *future* spiritual processes and events. To a mystic, each indication is a signpost with mystical implications.

After vast awakenings, you most typically experience phenomena in the form of *visions and auditions*, but as you develop you may also sense subtle energy via olfaction (sense of smell) and kinesthesia. Auditions, also called *locutions*, include hearing sounds, words, phrases and expressions. If you experience a corporeal locution in the form of a voice, you will hear words being uttered just as if a flesh and blood person from the material world is speaking them aloud. When you hear an interior locution, it will be experienced within your intelligence rather than hearing it out loud.

In terms of corporeal visions, you may see beings like saints, ascended Masters, angels and goddesses, as well as spirits and apparitions that appear to be standing before you in real bodies or bodies of light. You will see all manner of signs and symbols, representing virtually anything your consciousness is reflecting onto your perception. Interiorly, these same kinds of visions will be deposited within your mind's eye, your inner vision.

At first, you will tend to think that phenomena itself is the spiritual path, *but this is not the case.* Mysticism is not defined by visions and auditions and special abilities. Therefore, do not become hooked on the bells and whistles of enchanting phenomena that naturally accompany a highly-spiritualized mind. Remember, transcendence is a state of consciousness, not an experience, and phenomena are to be ultimately *grounded* within one's conscious, balanced and stable mind state.

Phenomenon range from being "gross" to "subtle." As Spirit descends into matter, for instance, it produces a *gross effect,* which leaves an imprint rippling in the material world of time/space. Most typically, gross effects create a physical *vibration,* a sensation you can feel, accompanied by audibly loud or low pitch sounds that seem to be coming from outside of you. As a process nears perfection, gross manifestations naturally lessen, and then *subtle ones* will begin to outnumber them. This is a sign of progress.

You are likely to perceive subtle effects as thought forms, finely tuned, high pitch inner sound frequencies, fine vibrations, and light and color seen with the naked eye. The gross manifestations appeal to the *corporeal senses,* while the subtle ones appeal more to *perception.* Visions, vibrations, auditions and sounds can be classified as being either gross or subtle manifestations.

As a result of gaining maturity and elevation, gross manifestations *transform to reveal their subtle aspects, signifying your vessel is becoming further refined.* Remember, the more polished your vessel, the more exquisitely tuned is the spiritual consciousness flowing through it. This means that with progress, phenomena, visions and mystical experiences will turn less obtrusive in nature, signaling that you are approaching the *perfection* of a current process *before the next one begins.* The appearance of the subtle does not chronologically follow the gross—they reflect one another, forming a whole, a continuum. If, years after your awakening, you continue to gravitate toward gross effects without noticing subtle ones, it could signal that you have attached to gross phenomena—the bells and whistles—and this tendency must be refined so that you move toward subtle refinement.

As you near the closure of certain processes, the number of phenomena wind down to become less frequent and dramatic. There is nothing you can do to prevent this adjustment from taking place, and you must resist the impulse to convince yourself to do so. The height reached during and immediately after massive awakenings is incapable of being sustained; it is not possible because it is the result of a great momentum of force. You will have been pushed upwards past the point of overflowing and over the brink of a curling wave, and although the water level will be higher than beforehand, there is only one direction you can go when riding over the curl, and that is south of the crest.

As you begin to experience less frequent occurrences of gross effects, it is only natural to at first miss those powerful outer visions and auditions and to value the gross above the subtle, for you will not know any better. *However, the decrease in the number of gross manifestations followed by the increase in subtle ones is actually a sign of tremendous progress,* and it does not mean that Spirit has forgotten you, but it is a signal that you are being raised into a greater scale of awareness. Once there, you are given the choice to elevate to the next degree.

You will not be allowed to ascend to celestial heights if you devalue the subtle, so do not make the mistake of trying to forcefully reproduce gross manifestations. The stages that produce gross phenomena are very thrilling ones, and it is difficult to remain emotionally neutral during these times because many phenomena and experiences are so amazing that you will be prone to crave their exhilarating effects. While this craving is natural, *unbeknownst to you, your spiritualized mind will soon learn that it can fabricate its own effects.* Real or unreal, do not become Alice in Wonderland, falling into the rabbit hole of mystical adventures. You must sacrifice your fascination with magical events and trust that the Real will sustain you.

Why perpetuate the known, when the Unknown is already moving within you and waiting for you to realize it? Why insist on clinging to the material representation of sound, when the non-sound of Silence is also available? He who has witnessed a Reality which is soundless and formless has truly found his immortal Self.

Why settle for the coarse outer lights, when the fine, inner effulgence is attainable? This magnificent, subtle Reality manifests itself as *the activated living stream of Christ Consciousness—the eternal, vibratory hum of the multi-verse and all creation—the living Presence of God!* It is the slightest, most delicate vibration. *It is the still, small voice of the Soul!*

In Sufism, the hum of the Unknown is called "*HU*," being both a holy Name of God and a sacred sound that calls to you and communicates a coded message. By entering into silence, you amplify your faculty of audition to receive and hear The Beloved's melodic Word. When you hear the HU current, it means The Beloved has made good on its promise to make its Presence implicit within you. The HU instantaneously draws the soul from its hiding place into the innermost mystical point of the heart. The HU intends to commune with you in order to lure the still, small voice of the soul out in the open *so that you may hear and recognize it.* And when this still voice speaks, it says, *I AM with you—the Presence of God is alive within you. That which you seek is present.*

Kundalini awakenings, Satori experiences and significant awakenings create openings that facilitate spectacular mystical events. Mystical traditions warn of this magical stage for very good reasons, for it is doubtless one of the trickiest passages to navigate without a teacher to guide you to embrace Reality over illusion.

Here is some insight:

☙ As the number of gross manifestations created by Spirit naturally becomes less frequent, accept that you are being reformed by a *subtle grace*—that of temperance and mercy. Although not as exciting, the subtle is just as powerful, *if not more potent* than the gross, and it is a *prime goal to sharpen your perception toward sensing it.*

☙ As gross material manifestations emerge, remember that an inner process is either creating or receiving such reverberations. Thus, while a solid object may appear to be melting in front of your eyes, the image is less about its activity of melting *than it is about showing you that an aspect of your consciousness is witnessing the transient nature of mind, the dematerialization of inner limitations and the action of energized consciousness itself.* Thus, the matrix of the material world itself may function as a wobbly movie screen displaying a three-dimensional projection— a composite of snapshots of "objects" that cannot hold solid form against a fourth (or higher) dimensional field of consciousness.

☙ It is important that you learn to honor mystical perceptions and objectively view their effects, for an alchemical process is not just being shown to you, *but most importantly, the effects themselves are working directly on your consciousness*, they are *spiritualizing your mind, energizing and greatly refining you.*

These effects include such things as:

☙ Seeing objects melt or disappear and seeing tracers (trails of light that appear to follow moving objects), along with orbs, symbols, energetic structures and light fields (energy fields that surround animate and inanimate objects).

❧ Experiencing coloresthesia, a phenomena in which your entire field of vision or aspects of it are colored in spectral gradients of light. This indicates that specific colors correlate to stages of inner attainment lasting from weeks to months to years. Temporary coloresthesia is related to the presence of transcendent, mind-altering natural compounds and psychoactive substances released by the glands that accompany self-limiting visionary states.

Varieties of Mystical Experiences

In the time period surrounding significant awakenings, much will transpire that is either Real, unreal, or both. Unless you receive Gnosis and attain discernment, it can be quite confusing to distinguish between that which is Real and truly spiritual and that which is decidedly not, especially since authentic mystical experiences are a byproduct and harbinger of awakening.

Discernment in the form of *sharpened acumen* is thus developed in the aspirant to deftly differentiate between the Real and the unreal (although one could also say that any and all manifestation of consciousness initiates from Pure Consciousness).

For the sake of discussing *discernment*, primary kinds of mystical events include:

1. Those which are Real and of a Supreme nature (genuinely numinous, delivered by The Divine). They include Gnosis, events and states that are generated by The Creator via The Holy Spirit/Shekhinah, the Ascended Masters, Gods and Goddesses, the emissaries of the angelic kingdom and others in the highest echelons. Supreme experiences can be rare, few and far between. The key is: Real messages and genuine numinous events greatly spiritualize your consciousness and intend to initiate, stimulate, refine, sustain, inform of, or complete a spiritual process, while *unreal, illusory experiences result in developmental dead-ends.*

2. Those which are genuinely mystical in nature (not strictly *Gnostic or Supreme, but Real nonetheless*). They arise within transcendent and heightened states of consciousness and super-conscious waking states. They occur frequently in the lives of awakened ones. Such real signs and messages kindle in the soul a sense of awe, deep humility and the desire for spiritual pursuits.

3. Those which are unreal, magical and illusory (generated by your mind or the "unreal" realms). First, keep in mind that lower entities from the unreal realms *cannot create Real experiences* (those generated within the God realm). Secondly, the mind itself is very crafty, able to disguise illusions to make them feel exceptionally Real. (In addition, other people may generate magic that affects you, creating energies and illusions which you may encounter.)

In this stage, you can be deceived into believing that magical and illusory experiences are Real and divinely inspired because at this juncture *it is easy for your mind to fabricate believable messages that seem as if they are being delivered by The Divine and the higher realms.* This is an exceedingly tricky stage in which you are walking a razor-sharp line edged with mystical states and experiences that must be lived, and yet the aspirant must not get stuck on their effects. To compound things, during this period the spiritualized mind is regularly under the influence of transcendent chemicals released by the pineal and pituitary glands and even the heart itself, all of which can create hallucinatory effects that further refine consciousness and aid the nadi system's energetic processes.

If you are not aware of these challenges, you will run the risk of becoming addicted to delusions which the mind wants to perpetually create, *costing you years in a holding pattern of little growth.* You may even push yourself to the brink of madness, unwittingly generating one dead end illusion after another, causing you to buy into traps that expose you to occult influences from the lower consciousness realms. Such seekers may attach themselves to certain occult powers they have attained that generate from the lower chakras rather than continue to seek mystical truths and develop the higher chakras, and these impulses pose big problems for more advanced spiritual development.

The seeker who remains too eccentric has not grounded his inner reality with his material experience and base mind—a crucial mystic objective. To a certain degree, *whenever energy or consciousness is continually in control of you, more progress must be made.*

If the aspirant is to truly advance beyond this stage to enlightenment, he must attain a certain amount of knowledge and keep to his spiritual practices to steer himself away from attachments and delusion, gain mastery over the workings of consciousness and eventually create the terms of Void and Abyss, for both of these states intend to duly strip the aspirant of his delusions and offer inner mastery. *If you eventually meet the Void, it is a sign that delusion, ignorance and the lower realms are ready to be discarded.*

Spiritual maturity must be developed in this stage. You cannot read the signs if you are blinded by delusion.

Here are some reminders:

☙ Unreal experiences arise *out of the requirement to develop the faculty of discernment.* If you do not develop discernment, then Reality will not be presented until you are more prepared.

☙ When discernment sharpens, the number of unreal experiences will correspondingly reduce. At this stage you must integrate the faculty of discernment with *judgment, intuition, discrimination and perception.* As you sharpen your acumen, mastery is approached.

Instead of generating uplifting feelings, experiences generated from hallucinatory states and the lower realms can result in emotions of extreme fear, confusion, anger, anxiety, disappointment and more. If a message urges you to do something that will lead you to fall back to unconsciousness, its source is non-divine.

Unreal experiences can inflate the ego with pride in an attempt to negate humility. When an experience results in desires that stimulate greed, corruption, degenerate or egomaniacal behaviors, emotions, attitudes and thoughts, its source is not divine. When words are spoken in ugly, threatening or profane language, and especially if a message urges you to do harm, it is a classic sign that non-divine energies are speaking.

Don't panic if you hear an unknown voice or a questionable event transpires because rather than coming from malicious factions, they may be originating from conflict placed by your own mind and psyche. These circumstances must be judged and evaluated to determine whether you are creating thought forms as obstacles, or whether you are instead dealing with interference from unseen, lower spirits.

Who Is In Communication?

Because locutions accompany awakening, how will you know for sure if it is truly The Numinous that is communicating with you and not your mind telling you a story?

The answer is *God does not equivocate.* Spirit thus enforces extreme measures to ensure you fully recognize that something amazingly supernatural is taking place, and forthwith all your ambiguity and disbelief is replaced by *trust in The Divine.* Therefore, instead of encountering a small, cryptic road sign that is fuzzy to read and understand, you will be met by a billboard spelling out an indisputable message in giant letters! When you later recollect such a sign, *a semblance of its original action will often reenact its vital power within you.* If Spirit blesses you with such an augury, *its immense voltage could trigger overwhelming feelings, or even create Gnosis*—knowledge so direct it overrides your own analysis and interpretation. The purpose of such bold measures is to lead you out of the dark wilderness and into the pastoral clearing of faith.

If your heart is awakened to divine love, *its power is so extreme* you would never consider it to be anything less than unconditional love that flows straight from the heart of The Beloved—*the love will be that radical.*

If you hear the blast of Michael's trumpet or Gabriel's horn, its roar will alarm and shake you, rocking your whole body in the process—*its rumbling sound will be that loud and vibratory.*

Here are some less extreme signs that Spirit may be speaking:

⊱ The message or sign remains indelible in your mind, and you are not apt to forget its image or verbiage.

⊱ The message or phrase is complete and requires no translation or filling in the blanks on your part.

⊱ The message is composed of only one word (often not from your own vernacular), that makes the message obvious or imbued with great meaning and power. Sometimes the word or phrase is spoken in a foreign language or an ancient way. Such messages put your mind and heart at ease, filling you with faith, wonder, tranquility, solace and inspiration.

⊱ The sign results in divinely-inspired interior effects, such as emotions of awe, exhilaration, reverence, passion and desire for God. Thus, Real messages create in the soul emotions of deep respect and feelings of humility as the soul's station is shown *in relation to the power and stance of God.*

⊱ The sign or message is so powerfully amazing that you may become somewhat fearful or sense your unholiness compared to God's holy immensity.

⊱ The message implies that you "be not afraid," or that "all manner of things will be okay."

⊱ The sign results in a spontaneous healing, leads to inner growth or creates the implantation of knowledge.

The Keys of Knowledge and Wisdom

Receive the precious metals to smelt the kingdom keys.
Sharpen the facets with knowledge and polish the angles with wisdom.
When you reach the secret gateway, Brahman cuts the final bevel.
Only then can you cross the threshold and latch the door behind you.

What is Spiritual Knowledge?

When you attain spiritual knowledge, it means you have captured an understanding of spiritual truths because their obscurities have been removed from your mind. Knowledge allows you to break the seals on sacred scrolls and understand the ciphers, sigils and encrypted codes within them. The acquisition of spiritual knowledge is a major key unto itself, signifying you have been entrusted with a powerful tool to access the meaning of symbols, theories, philosophies and universal patterns that *translate secrets of The Mystery.*

Gaining wisdom means that all of your knowledge to date has coalesced into a corresponding heightening and broadening of the mind's intelligence because *ignorance has been eradicated.* Wisdom, like a raw sapphire, emerges from the bezels of knowledge, becoming cleaved over time into a prized jewel until it transforms into a multifaceted and polished gem. And once your mind is embellished with the treasure of knowledge, it can no longer exist in the poverty of ignorance. You see, when knowledge increases, it causes ignorance to decrease. In fact, when any spiritual attribute within you increases, *its opposite correspondingly decreases.*

Knowledge and wisdom lead to the acquisition of spiritual intelligence, and this kind of astuteness is *prerequisite* for The Architect to impart sparks of consciousness that reform your mind. Without such intelligence, less reform is accomplished;

therefore, it behooves the aspirant to read mysticism and sacred books to gain basic keys of truth. Perception precedes understanding, understanding accompanies knowledge, and knowledge lays the foundation for spiritual wisdom that leads to intelligence. Please understand that such universal spiritual intelligence is, in actuality, *an aspect of God's Truth.*

Remember: Educating yourself by reading words on a page will not enlighten you—your goal is to *become a knower.* This suggests that words are only words until the seeker is sufficiently inspired to gain a deep understanding of their meaning. Conversely, each instance where your desire for knowledge remains unfulfilled, it points to areas of limitation where growth may be sought. Thus, each time you acquire knowledge it means you have gained a level of liberation.

Desire coupled with persistent seeking will eventually lead to the acquisition of knowledge. As you gain knowledge, your consciousness becomes eligible for expansion. Whenever spiritual wisdom is gained, it means that expansion has taken place. *Knowledge expands and wisdom elevates* and both arrive in varying stages via your perception and in accordance with your personal level of awakening.

Although consciousness is not linear, think of elevation as gaining levels of height, and expansion as gaining degrees of dimensional depth and breadth. Like points on a graph, each level of knowledge expansion has a correlating multiple, integer, or geometric degree of wisdom that is available to you. Outside of steps in growth, quantum leaps of attainment also take place.

Keys have two primary functions—the first is to open that which is locked in order to gain entry and the second is to lock out, secure, preserve and protect that which needs to be safeguarded. The most powerful passkeys are not handed to careless custodians, those who would waste their value, lose or throw them away. You must prove to The Creator that you possess pure intentions and that you are mature enough to handle the keys to the kingdoms of Heaven and Earth, for master keys are of such intensity and potential, they are only given to those who are authorized to safeguard and preserve their integrity. But not only must you receive the keys, you must also procure their instructions.

Mishandling the keys is considered to be a big mistake, an imprudent lapse of judgment, a willing disregard for the authority of The Absolute, and if you do so you will only experience setbacks. Should you purposely misuse a key it will be *retooled to lock you out of advancement—perhaps permanently.*

It is one thing to open the kingdom doors, but you must not forget to perform the critical action of *locking them behind you* to safeguard your attainments, meaning you must protect your inner station, *lock down, seal and make impassable those gateways that allow in unconscious darkness. You must lock in the maturity of your crystallization* and keep out of your awakened life any influence that would threaten your advancement. As you wisely fasten the doors, you secure a chance to gain instructions leading to knowledge and future attainments.

Keys to Mystical Study

Here are two important keys:

☙ Reading, reciting and putting into practice that which is Real and based on Truth will influence internal processes that stimulate growth and expansion.

☙ Reading and practicing that which is unreal will not stimulate a truly mystical process; some even result in illusion and dead-ends in development. Unreal practices do not lead to enlightenment.

When you read and recite scripture and literature written by the prophets and enlightened ones, *gems are mined so that keys are discovered which in turn distribute spiritual consciousness to your higher mind.* Recitation need not always be verbal, but repetitive sound *influences, purifies and encodes DNA.*

Just by exposing your mind to the teachings set forth by enlightened beings, *a personal transmission of consciousness, a shaktipat, is directed toward you.* Even if you read mystical language which you cannot yet understand, *a secret process takes place* that is being instigated *above your conscious mind.* Even if words or symbols seem cryptic, don't be so concerned, for you are still exposing your soul's heart to the teaching which may later decode its formula.

Understand that by reading this kind of book, you are being positively stimulated and influenced. Although I might be putting sentences together for you to read, *it is your own awakened mind that reveals the essence of The Word being transmitted by The Creator.* Thus, any deep knowledge and wisdom you receive is in actuality *consciousness itself being imparted by The Creator.*

If you grasp anything of depth in your reading, it points to the fact that you have made yourself *receptive* to The Word, that *you are ready* to hear the messages that Spirit is imparting to your awakened mind. As you grasp the complexity of mysticism and receive revelation, realize that the blueprint of your soul is most certainly in full operation!

As you read and grow, look to encounter signs of knowledge and wisdom arriving in the following ways:

➸ As spiritual insight coming forward to your conscious mind—suddenly you understand writings that were formerly cryptic or incomprehensible.

➸ As if a puzzle were suddenly falling into place to expose a deeper pattern, meaning a string of knowledge connects to form a bridge leading to secrets being revealed.

➸ As "aha" moments of insight and revelation flowing directly into your conscious mind with great comprehension of Truth, especially that which is due to contemplation.

The implantation of spiritual knowledge requires the rich earth of intellect, meaning intellect must be watered and fertilized so that mustard seeds of wisdom can germinate. Seeds will not sprout in the arid soil of unconsciousness—they will only sprout in wakeful moistness. In addition, *the root will not deepen, blossoms will not form and fruit will not develop from the seeds if you don't put into practice that which you are learning.*

Don't get frustrated if you don't understand every mystical key the first time you read it. Reading a passage once does not necessarily cultivate enough knowledge to understand its hidden mysticism because knowledge layers upon prior knowledge, meaning *it is designed to be seeded in increments, while wisdom blossoms in quantum leaps.*

As time passes and you keep studying you will find you have magically gleaned understanding. This is why important books are kept and cherished and its passages read numerous times, so that you may re-expose the soul to anything not fully grasped from the beginning and so that their words can continue to work on your consciousness.

When wisdom is gained it means that it has been granted by The Supreme. Like a benediction, you are conferred a blessing because you have demonstrated that you are worthy of receiving such grace. Each time you are lifted above incomprehension, it shows you have earned favor. Each time you are raised up in wisdom *acknowledge its divine source with your appreciative gratitude.* So that you attain the greatest progress, you should continue to ponder, contemplate, meditate and put into daily practice the insights you gain and apply the information that Spirit imparts to your mind.

Information is not supposed to remain dead to your mind. The point is to *find answers, to receive understanding;* by doing so, a tremendous inner operation ensues to make you *realize your personal consciousness is being stimulated, enlivened and brought into the light! Thus, knowledge and understanding are in fact prime methods of awakening.*

As knowledge is unscrolled, no longer is your vision obscured, for your sight is restored. Where once you were blind *you can see.* Where once the path looked wide and twisted, *it narrows and straightens.* No longer are you locked out of the principal gateways, for you locate the right lock and place the correct key in the tumbler.

Interestingly, your ego desire to accumulate loads of information can threaten to distract from advanced growth. Stay aware of any tendency to obsessively gather information, even spiritual facts.

Here are some keys to the action of reading:

⸗ Read on a regular basis. The method of applying consistent and frequent repetition helps to accumulate momentum toward building knowledge and assists to increase your capacity for advanced perception.

⸗ Begin each study session with an attitude of humility and read with a focused intention to gain knowledge. You may also read from a more contemplative mind state with an inspiration to simply expose the teachings to your soul's eyes. In both instances, a spiritual process is stimulated. Simply aim to connect your soul to Spirit via the medium of intellect, so that the teaching's gems, messages, keys, codes, secrets and meaning is embedded within your consciousness. Remember to inwardly acknowledge the source of any uncovered treasure.

⸗ Treat your books and the knowledge within them with respect, acknowledging that their content provides opportunity for awakening. Don't lay a scripture or important teaching on the floor or bring it into the bathroom, because those deeds also lower the reader and reinforce a lack of awareness of the teaching's power.

Not only is it important to acquire spiritual truths but one must *put them into action with spiritual practice*. The age-old keys to accomplishing multiple levels of attainment instruct the seeker to commit to daily spiritual practices, devote years and years to spiritual studies and training, and work diligently to advance the degree of his attainments. It is not unrealistic that you would apply these three keys for twenty or more years before significant spiritual realization is achieved.

The Ankh of The Veils - Is Spiritual Reality Hidden?
Gleaning the concepts and mechanism of the veils is a principal mystical key. Mystics say that Reality is hidden by filters, screens, or seals that are mechanisms of the veils that block one's perception of the closeness of The Architect and the totality of Reality. Veils are boundaries that designate the division between your mind and aspects of Reality that form the terms of duality. Veils infiltrate the individual's mind and heart as well as the collective's. Veils barricade your light against the brightness of The Architect as well as separate your fecund darkness from its Dust.

It is said there are inner veils and outer ones (those "below" and "above"). Inner veils exist within the innermost dimensions of your personal consciousness, while outer veils function on the exterior level. In essence, your mind maintains the inner veils below and The Source maintains the outer ones above, but Spirit is always interacting with the veils that surround your own mind and heart. The veils are like thick layers of substance that stand between you and The Architect, ones that block out the brightness of enlightenment and keep you far away from unification.

If you encounter Reality, do not think that your mind has created it. Beyond the veils Reality preexists, designed in its perfect wholeness by The Architect, but until you are sufficiently awakened, you will not be privy to its entirety. The deeper you awaken, the more access to concealed aspects and levels of Reality you gain.

Your expansion depends on one basic thing—the quality of your personal consciousness combined with that of The Architect's. As you cultivate your soul, you will at certain points become *elevated* (lifted up into higher realms of consciousness) and *expanded* (broadened in capacity). As you achieve more advanced levels of awareness and growth, *corresponding adjustments are made to refine the screens that grant access to Reality.* These adjustments facilitate the fine-tuning of your vessel, even affecting your material body.

As the inner screens perfect, select veils become eligible to be lifted and corresponding outer ones related to The Divine readjust. At any time, The Divine can spontaneously add or subtract adjustments, tuning your instrument and opening and closing veils. The closer you get to Reality, the thinner its veils appear, so that aspects of Truth are gradually revealed. As layers of the veils are eliminated, the closer you get to The Architect.

During extreme states of transcendence, you do not so much gain access to Reality as you temporarily *become one with the totality of it.* And within that union no duality, no viable separation can exist because Reality neither includes, nor needs, layers of heavy veils. As the veils become transparent, the reason for their thickness dissolves and dematerializes. This dissolution affords the Soul and its Witness a peek into boundlessness, into clear-seeing being-ness. The more transparent the veils become the more lucid your own consciousness becomes. *You see, it is your sheer exposure to Reality that awakens you.*

During enlightenment, essential veils that separate you from Reality are *simultaneously lifted.* Afterward, these veils remain paper thin for a time, but they thicken and close to certain degrees and reposition to different angles as time progresses, for you cannot maintain such extreme levels of transcendence for long periods and function normally in the material world. It is said that should every last veil be lifted at once, you would not be able to remain standing on Earth, for just as you cannot stare directly into the face of the sun before your retinas burn, your physical form could not survive God's unbridled Presence. Therefore, let's say that during enlightenment very particular inner and outer veils are lifted, temporarily exposing you to a tremendous degree of spiritual light.

The veils interpenetrate one another, and the higher ones maintain the ones below. Each higher dimension, or sphere, encapsulates the ones beneath. As you maneuver upwards past an existing veil, you enter a higher dimension and thereby gain access to every dimension that exists *below it*. However, until you reach full Self-realization, whatever highest domain you occupy is also being veiled by yet a higher one. Thus, you can move fluidly downward from your current sphere to lower ones and back again, but you cannot penetrate upwards past the limitation of your current sphere until such time as you are granted entry through its veil.

Can I Lift the Veils?

Yes and no. Just as you cannot manufacture your own enlightenment, you do not technically pry off the seal which authorizes access to Reality, for The Absolute is the one that ultimately conceals and reveals. However, you can *contribute to the terms* by which veils are penetrated.

Here are some keys:

⊶ It is not that you lift the veils of Reality; it is more like veils of your own mind/body/soul are temporarily stripped, exposing you to conditions that convert your inner and outer station, meaning you will "see" Reality, *and it will see and affect you*. Remember, it is your *exposure to Reality* that lifts the veils and spiritualizes you.

⊶ *Your unconsciousness—your "asleep-ness"—supports, maintains and contributes to the fabric of the inner veils.* Thus, your unconsciousness manufactures heavy threads that weave a dense shroud to separate you from the light, insulating you from it and causing duality. When you stay asleep, the veils remain dense, meaning you are the one who is largely responsible for their thickness.

⊶ Your mind and all its erroneous beliefs and your heart, with all its withholding of love, strengthen the threads of the inner veils. Thus, no one but you is responsible for your bondage or liberation.

⊶ Your willingness to keep yourself asleep only perpetuates the veils' density. There is nothing blocking your illumination except your own shadow, your own conditioning. As you take steps to awaken the veils will finally begin to weaken, but if you fall backwards into unconsciousness, you will re-harden the very same veils you hoped to penetrate.

⊶ Thinner veils equate to greater lucidity. If you want to attain remain as lucid as possible.

TWELVE

Intention, Thought and Deed

If you can't be real, you'll be deaf to the crescendo of Truth,
even if The Musician is standing but a breath away,
whistling his Empyrean hymn through the silver flute of your heart.

Become the Truth

There is nothing to fear in any form of truth, for truth never intends to harm. It is people's reaction to the consequences of truth that speaks of their relation to it. The foundation of truth is pure and its power is unchanging, so the only negative charges it holds stems from a reaction, as well as an attachment to creating an alteration to its basis.

If you want The Truth, you need to be authentic. Simply by being consistently honest with yourself and others, you demonstrate willingness to live and stand by Truth. At first, being sincere on a regular basis might feel foreign or difficult as you realize how often throughout your life you have allowed yourself options to detour away from validity. You will find, however, that the truth is equal to a type of unsequestered freedom, and this kind of unbridled liberation cannot be fettered or discounted by your efforts to change or control it.

What if you don't know your truth? What if you wouldn't feel it if it crash landed on your head? This is a conundrum only you can solve, for The Absolute has given you a mind to unravel such enigmas, to snap out of any stupor. If, for no other purpose than to sharpen your own insight, *then awakening makes it impossible for you to feign ignorance and live a self-constructed charade.* Once you have exposed your own imperceptibility, once you have seen through your opaque paradox, *once you have penetrated your*

127

own void and have been stripped of blindness, there is no going back to darkness. Once you see The Light, it cannot be unseen.

Watch your tendency to lie by becoming aware of your impulse to bend facts. When you tell a story, it is very easy to spin a better tale, one that is more spellbinding, tragic, funny, scary, or any other alteration of the real deal—this only demonstrates your discomfort with realism, your addiction to the unreal, your conditioned comfort with being deceptive and fake, or even your need for attention that gives you an ego payoff. Who do you think is exaggerating the truth? It is the false persona perpetuating its agenda of pretense, that's who. Manipulating a story by stretching the facts and telling white lies or even big fat ones only displays your consciousness as being false and invalid.

When you begin to deeply desire the mystical Truth, expect to meet frank people who will honestly express their views about you and your behavior, sometimes brutally so because authentic people can clearly see through baloney. Although disquieting, this is a very good sign of progress, but at first being confronted can feel intimidating, especially if you have lived your life being largely unaware, routinely fibbing, concealing truth or suppressing it.

If you aren't used to being around honest people, if you grew up in a household where fakeness was reinforced, deception was rewarded and authenticity was squelched and stomped on, then these new relationships will be eye-opening. At first, if there is much falsehood within you that needs to be deconditioned, you will tend to think candid people are being ruthless, cruel or way too blunt. You might be embarrassed by what they say about you. Your skin will be thin and your feelings raw. You will want to be spared from criticism, but there is little room for growth when you are engaged in relationships where others won't share their truth. Understand that offering truth is a gift, a favor; it is not a punishment.

Nobody is suggesting you need to be tied to a whipping post to be subjected to abusive people who want to lash remarks that are really intended to injure you instead of bring light to your condition. It is up to you to hold up a mirror to such people who use the truth as a ruse to be mean, to expose their tendency to shame others based on their own insecurity, frustration and power issues. It is up to you to voice your own candor in diplomatic ways so that the truth illuminates rather than darkens another person's spirit.

Perhaps you are apt to penalize others for being direct and honest, making you shut down their opinions and prohibit their freedom to deeply relate to you. Perhaps your personal connections have been built on your terms of evading reality, causing others to walk on eggshells around you because they dread the backlash of your defensive anger, resentment, disconnection, wrath, dramatic tears and histrionics. Instead of building mutual authenticity, these relationships atrophy into ones in which the players in your life are rewarded for stroking your false ego and keeping everything "nice." These connections are not vessels for sharing—they are fragile, tin row boats teetering on the illusion that they're forbidden to rock. But if you're going to wake up, then your boat needs to rock—it might need to capsize and drench you in the chilly waters of truth in the process.

What of recognizing the truth of your own suffering? Since life holds sweetness and disappointment, the emotions you experience are there to be noticed and experienced, taken into the heart and ultimately witnessed. It is a form of self-deception and denial to continually run to the periphery of your honest experience rather than commit to the act of bringing your presence to its nucleus.

Become aware of your habit of fleeing far away from discomfort. For example, if you experience loss and think your grief is too bitter to taste, watch your tendency to doctor it up with sweet or spicy activities. You can disguise pain any way you like, but if you don't face it you will only push it deep in the cellar of your mind to fester and one day grow toxic mold. By chronically shielding yourself from experiencing pain, you are nailing the door to your heart shut. By running from pain, you forfeit the chance to discover that hidden within the wound is the hard-earned gift of compassion. By armoring yourself against grief and suffering, you wall off your chance to see that scars are evidence of healing.

By fearlessly approaching the wounds held in the abrasions of your heart, you will recognize that pain is the sensation that cures you. You will find that your sickness is the perfect vehicle to carry you deeper into the nature, cause and effect of its affliction. You must face the bloody flesh of your own stigmata in order to overcome its control over you. By courageously attending to your failures and injuries, you will begin to understand and relate to the suffering of all beings. As you compassionately attend to your excruciating hurt and the disfigurement being held in the wound, your attention will begin to desensitize and repair it.

What of recognizing your fear? You might be scared to speak your mind or be reluctant to display your authentic self. You could deny your own sensitivity because you are unwilling to expose your vulnerability. You only want to protect yourself and avoid repercussions of telling the truth, *but you are in fact avoiding fear.*

Achieving a semblance of fearlessness is part of the path. If you want to evolve, you need to have the guts to deal with conflict, threats and dangers and bravely tackle obstacles. You must gain courage to face your terrors because when you are confronted by The Mystery, you will need every ounce of valor to stand in its Presence! To surrender to the Void, you must be secure enough to enter into the ambiguity of your own darkened heart.

Here is the message: *You must live your own truth before you will be allowed near The Ultimate Truth.* You see, the mystic doesn't cling to half truths—he wants The Truth, the whole Truth and nothing but The Truth. You cannot cross through the portal of Reality through a deliberately inauthentic doorway of unconsciousness. *Thus, if you want Reality, you need to be real.*

As you progress on the path, your impulse to lie to yourself and be deceitful to others will lessen. You will notice when *an impulse* to bend the truth arises. *When it doesn't even occur to you to be deceptive and guileful or do things for the wrong reasons, you will know you've made excellent progress.* Look for this auspicious sign.

You Cannot Hide

Now that you know that Reality may be hidden from you, understand that you are not hiding anything from Reality. *Nothing is concealed from The Architect.* Whether you are making soul advancement or whether you keep yourself in bondage is evident from across the veils. Just because you cannot yet see beyond the veils, it doesn't mean that The Creator cannot already see everything about you.

Based on the assumption that The Creator's view is unlimited, *it is impossible for anything whatsoever to be missed from His all-seeing eye.* From across the veils everything is apparent, so any option you exercise to hide, fake it, be deceitful, or escape from the truth is always noticed. You may profess to be as sleek as a sperm whale spouting up tales from the Indian Ocean, but The Creator can see whether or not you're just a little gray guppy who has never made it out of the pond.

Your true self is the one whose character you display when nobody else is looking. Hence, The Almighty spots every impostor who is hiding like Oz behind the curtain, pretending to be beneficent and all powerful. It is like you are peering into a looking glass, assuming that only you can see your face, but The Creator is always watching your expression from the opposite side of the mirror. The only person you can fool is yourself. You may think you can run from The Creator, but it is not possible.

The only one you can lie to is you. The Creator not only sees every aspect of your reality, *He is ahead of your thoughts and deeds, always anticipating every single aspect of consciousness.*

The Architect notices all of your progress toward enlightenment. Likewise, any transgressions you commit are obvious. Every aspect of each lifetime you have lived is written into your consciousness, and each instance of placing conditions on your experience registers within its memory banks. Similar to the way a computer works, the hard drive of your basic consciousness has been built and wired by The Architect, but you are also contributing to your personal software program—*you are the one who is coding your own life.*

Your program works almost like a binary number system, so that each transaction you cause subtracts, maintains and adds to consciousness. Just like wrinkles engraved on your face shows evidence of having lived a long life, all of your past history—positive, neutral and challenging—registers in your individual record. You broadcast the wavelengths of your intentions, emotions, attitudes and thoughts by virtue of what *you do and do not do,* demonstrated in every willful action and deliberate inaction.

It is not like some unseen referee needs to keep score of your hits and runs and fouls. *The scorecard is your own consciousness, automatically crediting, debiting and balancing itself,* for millisecond by millisecond every consequence of will you project onto your intentions, attitudes, thoughts and deeds is being recorded.

The Architect is attuned to the quality of heart you develop, as well as *your mind's intention.* When your heart's capacity increases, you are gaining favor. Each time your loving intention matches a positive deed, you are making ground. Do not deceive yourself by thinking that the credit of good deeds outshines your destructive ones, for intentionally doing harm actually debits your growth.

All of this means you cannot fake your way into Reality. If you choose to be false and deceptive, then by default you will choose fakeness and you will manifest a fabricated, *small* reality. Since The Creator sees all, you cannot hide behind a gesticulating puppet acting out lofty behavior, when the intention of the puppeteer is so obvious. If you want to be an authentic human, then be truthful. But don't be an actor, disguised as a person who thinks he looks authentic. Who do you think you are hoodwinking? There are no secrets you can keep. If you think you can trick The Master Builder and use a counterfeit key to sneak through the door of Reality, think again—for whom do you suppose constructed the door and tooled its lock?

The Reciprocal Nature of Intention, Thought and Deed

In spiritual terms, that which is *stationed above* is rooted in what *lies beneath*. Each depends on, includes, is equal to and returns to the other. It is up to you to choose the nature of consciousness being promoted, sustained, or withdrawn, for it is being reflected in your inner and outer reality. In this particular way, you and only you decide with your free will who you intend to become in this lifetime, for your intentions will always project into deeds, thoughts and attitudes being generated by emotions and feelings.

Let's explore the inter-relatedness of the following three factors:

Intention - *The motivation, purpose, plan and goal* that is driven by desire. Intention is the "*why and reason*" behind your deeds.

Thought - *The idea and impression* produced. Emotions color attitudes, which in turn influence thoughts.

Deed - *The act* that is influenced by intention, thought, attitude, emotion and desire. Deeds are fulfilled by exercising human will.

Independently, intention forms the most powerful note, but its power is multiplied when it is infused with emotion. When you *harmonize* intention, thought and deed, your growth is enhanced; to begin to make the biggest leaps in spiritual growth, all three should be *consciously* aligned to deliver your goal. But more than that, you must also notice any disharmony in their connection, and then *unearth the conditions that provoked it.* In other words, when the trinity becomes unglued, you must ask yourself why it happened and work to become aware of the factors that caused it. *More importantly, you must uncover every single hidden reason that makes you do unconscious or even wrongful things.*

The problem is, before you are awake there are many times you are unsure of your intentions. Memories and emotions may be repressed, you may have no idea why you feel certain impulses, or you don't have a clue as to why you commit certain acts. In order to grow spiritually though, it greatly helps you to understand *why you do what you do, why you say what you say and why you think the way you do.* For when you are conscious, you will no longer be confused as to any of these reasons. Enlightened persons don't walk around saying, "I am completely in the dark. I have no idea why I just said that. I wonder why I behaved that way," *because aware people are cognizant of every inner causal circumstance.*

Whenever your intentions are in direct opposition to your deeds, you will fall short of your goal. It is like saying, "Deep down in my heart I want to be an awakened person, but nonetheless I will continue to inflict unconsciousness on myself or others." If you want growth, then you will need to keep your deeds and behaviors in line with your spiritual intentions. In fact, *since you strive to be awake, you will need to forsake unconscious deeds.*

Acts based on greed, hatred, vengeance, arrogance, punishment, ridicule, cruelty and remorseless, self-serving disregard for others constitute the type of unconsciousness that is very often more obvious to eliminate. Meanwhile, passive-aggressive acts of withholding love and forgiveness are more driven by hidden unconscious reasons that are harder to detect and uproot.

Since behavior demonstrates your inner impulses, if you were to try and discipline behavior, then you will want to select "right actions," those deeds that are aligned with well-being and the highest good of mankind. Right actions are generated by the desire to do healthy and productive works for yourself and others. When you give up your self-destructive tendencies and exercise your will to help others and act in positive ways that are supportive of growth, you will have made some decent progress.

Thought is the last thing to change. Bring your awareness to the *quality* of ideas and concepts that cross your mind. What kind of thoughts are you regularly generating? What kinds of attitudes are you stuck on? It takes persistent attention to uncover patterns that your mind wants to keep reinforcing.

In particular, begin to notice your predilection to fashion pernicious, false and negative mindsets. *By continually obsessing over counterproductive thoughts, you are littering the interior path with factors that impede progress.* It takes careful attention to catch yourself overindulging in corrosive thinking that breeds attitudes that are not doing you any good at all—ones that can hold you back and contaminate your growth.

Here is a valuable key: You will know you have advanced *when your thoughts and attitudes have been changed for the better.*

Heart is intimately linked to spiritual growth. For example, you make steady progress when your helpful deeds carry out a *corresponding, emotionally heartfelt intention.* To advance, you must on one hand plant the garden of your spirit with enough heartfelt intentions, and on the other hand demonstrate your growth in corresponding acts of loving and helpful behaviors. *Thus, when you do things for the right reasons you are going to*

make spiritual progress. Heart states based upon mercy, compassion, tolerance and loving-kindness aid your progress because they influence productive thoughts and healthy emotions.

Here is another key: You will realize you have made enormous progress *once your sense of compassion and tolerance increases. You see, it is the heart that reforms the mind.*

Once you are awake, you will no longer do harm. It will not occur to you to harshly punish or shame another person; this happens due to the *emergence of compassion as the main reward of awakening.* No matter your former patterns of being impatient, harsh, critical and unfeeling toward others, as a result of awakening, you will simply select merciful and loving words and deeds, thereby avoiding damaging ones. You will not harshly judge, ridicule, belittle, laugh at, take advantage of, or callously berate another person. Conversely, if you find yourself reverting to former negative patterns like being critical, spiteful, sarcastic, or mean at another person's expense, it is a sign you are falling back to sleep, so you must notice any reemerging pattern and lift yourself from it. *This stage nears fulfillment once you extend to yourself the same level of compassion you offer others, for without offering loving-kindness to your own heart, your perfection will remain incomplete.*

As you become awake, you will find yourself automatically acting in the highest accordance to your ideals. This accord arrives as a byproduct of awareness. Look for this admirable sign.

Become Transparent

It is requisite that you see with extreme depth of clarity the motivations behind your impulses, for if you consistently watch your intentions, there will come a time when inner translucence naturally emerges. You will in turn begin to lucidly see into the motivations of others.

At one critical juncture on the path, your mind and your heart will become constellated, and then you will be ready to view your past mistakes. You will become *transparent to yourself.* No longer will you own a ticket to run away from yourself because all of your excuses to do so will be useless—by virtue of awakening, those old stubs are cashed in. You will then have dived into knowing yourself. You won't scratch your head and question why in the world you spoke the way you did or acted in a certain fashion. If you are not aware of their exact *reasons,* then you will be alerted to their *influence.* You will be conscious of your own truth. This is clarity. This is progress. *This light of transparency* is the mark of a truly progressed soul.

At first it might not feel like you are making progress because a tsunami carrying evidence of the opposite will flood over your past deeds, washing to the surface the wreckage of poor choices you made, like all the times you were stingy, moments when you kicked someone who was already down and instances of harshly judging others. You will be made aware of the times you manipulated, deceived and lied to people. You will cringe recalling all of the erroneous, misguided, ridiculous, foolish and dumb things you said and did that simply spawned from being asleep.

The light of truth illuminates past situations in which you were blatantly self-serving, arrogant, entitled, ignorant and uncaring. You will know you purposely hurt people and remorse will swamp your memory. You will regret that in the past you chose to act like such a harmful or needy person, such a bully, such a pest, such a pain in the ass—such an asleep human being. You will see how many times you shot yourself in the foot, closed your heart, sabotaged relationships, set your own life back and violated your deepest values. The truth of your unconscious and damaging motivations will do more than sting—you will feel ashamed and mortified when you recognize how often you brutalized others, broke their hearts, or withheld love out of fear and malice.

But more importantly, the pain you inflicted will rush through your consciousness; you will feel a semblance of its consequence and ache from the wounds you caused. As demonstrated in the revolving karmic wheel of fate, consciousness always returns to its source. By the time the pain comes back around, the injury you caused will have gained momentum, and you will experience self-recrimination blended with personal suffering.

When you cause suffering, you set into motion the ancient law of karma. For karma to be purified you need to vow to never again willfully harm yourself or others, *for consequentially any harm you intentionally commit imprints your own karmic record and undermines your growth.* In this regard, an aware person who forgets himself and commits a transgression does not say, "What will The Universe do to reprimand me?" Rather, he asks, "What have I done to myself?"

Nevertheless, when you deeply change you will rise above such conditions, for no one is condemned to their past. You won't be held hostage by past mistakes. Instead, because light is shed on your errors, you will gain humility and clarity. Going forward you will pledge to keep your heart open, strive to accept and understand yourself and others, and commit to the task of keeping your intentions, thoughts and deeds elevated beyond your doubts and insecurities.

You may find that the effects of your own unconsciousness will need to be forgiven and atoned. First, you must forgive yourself and realize that your behavior stemmed from being asleep. Secondly, offering no excuses, you must bravely admit to mistakes and be wise enough to ask for the grace of forgiveness. The truth is it is never too late to ask for forgiveness, both from God and the people you harmed or slighted. In exchange, you are offering someone else a beautiful choice, a chance to extend compassion. The exceptional quality of energy that results from extending loving-kindness and forgiveness allows a person the opportunity to pierce his personal veils, *for compassion is a vehicle of such strength it alone is capable of edifying the soul and purifying karma.*

Now that you are waking up, there is no excuse that warrants injuring yourself or others. There is no justification for turning the blame on other people who were only trying to lure you into your own heart in order to show you your concealments.

When you fully understand your impulses, you will begin the process of selecting deeds based on honest and honorable intentions. You will now deliberately *walk the walk of the heart*, not pompously, conveniently, haphazardly or unconsciously talk it.

When you attain this level of clarity, you will finally display a transparency within your consciousness. *You become a light unto yourself.* You then turn into a clear pool, a *still water*, a smooth and conductive medium for the purpose of divine reflection. You will then embody and mirror the skyless sky, The Clear Light.

You must make a choice. Do you want to commit harmful acts or do you want to attain growth? Because each one is mutually exclusive of the other—you cannot have it both ways. You cannot attain enlightenment while at the same time remain a harmful person. You cannot stay awake while you select out times to fall asleep. Thus, you will watch even the small things. When you cash your check at the bank, you will not pretend to be unaware if the teller mistakenly hands you $100 extra. You will not feign ignorance if you notice that the cashier at the grocery store has undercharged your bill. You cannot become translucent while concealing crimes and misdemeanors—it is not allowed, it is not possible.

The more transparent you become, the more awake you remain. At this stage of transparency, you are utterly alive, awake even during dreamtime. The constancy of lucidity runs in a continuous thread, and timelessness is experienced. Watch for the occurrence of lucid dreams. It is a good sign of the arising Witness.

Watch for the elevation of your integrity—when it doesn't occur to you to take the low road, this is an excellent sign of progress. When you no longer need to use your judgment to make a choice between participating in moral versus immoral things, you will know for sure you are attaining because attainment eliminates immorality.

The Kaleidoscope of Reflection

Picture a kaleidoscope. Inside the barrel are three elongated mirrors that face one another, joined along their long edges to create an inner chamber. When you look through the lens and rotate the tube, an internal image is manufactured to reflect in the mirrors.

Perhaps upon the first turn of the barrel you would find a collage of hearts and diamonds tinged in a field of scarlet and blue but if you twist the barrel again you might encounter clubs and spades suspended in a pool of amethyst and white; the inner scene all depends on the position of the pretty colored objects encased in the kaleidoscope.

Imagine that one mirror holds your thoughts, the second your deeds, and the third your intentions; when you gaze through the lens, *it is the consciousness of all three combined that is actively being projected inside the chamber.* This combination is being further imprinted by *the nature of your behaviors, attitudes and emotions, and it is being vitalized by your desires.* Thus, captured within the kaleidoscopic reflection of every desire, thought, behavior, attitude, emotion and intention you generate, you are projecting a conditioned image of your inner reality. Each time you desire, feel, judge, think or react, you generate the terms of your consciousness in the positional form of hearts, clubs, spades or diamonds that color your objectified kaleidoscopic experience.

There is something more.

If you gaze into the kaleidoscope and then cover its end with your palm, you'll find only darkness inside the chamber. When you take your hand away, the light of The Architect infiltrates the chamber, entering by the opposite lens to provide the source of illumination, showing you that *the light of the Architect continually mixes with your interior consciousness to offer luminosity.*

Light is always being offered in response to your viewpoint, and the density provided *is in direct proportion to the nature of consciousness you are bringing to the inner chamber.* How *clearly* you can see depends on the degree of illumination that is made available by The Architect from outside of the lens. The more restricted the volume of light provided, the less illumination is present within the chamber. The Architect brings light out of darkness for you to be illuminated, but not before obstacles in your mind and conflicts in your heart are first made glaringly apparent. If a vast amount of light is being provided to you, then your inner vision, lower world view and upper realm view will be extremely well lit.

There is something else.

That which shapes and colors your interior world conditions your outer experience, meaning you project your imprinted inner light onto the material world. To the mystic, the representation of the exterior mundane world is a microcosmic reflection of his particular *inner level of soul development.* This perception demonstrates that the universal consciousness that is "outwardly" present penetrates the interior self, whose penetration doubles back to project outwards.

Your task is to desire to encounter an immaculate Reality that is uncolored, unshaped and un-conditioned. For example, were there no thoughts placing conditions within the looking glass, no "objects" would appear. Without objects, the only thing that can arise is the essence of transparent lucidity, the original nature of the Self. Since it is your pristine interior consciousness that provides the milieu by which you perceive Reality, you must really "look" for the reflection of your own sheer emptiness.

THIRTEEN

Dragons at the Gates

Do you think there won't be crocodiles
spying above the water line, slithering toward Eden?
No hyenas gnarling at the fraying heels of your sandals?
No dragons chained before the castle moat
spitting out cinders and breathing a menacing fire?

Encountering Impediments

It is unrealistic to think that nothing would create friction against spiritual growth. Impediments in the form of spiritual resistance are seen as factors and forces that pose opposition to progress. Just the way the tiny acorn needs to drill through the boundary of its own shell and then push against the overbearing weight of soil and rocks in order to sprout, your desire to progress will also be met by some form of inner and outer conflict. Resistance helps you to develop qualities like valor, courage, strength, persistence, determination, discernment, judgment and more—virtues that assist your growth and attest to your progress. *If not recognized, resistance can very effectively hinder your progress.*

Impediments arise out of a need to recognize them as being conflicts that pose challenges to growth. Conflicts arise internally and externally. The quality of resistance relates to your degree of awakening, meaning to the level that you are awakened expect to encounter its sibling of resistance. Thus, if you achieve a little bit of growth, there will be a little bit of resistance present. If you earn a large degree of growth, then don't be surprised if at times you are met with a great amount of resistance. Therefore, the steeper the path the more challenging the conflicts met. When you reach landmark vistas, the path will plateau, and internal resistance is no longer such a big factor.

When your mind and thoughts become less of an obstacle, you

will become more adept at climbing the mountain, and the path gives way to fewer inner obstructions. However, once you solve your internal conflicts, external ones posed by outside forces will still arise. Each stage of growth provides opportunities to experience, push through, and overcome different types of challenges.

Challenges present very specific spiritual tasks that the aspirant needs to accomplish and master. The higher up the mountain one advances, the more intricate and involved the task. In effect, as the mountaineer scales higher and higher grades, he endurance trains his heart and lungs to adapt to a new altitude. *When you master the task, you are harnessing, controlling and directing consciousness to influence energy, training yourself to recognize and navigate perils and function within the spiritual realms.*

Forms of Resistance
 1. External resistance originating from other people
 2. External resistance originating from your environment
 3. Cosmic resistance influenced by universal, planetary, solar, Earth and lunar factors
 4. Positive resistance originating from The One Source and upper pantheons
 5. Negative resistance originating from maleficent factors
 6. Internal resistance originating from your mind and lower personality

External Resistance Originating From Other People:
 Certain others will wish, deliberately or not, to hold you back from growth and change. This kind of resistance pulls you off the path due to the conditions others impose upon you. Expect that those closest to you will unconsciously try to stop you or get in your way. These are the people you love and feel the most responsible for, obligated and tied to.

In terms of those who love you, think about it—if you become too elevated, then won't they worry you'll be out of reach or disappear from their lives? It's normal that family and friends will distract you and impede your growth, especially since every one of us is going to need help and support from time to time. This type of normal distraction is not necessarily resistance, but it is part of life.

As you begin to trust yourself, expect that other people are going to notice. Reflecting back your inner conflict, some will tell you to turn back on the path, saying it's too thick with brambles for anyone like you to traverse. Others will say the way is too dark, that you'll get lost, or surely stumble, fall and fail. If they know they can't stop you, they'll try to detour you or slow you down.

Some will go out of their way to sabotage your growth. They won't take you seriously. They'll doubt you, shun you and chide your effort. They'll suggest you're just a dreamer. They'll try to make you feel that the journey is frivolous, senseless and hopeless. They'll ridicule your insights, attempt to dehumanize you, intimidate and control you, and question your sanity. They will want you to think it's too late. They'll say you're too weak, too old, or much too rigid to start a new life. They will guess that since they cannot deeply change, then you are incapable of radical transformation. They will bitterly complain to you and dominate your time with their drama, broken record tantrums, threats, cold shoulders and crazy personal calamities.

Or perhaps they will promise to make your life far too easy, lavish and predictable—so safe and cushy you won't want to take a chance and follow your heart. They will vow to fulfill your every wish and need. They'll throw piles of money your way and try to convince you that happiness is found by owning hundreds of inanimate objects. Or they will romance you—shower you with so much affection that you might forego your search for The Beloved's touch.

There are those who want enlightenment only for themselves, and they will be envious of your progress. Some who claim to be spiritually advanced will need to appear brighter than you, so they'll try to pull the wool over your eyes, throw a wet blanket on your development or hold back guidance that could help you.

These people assume to know who you are but because they are asleep, there is no way they could. All of them will underestimate you. Nonetheless, acting on a higher impulse, you will gain the guts to walk away from worn out roles, soul-obliterating friendships and degrading relationships. Your inner voice will remind you that deep down you've always been a light-bearer. So even if the path is lined with whiners, control freaks, pessimists, enemies, punishers, naysayers, fibbers, hecklers, bullies, haters and throwers of stones, you are the one to whom The Way will be shown.

Ongoing spiritual resistance due to others is compounded *when their conditions cause you to develop personal internal resistance;* this kind of resistance can become chronic, especially because certain relationships reenact psychological patterns of unhealthy enmeshment that imposes co-dependence. Such powerful resistance creates an unconscious cause/effect loop that feeds you persuasive messages, such as, *"I'd be lost without them. I'd feel guilty if I were to leave her. I'd receive bad karma if I shut him out of my life. I must fix, help, rescue and give up my inner life for them. I must stay at any personal cost. I must submit to their abuse. My life would collapse without him. They would die without me."* All of these statements mean, *"I doubt my ability to stand on my own and wake up. The path is not worth it."*

The loop suggests that external resistance is not all about what others are doing to you, but that it ensnares you, triggers personal internal resistance and demands your ongoing attention. Sometimes the loop of resistance leads to *an internal payoff to your ego.*

Here are some signs and symptoms of external conflict that mirrors or encourages internal resistance:

❧ You sacrifice so much for others that you have no physical energy and zero clock time left for meditation or spiritual pursuits; however, you secretly *need to be so desperately needed by others.*

❧ Your identity and livelihood is coupled with your ability to save others from themselves. You feel a need to take control of peoples' crises, to fix their constant stream of problems; *thus, you become so adept at rescuing people and solving their issues it helps you feel gifted, powerful, virtuous, indispensable and useful.*

❧ You choose harmful relationships that damage your self esteem; *however, you think if you can just redeem yourself in their eyes, you will be loved, cherished, respected, desired and valued.*

❧ You are addicted to drama-obsessed people because *you are addicted to drama itself.*

❧ Your relationships are based on you being the savior or hero because *it is the most powerful way you feel connected to others.*

❧ You lose yourself in relationships because *inwardly you are running from the contents of your own inner world.*

As much as possible, surround yourself with people who strive to stay awake, and avoid selecting relationships with people who intentionally aim to create drama, bedlam, harm and havoc. You need to make a choice. Do you want to allow other people to dominate your life and pull you off the path or do you want to wake up?

External Resistance Originating From Your Environment:

Your environment can present a number of obstacles to progress. At this juncture, you need to be highly selective about the quality of the company you keep, both personally and professionally, and select healthy work, group and living situations. Since you are not separate from the company you keep, it is helpful to find your spiritual tribe, groups that are dedicated to humanity and growth and those that are interested in contributing well-being, love, innovation, inspiration, beauty, progress, peace and collaboration in the world.

If you are working with those who are invested in generating negative actions, this will delay and prevent your growth, most particularly if harmful intentions are directed toward you. Companies best suited to enhance your spirituality are ethical ones that support the Earth and its inhabitants rather than ones that cheat and rob people or contribute to addiction, debasement, enslavement, ecologic, human and animal exploitation, degradation, suffering and abuse.

You may think that one person cannot change the entire world. But think about it—*if individuals simply refused to work in industries and do business with organizations that are wantonly creating harm and capitalizing on suffering, then those unsupported entities would collapse.* Yes, some businesses are deceptive at the top so their unknowing customers and minions will not always be privy to the extent of harm being generated, but you cannot wake up to such activity if you do not make it your duty to educate yourself about such dealings. If you choose to keep a blind eye to a company's unconscious, immoral and harmful affairs, *then you will remain blind to the light of awakening.* Hence, people who select to work for and do business with entities they know are doing harm are quite obviously asleep. The Creator sees such individuals as being complicit, for it appears as if they, too, wish to inflict harm.

Some environments, both ancient and contemporary, like certain places of worship, shrines and temples are charged with spiritual energies that over time have been deliberately fostered and built, and it can aid your growth to spend time within them.

Many locations in nature and certain geographic areas of the world are similarly charged. It stands to reason that places known to foster evil doings and those conducive to satanic, profane, addictive, illegal and inhumane activity are infiltrated with lower frequencies and forces *that are destructive to your growth.*

Here are some signs and symptoms of environmental resistance:

֍ You live in household where you have no access to solitude, tranquility, quietness and well-being.

֍ You exist in a figurative or literal war zone where others are creating ongoing pandemonium and ruination, and it takes much of your energy to survive it.

֍ You work for a company whose product or service is dangerous or threatening to the well-being of individuals and the world at large.

֍ You live in an unpleasantly chaotic, noisy and busy geographical environment that prohibits peace and quiet.

֍ You live close to areas that are affected by chemical poisoning, pollution, nuclear fallout, high tension wires, cell phone towers and power plants.

֍ You live in areas that have endured man-made catastrophe, scourge and ruination that makes well-being impossible.

Again, make a choice. Do you want to associate with a company which is founded on violence, greed and avarice, one based on swindling others, destroying the natural world and adding to the suffering of sentient beings, or do you want personal growth? Do you want to continue to spend time in lower environments or do you want to be raised up? Because you cannot have it both ways.

Positive Resistance Originating From the One Source and Upper Pantheons:
Spirit will always contain your progress to certain degrees to

maintain you at a particular level and create a boundary to support a process. You cannot always run before you can walk, so Spirit will adjust resistance and position the veils depending on your inner progress. It is said that benevolent spirits, guides, angels and Masters that reside in the upper pantheons and higher dimensions also help to guide, check and protect you.

If you are working to refine your life, you are proving to The One Source that you are "worthy" to be allowed entry into the upper realms. Worthiness decreases positive resistance so that veils are thinned and penetrated. Each time you are elevated or expanded, it means you have been granted entry into higher consciousness because you exercised your will to push against the resistance of the veils, making penetration possible. Just as the veils can be dramatically opened during an expansion of consciousness, they will close back down to certain degrees afterward, offering positive resistance.

Here are some signs and symptoms of positive resistance:

⊷ Vast expansions of consciousness due to significant awakening, and especially enlightenment, are counterbalanced by degrees of compression (contraction). Thus, transcendent and enhanced states of consciousness resolve to a more balanced and "normalized" state of consciousness.

⊷ Gross manifestations of consciousness reveal their more *subtle* nature.

⊷ Your mind, if temporarily destabilized by massive awakenings, is apt to naturally re-stabilize over time.

Cosmic Resistance:

Influence of Astrology - This type of resistance is found in your astrological chart, a kind of elemental soul map that illustrates your personal spatial relationship with concentrated energy dynamics of the Sun, moon, planets, stars, and celestial bodies. Factors like karma, fate and destiny are geometrically constellated within your chart, and astrology is used not only for predictive purposes but also as a tool to understand your personality, patterns, cycles, strengths and weaknesses, potential, obstacles and challenges.

If you feel cosmic influences are creating roadblocks or setbacks, consult with a professional astrologer who can help you understand how intensely concentrated energy patterns in your chart shape restrictions and contribute to your inner and outer picture. Depending on the parameters of the 12th house, for instance, your chart can spell obstacles such as illnesses, ordeals with enemies, undue hardships, extremes of solitude and secrets. Related to the soul's spiritual development and the travails of one's inner life, this house is a crucible of confinements, inner crises, tests, grave predicaments, major catalytic events, strengths and weaknesses, potent karmic imprints and ancient entrapments.

Whenever the 12th house is inundated with difficulties it offers insight into your deepest, darkest holding places, wherein the soul is faced with bearing the cross of surrender and sacrifice or is being suspended in purgatory. Since the 12th house encapsulates causes that are hidden from awareness, by becoming conscious of them the soul can cast off the shadow of concealment and become illumined. For some, the 12th house creates the perfect storm for the soul to crash to its knees and loosen its own binds, for grace to descend under fire, for mercy to transfigure the stigmata, transform the wound and resurrect the life.

Influence of Cosmic Forces - Factors like the full moon are well known to influence human behavior. The Earth itself has a personal astrology that acts and reacts in concert with the behavior of the galaxy. The Sun's solar flare activity has an effect on the Earth's elements, and since your body houses elements, you will in turn be affected.

The truth is that the soul part of you is not necessarily dependent on conditions set forth by the local solar system's whims or control. Rather than remaining strictly relegated to the solar system, your awakened higher self is *non-local*. Once you fully awaken, you will expand past your solar-centered self beyond the strict influence of the local universe, so that whatever cosmic condition may be manifesting, it will no longer so forcefully dominate *your inner state*. Instead, you will see yourself as being one with the entire cosmos.

Here are some signs and symptoms of cosmic resistance:

☙ Imbalances are present in your chart that weigh it in one or more elemental directions (earth, fire, water, air) or sign mode (mutable, fixed, cardinal); there is a concentration or absence of factors in certain houses.

☙ There are difficult dynamics, angles and aspects present; there is a polarity present—an "opposition" or "square"—that gives you particular trouble.

☙ You are being influenced by "transits"—motioning planets. Celestial bodies that return to their natal position or progress to a degree position in your chart signal change. Planets appearing to move backwards can form a difficult aspect that may hinder you.

Negative Resistance Originating From Maleficent Factors:

Since shamanic and religious paths prepare their aspirants to deal with predators, enemies and evil, it is worthwhile to touch on the subject. Negative spirits, lower life forms, inorganic beings, shape shifters, disturbing entities and malicious forces are discussed across a wide variety of mystical traditions, warning of factors at play that would interfere with your growth and create disturbances, vulnerabilities, imbalances and illnesses in order to test and distract you, block your progress, neutralize or steal your power, harm you, and avert the assertion of wakefulness. Knowing this, it is unwise to mock, dismiss as insignificant, provoke, dabble or toy with anything that encourages and perpetrates evildoing, which is a dense form of unconsciousness that projects itself upon the subconscious mind.

The terrible and horrendous effects of evil show you the dire consequences of unconsciousness. If there are purposes for evil, then it would be to teach the value and power of its opposite and to reveal the darkness residing in the recesses of the individual and collective heart and mind, a dimness that stems from the misconception of Reality.

Why would malevolent entities interfere? For one, a single greatly awakened human has the capacity to illumine the path for thousands upon thousands of others; his very presence infringes on the reach and influence of evil. Understand that when you awaken your light will shine like a beacon from across the universe, attracting all kinds of attention, for the bigger the star, the greater its powerful globe of luminosity.

It helps you to be prepared to meet anything you may encounter on the path. Would a Shaman go into the underworld untrained? No, in fact he expects to confront energies that appear in trance, dreams and outer reality. He is trained to remain vigilant, keeping his enemies on his radar, stalking and tracking their every movement.

The building of protection is an enormously valuable spiritual key. There are hundreds of religious rituals and methods that have been used for millennia to increase one's level of purity, attract in beneficent help and offer protection from paranormal and negative energies. Entire books are written about the subject and I would guide you to find the measures that ring true for you, especially those associated with your religious or mystical path.

For example, you may employ protective prayers, specific mantras and visualizations. In Hinduism for instance, Hanuman, the Monkey God, is worshiped for his ability to armor against and remove demons, the evil eye, negative demigods, uncooperative spirits and negative energies, as well as make peace with their influence.

The real point is to be ready in advance, rather than wait for things to hit the fan. Think about it, if a castle were being attacked, would its queen start building a moat and recruiting an army on the same day?

When you encounter questionable activity, *the most powerful thing you can do to protect yourself is to invoke the perfect presence of God within you.* As you consistently invoke and glorify The Absolute, a protective shield of light is activated within and around you. To be ready in advance, you must commit to the effort of building your defensive shield on a *daily basis. Each time your garment is activated it thickens in strength.* Conversely, the less effort you make, the flimsier your protection will be in times of chaos, confusion or need.

Evil will always succumb to the light, but if you are caught up in the world of illusion, corruption, immorality, malfeasance, substance abuse, wanton decadence and depravity, you are more vulnerable than you realize, meaning evil can dominate those who willfully endorse its foundation.

Here are some signs and symptoms of malevolent resistance and negative interference:

☙ You experience unforeseen or sudden physical, emotional or mental illness or disability with no definite, underlying cause.

☙ You experience uncommon aches and sores or are overcome with nausea, drowsiness or physical exhaustion that is not related to a known physical condition.

☙ You have illogical accidents and injuries, like taking a sudden fall for no apparent reason, or you have a freak motor vehicle crash with no known cause.

☙ You are drawn to participate in uncharacteristic behaviors like violent, aggressive and deviant thoughts and behaviors.

☙ You encounter unpleasant paranormal activity traced to the occult, such as poltergeists, peculiar life forms, discarnate spirits, lower entities or other creatures.

☙ You hear threatening voices urging you to do harm to yourself or others.

☙ Your dreams are disturbing and nightmares suddenly increase or become relentless. You are attacked or chased within dreams by monsters, assassins, aliens, or other negative entities. You meet animals in your dreams that provoke a fight or try to poison, kill, maim, or paralyze you or other dream animals.

☙ Your intuition is blocked or completely shut down.

☙ You are uncharacteristically teary and overly irritable while feeling like your mind is being controlled, manipulated or disturbed by outside forces or entities.

Of course, just because some of the above things might occur, it does not mean they were definitely created by an evil source because *during rapid spiritual expansion your own mind manufactures a fair amount of delusion.*

If you feel destabilized by frightening things during this juncture, it means the structure of your mind is expanding and fracturing open but in doing so all manner of hallucinatory and illusory substance is seeping through the cracks, warping its presentation. This is a sign that your consciousness itself warrants further refinement or may in fact be engaged in that process.

If you feel your mind is spinning out of control, you can take grounding measures, such as eating meat, placing your bare feet on the earth or dense rock, performing rigorous labor, taking a sea salt bath, and temporarily avoiding spiritual practice that accelerates development.

Listen. There's a difference between darkness and evil, meaning there is a distinction between carnal and libidinous devilishness and Satan himself. Since from out of the primordial blackness comes the light, all darkness can't be evil.

Let me explain. You naturally possess a dark side, the subterranean part of your life whose shade and rich fertility you tap for creative and expressive means, such as birthing inspiring works and ideas. Your subconscious shadow side is essential to your life, for it lives inside your libido, ambitious drive and inner potential. You cross into your shadow to get sensual satisfaction and to fulfill healthy sexual desire. You access your shade when you delve into your own clandestine, secret interior and strive to understand the mysteries of life.

This wild and mystifying landscape is not meant to be laid bare by willfully choosing wrongdoing and succumbing to fatal temptations that will only decimate your life. Don't poison this succulent terrain with obsessive, unconscionable, or destructive attitudes, behaviors, thoughts, emotions and deeds that kill its creatures, ruin its ground and leave it withered.

Your shadow side is best sown with your untamed imagination and then nourished with your searing insight, the wish to thrive and the will to create a juicy, inspiring life. As you plant this inner field with productive fruits and spiritual labors, you shall *reap the ability to differentiate* the subtle roots of your drives and impulses, such as those that define goodness from depravity, love from hate, peace from unease and free will from control.

However, it stands to reason that consciousness which has been grossly darkened can amass enough force to infiltrate your subconscious mind and contribute to seriously unconscionable acts.

But exactly which force is responsible for imposing over-the-top, menacing, unwholesome and unholy circumstances? *Is your mind manufacturing them, or is some outside being or force interfering?*

In order to make that determination, you must gain the acumen *to discern the difference between the two*, and you can make that advancement *based on judging their effects on your mind*—most especially judging impulses that urge you to commit harmful deeds. Thus, one function of "darkness" is to give you the option to learn *discernment itself*—to conclude whether or not such impulses are arising from your own subconscious mind.

You and you alone possess the power to bring light out the darkness of your subconscious, to maintain the balance of shade and light within you and see their interplay. Should you willfully act to destabilize this balance and weigh down the negative side of the scale with unconscionable actions your subconscious mind will only be vulnerable to outside control.

There is something else. Something much bigger.

If you encounter evil, scary or immorally tempting things, it indicates you have encountered *a critical stage, a threshold through which you must valiantly and shrewdly maneuver*, for at this point your mettle is being greatly tested. It is due to this arc that *Spirit confronts your unawakened mind with aspects of personal and collective "unholiness,"* bringing to the surface your repressed consciousness and unresolved shame.

To compound matters, your mind can become destabilized by rapid spiritual expansion, exposing you to not only the higher realms but the lower ones as well, prompting sometimes terrifying and chaotic circumstances.

In this stage, the soul must face darkness that is packaged in any way, shape or shapeless form so that you can overcome any vulnerability and be ready to conquer each and every encroachment, whether it be met as a result of mind-projected delusion, by black magic and voodoo, by the nebulous blackness Spirit imposes upon the soul to strip it of its sensibility, or by imaginary or even tangible outside assaults.

Evil can fluently traverse the astral dimension—the murky subliminal realm alive with the collective darkness, energetic imprints of ghosts and spirits and all kinds of interesting and peculiar energies. Don't become entranced by the astral realm, for the highest levels of awakening are not seated in this dimension.

The challenge is as the mystic rises up in awareness he may find himself crossing *through this realm so that he can exist in the transpersonal ones above it.* Interiorly, he needs to be equipped to fluidly maneuver through and around the astral dimension *rather than be controlled by it or remain stuck there.*

Since each sphere encapsulates the others, there is no way around the astral dimension. In order to become super-conscious, you must enter the underworld and master the subconscious domain—*you must walk through the valley of the shadow of death and fear no evil. And you must firmly know that God is with you and trust that His rod is protecting you.* You must traverse your shady interior and know its ins and outs. *You must learn to shut down the inner gateways that allow in the darkness. You must lock the doors behind you and make it impossible for forms of lowly unconsciousness to follow you.*

At this point, base ego tendencies can be further purified, but not before they come up or literally rise from the dead. This stage is the place wherein you discover whether or not you are fighting your own subconscious mind or battling that which is located outside of it. You are being called to slay some inner dragons and make others your servants before you may move forward.

Thus, for a time you may feel threatened by visions of gruesome monsters and horrible beasts, experience nightmares and waking visions fraught with things like snakes and vermin and black flies, hear voices giving you perplexing or worrisome instructions, encounter entities and certain animals, run into counterfeit humans dressed in sheep's clothing, meet beings disguised as saints and benevolent ones, see specters that appear as ghosts, or attract in beings who identify as aliens.

It is under these conditions that your faith and confidence in your higher power is tested, where you must accrue discernment, apply solid judgment, and thicken your protective garment of light. In addition, if you do not manage personal inner demons and tame your beastly temptations, *you shall not pass*—you shall not progress beyond this juncture.

Several factors are presented in this stage:

᛭ *The unreal is being projected through your mind*, requiring you to discern Real from unreal and to identify illusory substances that are filtering through the subconscious.

◦┐ *Situations and circumstances are arising from the lower realms and manifesting in the material world,* requiring you to discern whether or not they are genuinely coming forward as threats from the outer realms of existence, whether they are Real, or whether they are the stuff of illusion.

◦┐ *The Real is being presented by God—both directly in your outer experience and through the medium of your awakened consciousness,* allowing you to perceive the difference between the Real and the unreal.

Buckle up, because this is a thoroughly challenging stage that is filled with tests. This is where your rubber hits the road and the impure is burnt from the tread of the wheel, where you learn the truth of whether you are riding in a clown car made of flimsy fantasies that will crumple at the first signs of pressure, or find that your chassis is forged with the tempered iron of the Real, built to withstand the hellish flames of divergent forces.

Such a rite of being burnt is designed to intimidate and confuse only those aspirants who, out of delusion, inexperience, lack of knowledge and ineptitude, will be unprepared to pass through the stages of heightened refinery. Out of fear, many turn back on the path in this stage and/or medicate themselves with psychiatric drugs.

Rest assured that your partnership with God and the proper employment of spiritual light will effectively put evil out of business. Since the force of evil can be stopped, it means that it is finite and limited, and since it is terminable, it holds no real or lasting power. Remember, *there is only one interminable power— the Real and limitless power of the God Force.*

Interestingly, one's awakened super-conscious mind can manifest beautiful visions of faeries, Devas, Masters, angels, deities, gods and higher beings. So how will you know whether they are benevolent ones instead of impostors filtering through the lowly subconscious realm to trick you? Again, you must employ discernment.

Human ignorance, in its most distorted form, produces atrocities of evil. Even a small amount of incomprehension of Reality on your part, such as the notion that the God Force is something that is separated from your soul, will concoct the idea that darkness possesses some kind of power that can dominate you. This illusion only lends energy to darkness that feels an awful lot like power. But it is not real power. It is only your illusion and fear generating energy.

Evil has no real influence over those who have attained the light of non-duality. Knowing that an illusion is but a vague mirage will dismantle its substance. You see, once your inner flame is lit, then its brilliance will dissolve every trace of misconception, every semblance of distortion. Once you achieve recognition of your "I" Self, then you will firmly know that the Almighty power of God is with you, superseding all other forms of power.

Remember that nothing Real—nothing of God—can endanger your life. That which is unreal *will always submit to the Real.*

Internal Resistance Originating From Your Mind and Lower Personality:

As the biggest obstacle, this type of inner resistance is *false* resistance because there is nothing Real standing between you and The Absolute. The unawakened mind unknowingly propagates the inner veils that contribute to duality.

It is your notion of being far removed and separate from The Absolute that creates conditions that skew your view of Reality. Also, if you believe that you are limited to your body, you are encountering inner resistance. You must repeatedly look beyond identification—past the identity of the "I" that you think is doing your thinking, for it is beyond your identity that non-duality exists. As contributing factors, your relationship to fear, harsh self-judgment, self-doubt, lack of faith and disinterest in the path stands in the way of progress.

Since overcoming personal obstacles of the mind and heart is the basis of the path, every religion has age-old practices that aid in their resolution and increase your level of strength and inner purity. They incorporate methods such as meditation, prayer, chant, invocation, yoga, mantra and mudra, along with songs and divine hymns, dancing and movement, reciting verses, employing sacred instruments and tools, using sacred herbs, plants, incense and aromatic plant oils, making and gazing at special designs, lighting lamps and candles, as well as worshiping gods, goddesses, deities, Masters, The Creator, and others. For example, Hindus, Buddhists and Jains may worship and call on Ganesha, the elephant-faced deity who is most widely known as being a remover of obstacles. (Interestingly, Ganesha also places upon the aspirant positive resistance to test and check his growth.)

The key to invoking the presence of a Supreme or beneficent one and evoking the principles it represents is to cultivate an internal state of prayerful intention, adoration, respect and glory. Even if you do not perform a method or ceremony perfectly, it is *your intention and desire* that is the most important factor, so that something as simple as consciously lighting a lamp can exemplify your deep wish that your ignorance is illuminated with wisdom.

Here are some signs and symptoms of personal inner resistance:

☛ Your sticky ego identifications bind you. Your sense of self-importance limits you. The more of a "somebody" and big shot you are in the world, the more it can pose a block to progress. How hooked you remain to your persona, possessions and worldly future results in bondage. What inner and outer moniker is your identity tied? If you are not willing to let go of who you think you are or will be, you will limit your potential to become more than you could ever imagine.

☙ Your ego makes demands. It complains, *"I need what I want!"* You are tempted by base desires to pursue unconscious activities, accumulate too many material objects and chase sensory satisfaction and endless amusement which distracts you and takes precedence over spiritual pursuits.

☙ You let the path overgrow and find reasons to neglect spiritual practices. Suddenly you are uninspired, unmotivated, impatient, dispassionate, too tired or too lazy to sit in meditation or engage in contemplation. You decide your progress is not a priority because the material world is so much more exciting, fun, interesting, easy or important.

☙ You fall in love with your mind's delusions. You are fascinated with your own power and your locutions.

☙ You are romanced by occult or magical activities that you think will get you somewhere, but in reality they will ultimately lead you to a dead end. (This is where many people become entranced with and get stuck in the astral realm and don't progress beyond the lower chakras. Aim to develop the chakras above the solar plexus.)

☙ Your faith wanes and you become disillusioned by the path itself. Since you have not yet made significant progress, you think you never will.

If you feel that your faith is dwindling, then bring your awareness to the absence of spiritual desire and then *pray for faith itself to be restored.* Contemplate, and ask that Spirit renew its uplifting essence within you, and it will only be a matter of time before faith returns.

Temptation as Resistance

Temptation is an inner form of resistance that presents you with choices to either elevate yourself or succumb to lower activity that is counterproductive to growth. Because every deed, intention, emotion, attitude and thought is imprinted upon your consciousness, The Divine is always watching, always listening, always expecting you to maintain the station befitting a mystic.

Temptations are seen as tests and obstacles. They are food for awareness of the nature of your desires, and until you become conscious of them as such, you will not be able to effectively address them. To make progress, you must first recognize any destructive patterns and then act in your highest capacity to overcome them. Expect your patterns to repeat themselves, for this action serves to draw your attention to embedded road blocks. The day you wake up to your patterns as being obstacles and then act in your best judgment to change and refine them, it will be an auspicious day for your soul.

If you cannot transform your destructive tendencies into healthy ones, you will hold yourself back from growth. Anything that prompts you to act from your lower, unconscious self instead of your higher, conscious Self will prevent your full awakening. Anything to which you are addicted, whether it is an attitude, emotion, role, thought process, substance or behavior will hold you back from progress.

When you encounter temptation, weigh your prospects in the following ways:

ᴂ Before you impulsively react to circumstances and succumb to temptation, choose to first bring your *presence* to the situation. In other words, just notice that you are being tempted.

ᴂ Next, weigh the consequences. Judge whether or not the deed is worth the cost and if its price—that of spiritual growth being subtracted from you—is one you can afford.

There is something else.

Each time you are greatly elevated, the scale of balance will have been tipped in your favor, creating expansive awareness. Paradoxically, it is after this rebalance takes place that your ego may try to slip you up and bring you back down to your previous level. Watch the quality of your ego desires after positive leaps of consciousness, keep elevated, and do not succumb to falling back to sleep.

When there is an absence of the need to weigh consequences it means that you have consistently chosen positive measures over negative ones. *When the need to weigh consequence permanently vanishes, it is a sign you have made great progress.* Each time you act to recognize and then resist the pull of temptation, you are making progress.

When an offending circumstance loses its attraction and charge, you will know you are making solid gains. *When you no longer possess the impulse to cave in*, when a lower temptation no longer poses a threat to your advancement, then you will know for sure you have attained growth. Look for this good sign.

Overkill as Resistance

When you begin to wake up, you'll notice that certain people in your life deplete you, seeming to siphon off every last drop of your life force. Often, they are the chatterboxes, the ones unable to cope with silence. They unconsciously believe, *"As long as I keep making noise, no one will notice I'm afraid of being invisible, terrified of being unheard."* They hate those awkward lapses in conversation, so if they keep on talking and talking then they won't feel so disconnected, irrelevant, or alone. Yet quietness and solitude is needed to approach Silence.

The people who seriously deplete you admire how they can multitask by simultaneously juggling four or five things. For them, slowing down is not an option because their lives have sped up to a furious pace and doing one thing at a time is no longer a viable option. As long as they keep up with this hurried tempo, they will stay in control and be much more productive, but deep inside they know they are always out of breath. To them, scheduling time to replenish the heart seems a luxury, a distant dream. Except peace is needed in order to wake up and serenity is required to breathe life into living.

The ones who drain you the most will cram every waking moment with busyness. They can't tolerate the absence of entertainment. They are always rushing out the door for errands and visits and games and activities, but mainly they do not see they are abandoning their hearts. It seems they can't sit still because they've unknowingly grown too used to agitation and chaos. The busy doers of the world are those you spot in quiet outdoor settings strapped to electronics, addicted to a continual scratch of news and music or any virtual contact because for them, listening to the soft sound of nature is too deafening to bear. They'd rather disconnect from the natural world rather than unplug. But by perpetuating such constant outward activity, it thwarts the simplicity of *being*.

Wait a minute. Maybe you're the one kicking up all that dust, the person who can't tolerate stillness. Maybe you mistakenly equate peace with boredom. But peace is never monotonous. The experience of monotony is only your mind boring itself.

Maybe you are your own enemy, your own tormentor. It is time to wake up and see that all this chatter, all this crazy, extraneous activity, the racing and panting all day long—*it is all overkill*. Overkill is a form of self-harm, one in which you unconsciously sabotage wakefulness. *Overkill is a perfect excuse, a very effective obstacle to awakening.* As long as you keep whipping your mind into a manic frenzy you will only create a thick smoke screen to hide behind. As long as your mind stays amped up you will kill your spirit with busyness and deliberately shun your own presence. As long as you keep reinventing your own agony you will snuff out your chances to stay awake.

Watch your intention to commit overkill, because any degree of needless, exorbitant, unhealthy activity and hyping up of the mind is a symptom of an underlying malady. *Overkill amounts to violence—it is a soul-annihilating act of aggression.* With so much overdoing, overdosing and over-the-top obsessing, is there any wonder there is no time to *be*?

Understand something. You have been *conditioned* to stay asleep, and a prime method to accomplish this is to keep amusing yourself with busyness. In addition, modern-day culture has monetized your slumber; it is heavily invested in keeping you asleep—forever, if need be. Those who choose to remain unconscious are only contributing to a walking dead, zombie world. To *come to*, to lift from your coma, you must recognize your tendency to flee from your own actuality.

Here are some symptoms of fleeing from presence:

⊶ You are prone to obsessive-compulsive behaviors and thoughts.

⊶ You are experiencing an addiction or you self-medicate to the point of getting loaded—thereby fulfilling the mission of knocking yourself unconscious. You overdose on substances, work, food, reading, television, exercise, sleep, or other behaviors. You fall into the internet for too many hours, craving news, endless texting, gaming, social media, or other online stimulation.

⊶ You spend far too much money, and you might inflate that symptom to amassing collections and hoarding objects.

⊶ You are over-scheduled. You tend to over-commit to work or volunteer activities.

⊶ You give too much and sacrifice everything for others so much that you resent it, or, so much it has made you physically ill, exhausted, or deprived of your own emotional and spiritual well-being.

When former significant obstacles are more or less nonexistent, you will have resolved much inner conflict and attained superlative inner growth. Look for this excellent sign of progress.

FOURTEEN

The Gems of Spiritual Power

When you receive a stunning gift of insight,
tend it like a jewel, for it means your soul is being refined.
Each polished bead of wisdom conferred is proof
that you are being led to the pearl of your magnificence.
Therefore, do nothing that would cause the mercy in the gem
to fall from the grace of the bezel.

Can Spiritual Growth Be Reversed?

Until you reach a certain level of attainment, yes. When you willfully engage unconsciousness, that very darkness threatens to erode progress and re-form the veils that obscure The Truth. The simple spiritual mechanism of *subtraction* is the reason why aspirants take backward steps in progress.

Just as you contribute to building higher spiritual consciousness to make progress, you can dismantle the terms of growth, power and perfection when you willingly abandon the path by participating in unproductive activities, thoughts, behaviors, deeds, intentions, attitudes and emotions that undermine the very progress you aim to attain. Thus, as you take one step forward followed by one step back, you can remain stagnant and stationary on the path.

There is another reason. Throughout your development, and especially in the early years, you will achieve many lesser elementary awakenings that don't necessarily amount to lasting or high level spiritual realizations. *These rudimentary awakenings are reversible*, meaning their process seems to be limited by time and other contributing factors; you will therefore enjoy their rewards until such time as they diminish or vanish.

Even shaktipat transmitted to you by a guru can reverse over time if you do not maintain or advance the degree of that attainment.

Here is a key to prevent the action of reversal: *Elementary awakenings are given so that you continue to seek, study, train and practice, so that you achieve even greater degrees of attainment.*

Where there is one such significant attainment, there can be more to follow! Where there is a single raindrop, there is always the cloudburst. Where there is the downpour striking the surface of the sea, there must be the ocean and its sprawling floor.

Don't assume that the single raindrop could never evaporate or get lost in the wind; you must moisten its sphere and protect its wholeness and guide its descent past the cloud so that it is delivered into the sea. Don't turn your back on The Divine. Don't let the atmosphere become arid due to neglect, spiritual ignorance, distraction and lack of desire to study, practice and receive training.

It is very tempting to try and rush your process, and this stage requires patience, skill, keen observance and discipline. After you become awakened, the choices you make influence your future growth opportunities and determine if even higher levels of spiritual mastery will be offered or denied.

When you exercise wisdom in your choices, positive forces are set into motion, increasing your options to attain greater realizations. Those who foster the light will be more prone to advance than those who wantonly discard their lanterns. It is your responsibility as an enlightened one to cherish your inner flame and not reject its Source.

To increase your chances to deepen your future attainment, don't rush to broker a newfound power for fortune and fame, because misusing power for lower purposes will make you ineligible for much greater attainments. In addition, relinquish behavior that is unbecoming of a conscious person, for each time you reach for that which is beneath you, you only "dis-grace" yourself. When you assume an inferior stance unbefitting your station you fall from the heightened Way.

Should you participate in things that are beneath the stature of a conscious person, *you will be the one hindering your own advancement.* By lowering your station, you place it in a cesspool of corrosion, and sooner or later the rewards and benefits previously garnered by your elevation will disintegrate, leading you back to square one.

The law of justice determines the scale of balance. This law has been set up in advance to respond automatically based on your unique consciousness configuration. Thus, Spirit is ever able to bind (connect), unbind (release/subtract) and neutralize (sustain) energy for the purposes of consciousness growth, withdrawal, coalescence and stabilization. Just as prior consciousness is first dissolved, shifted, or expanded so that innovations take place, advanced consciousness can be removed and put on hold.

If you intentionally participate in irresponsible, foolish, or negative actions known to jeopardize progress, *you will either not be allowed to advance, or attainments will be veiled from your awareness.* If you deliberately misuse Tantric energy, for instance, you will place a limitation upon it.

Depending on the severity of your infractions, progress can be dismantled and reversed, or you may be held back for a time from taking further steps forward. If the violation is severe enough, you may disqualify yourself from making appreciable progress in this lifetime, or you will greatly impede your growth. You see, the more your unconscious actions skew your view of Reality, the more you will be prone to gamble with your growth, leaving you and your gifts exposed to bankruptcy and making your progress vulnerable to theft and erosion.

Power is withheld for your own good. If The Creator deems you irresponsible or needing protection from yourself, your power is contained, unplugged or neutralized. Think about it; why would additional power be given to one who mistreated or abused it in the past? Why give a pack of matches to a toddler who wants to light a candle, but instead he unwittingly torches the whole neighborhood? This is an example of positive resistance originating from The Creator.

What if I make a mistake in judgment?

Being human, you are not totally immune to the challenges of pride and egotistical mistakes. Though you cannot be made "unenlightened," you will still need to watch your intentions until such time in the future that your realization *creates an irreversible inner condition.*

Thus, until crystallization is established as a firmament within the soul, you are at risk of forgetting who you are. Every religion has its awakened ones who have fallen from grace. You must endeavor to become crystallized so that humility, compassion, tolerance, kindness, selflessness and similar higher motivations turn to bedrock that naturally thwarts the destabilizing effects of lower temptations.

Spirit thus acts as a shepherd to bring its most cherished lambs back to The Fold, administering such a dramatic and authoritative influx of spiritual light that you may suddenly experience visions and auditions along with interior adjustments that expand you well beyond the confines of the material world. In such a case, you will be forcefully evicted from Babylon and returned to green pastures *in order to remind you that the verdant riches of Spirit produce far greater comfort than any materialistic dream which your ego may inflict upon your mind, to reinforce that God's gaze is riveted upon your Soul, and to remind you that the staff of Spirit remains an ever-guiding force.*

If your mistake is grave enough, then Spirit may decide to temporarily prevent your base mind from operating efficiently in the material world, expanding your consciousness so wide that it is nearly impossible to think and function in the grossly narrow material realm.

Repeated big errors on your part indicate you are *choosing* to fall back to sleep, that you are willfully turning your back on The Beloved. Spirit will still hope to offer you some form of salvation, but your continual choices *to dampen your own light will ultimately become a serious problem.*

Here is the message: If you are not careful, if you undervalue the most prized of your treasures and sell them cheap at auction, you will forfeit the benefit of the doubt that Spirit provides to remedy mistakes.

What is Spiritual Pride?

Spiritual pride results from over-identification with status, experiences, powers and gifts *that leads you to become distracted by their effects.* It is very easy to fall into this trap because along the way of awakening, the spiritual world will have opened for you a new source of desire, but one in which you could erroneously want to accumulate spiritual wealth that the ego will love to solicit.

You will want to bring your attention to this condition, for spiritual desire that makes you hoard spiritual power or achieve fortune and fame at the expense of Soul is seen as being a deviation from the neutrality of the Witness. (Some mystical traditions advise the seeker to drop *all* desires—even spiritual ones—for this reason.)

The truth is that although spontaneous enlightenment occurs for some individuals, realistically expect that it may take you years of inquiry, study and practice before you might achieve significant spiritual realization. Understandably, there are far more people who want to achieve stations of conscious awareness, who want to learn how to become loving and compassionate souls, but who do not want to commit so much of their lives to the path of enlightenment itself, and to endeavor to become such a person is quite a good decision. However, upon reaching certain stations, countless seekers fall in love with the transient power that accompanies them.

Power is a natural outpouring of advancement. *It can lead you to greater consciousness or pull you down a meandering road to absolutely nowhere.* It is like receiving a sparkler on the fourth of July—you think you should keep lighting its fuse only to watch the sparks flit away while you completely ignore who or what gave you such a gift. Perhaps while waving the stick in the air, you want to draw attention from others. Maybe you are proud of yourself for lighting it and are infatuated with the dazzling sparks. Meanwhile, the reason for the existence of the sparkler's base and true action goes unattended, and you will only want to keep striking the fuse until the whole candle melts to soot—its intended power slipping between your fingers for good.

Don't become infatuated with power, or it will keep you seated in a self-limiting state from which you may never progress. Stay alert to the nature of demands your ego is invested in making surrounding power. Whenever you feel some kind of emotional kick or payoff to the ego, you are in danger of succumbing to spiritual pride. By attaching to the residue of power—to its *outward* elemental effect—you will overlook its *source and cause* and you will *differentiate from its essence.* You will want to turn power into an ego-based object that you take credit for creating, and as a result you will miss a critical key—the fact that *the sparkling light is shining something back to you.*

The mystic does not cling to anything. He sees power and special ability as being a natural extension of awakening. The mystic understands that the sparkler and its light-action are reflections, and his experience is not solely dependent on outward effects. The mystic witnesses the entire universe and each and every form within it, including his own, as being fully soaked with the splendor of light-consciousness. He knows that whatever consciousness he perceives is, at its ultimate foundation, also *perceiving him*, that the wholeness of the Self is not extracted from any level of Reality, *but is equivalent to it.*

And this is an essential point; *that the individual soul is not separate at all from The Supreme Consciousness.* Thus, The Observer ceaselessly observes the subject of its observation until that subject wakes, again and again, to the point of *knowing The One* that offers *the sight to see that Observer and observed are one.* The mystic—*the knower*—conceives that *he is always being responded to. And this is the Real point.*

Remain Cloaked

Protect and value your growth and always prevent its loss by doing nothing that would damage your image in the eyes of The Creator. The mystic is by nature a private person, safeguarding hard-earned secrets beneath his elaborately embroidered cloak. Only he is aware of what is written on the rich inner lining of his robe. He knows that others might think to interfere with his work and progress, even encountering those who wish to undermine or steal his spiritual power.

Outside of sharing your inner condition with your teacher or spiritual director, it is not wise to discuss your spiritual states and experiences with others. Aim to gain wisdom, rather than entertain or try to impress others by relating stories of your spiritual process. Especially early on, telling too many tales marks an aspirant as being immature, and those who are so underdeveloped are never given spiritual authority. Also, without having first gained wisdom, you may mistakenly throw out a tale of a true experience or inner state from the basis of an irreverent mindset.

If you want, detail your progress in your journal, dating each entry and recording it in the present tense. As your legend unfolds, you will one day be able to look back on your own evolution and appreciate that you did not disperse its power by immediately relating spiritual events, or worse, assigning a random meaning to them.

Esoteric orders have always preserved secrets so they don't fall into the hands of the evildoers or black hats. Secrets are only taught to those who are ready. They are not revealed to the immature or those who would improperly wield power; therefore, the most advanced keys and their intricacies are not entirely shared with the public. Some keys must be personally transmitted from teacher to student.

Many advanced mystics tend to stay off the public radar to avoid attracting unnecessary attention. At some point in the future, you may reveal some of yourself in order to teach or help others, but even then you will need to be discriminating about how much personal information you reveal. Intriguing stories may someday be told, but you may risk diluting their essence if you speak too soon. In revealing your story, be prudent about the details you share, for the mystic does not cast pearls on the unappreciative sow's ear. Protect your inner mystical potential beneath your cloak and wisely conceal your discipleship, knowledge and identity.

Here are some ways to stay cloaked and avoid spiritual pride:

☙ Let go of your need to tell stories about your mystical experiences and states. The impulse to spill tales marks you as being green—spiritually immature and an obvious target for those who would want to spend down or steal your power. Except for your spiritual director, leave most spiritual events unspoken.

☙ Don't brag. Soul does not brag; your ego does. Boasting portends of an attachment that obscures Reality, and it suggests you are deluded and caught in an *illusory phase*. Bragging means you are hooked by the effects of your own process, and it implies that you might enjoy being recognized as someone who is special or somehow divinely chosen.

☙ Don't make a spectacle of yourself. Instead, display dignity and grace. You are not the village fool, indiscriminately dribbling over your chin your secrets to everyone. You are not a circus performer, juggling and swallowing swords, showing you can do something the unawakened person cannot. If you want to receive grace, you must display grace. Since The Creator ever watches, *your consciousness is being measured against your judgment and discernment.*

᛫᛫ Be careful of your need to work "miracles" in public for the sake of proving something. It is not your job to convince or convert anyone else, for *only God owns such a power to convert someone into a knower and believer.*

᛫᛫ Stay willing to let go of rewards associated with being seen as a big-shot. If you grasp onto being special, you are facing an obstacle. If you stay glued to your public brand, you are a dead ringer for one who is caught in the web of illusion. If you keep a death grip on your status, it is a sure giveaway that you are stuck. Capitalizing on your awakening to achieve fame, fortune and public acclaim is an incredibly intoxicating trap. The mystic is ever willing to walk away from any identity and every attachment that might block his access to The Supreme.

᛫᛫ Don't become needy. Avoid garnering admiration from others by demonstrating power like an illusionist. You are not a trickster, you are a mystic.

If you would like to be a true magician, that is quite a valid endeavor, but be aware of the risk that you may mistakenly chase the intoxicating effects and rewards of power and thus forego attaining mystical knowledge and seeking union with The Divine. In reality, managing power is part of the magician's task. It takes the heart of a clear-headed wizard to masterfully handle the wand and the scepter, to walk the magical path and avoid power's pull on the ego.

Handling Power

Although one could say that The Creator is the provider of all power, there are two main types—*power you work to develop yourself* and *superlative power that is gifted to you by The Creator, bestowed as a result of enlightenment and vast attainments.*

Both types of power are not considered to be equal; God-given power trumps the self-administered. Although you may own a power, you cannot possess the full power of God—it is simply too big.

In terms of self-developed power, everyone can develop special abilities. However, just because you have accrued an impressive list of intuitive gifts and occult powers does not mean you have reached a pinnacle of spiritual realization or have attained significant aspects of The Truth. For instance, a person can be psychic, but it doesn't mean he or she has also attained spiritual realization. Every psychic is not a mystic; there is a difference between the two.

It is quite okay to possess and exercise self-given power, but don't get waylaid in the stations of the occult, paranormal or psychic when the mystical region is expecting your arrival. Remember, just because something feels paranormal in nature, it does not mean it is also "spiritual" (meaning "of God, of The Holy Spirit, of the awakened Soul").

In regard to spiritual gifts The Creator bestows, advanced and even miraculous powers naturally emerge as a byproduct of enlightenment and vast attainments. This kind of power is further perfected by applying the secrets of working with the alchemical and elemental properties of energized spiritual consciousness. It is only natural to be curious about these newfound, amazing gifts and abilities. You will want to test your skills and use gifts to help others but be aware of the traps associated with doing so. Until you reach the wisdom stages, you can easily become deluded by power, particularly if you are not aware of its source and purpose.

Instead of identifying with power, explore your intentions around accumulating it. The aspirant does not seek with an impulse to stockpile spiritual wealth merely for the sake of his ego, and he does not become attached to owning and wielding power.

If you get derailed by ego rewards, you will threaten to eject yourself off the higher path, and you will risk wasting years steeped in delusion. The world is flooded with would-be mystics who, out of spiritual ignorance and lack of seasoning, training, practice and study, unknowingly veer off the path too early to speed onto a quasi-spiritualistic dead end, one that hastens them to exploit elementary awakenings. Erringly thinking they must have arrived at a pinnacle station after having attained only rudimentary states of awareness, they have little knowledge that unless mystical states are fostered, they reduce over time to the "psychic" level of power which may one day simply burn out.

Although The Creator may wish to bless you with abundance, remember this: The path is humble; it is not ostentatious. The path humbles; it does not inflate the ego.

If the gift you give to the world is all sizzle, all special sauce with no secret ingredients and not enough manna to lead others to want to discover their own recipe for awakening, then I wonder which path you are on.

Do No Harm

The manner in which you commandeer power is an important determinate of growth. If you value advancement, then you will need to position yourself above any mindset that imperils it. You must know and firmly believe that it is beneath you to do harm to others, yourself, the Earth's creatures and the world at large. Do not create your own debasement by using power to inflict suffering, and do nothing that contributes to injuring, controlling, or intimidating others. If you want the benefits of rudimentary attainments to be a flash in the pan, if you want to quickly spend their wealth down to pennies, then by all means squander the wealth of power.

Take a good look at your inner condition. What do you stand for? Do you want to abuse or flash your power, or do you want to know your Soul? Do you want to defame another person's character and control his life, or do you want to wake up? Make a choice, because you cannot have it both ways. When you misuse power, your own is automatically subtracted.

What of revenge? Watch your temptation to get even with others and create retaliatory wrongs. By giving someone the evil eye, it signals that a malady has infected your heart, one that can only be healed by *mercy.* Wishing illness on another will only multiply your own affliction, while offering mercy will cure anything that ails you.

Regardless of whether a person does you wrong, be aware of any internal desire that he be destroyed and ruined. Do you think anyone's deeds or intentions go unnoticed by The Creator? You are not a vigilante, so whether another human deserves to physically, spiritually, emotionally or financially crash and burn is out of your jurisdiction. Who are you to inflict extreme punishment upon another, *when all karma is already being judged and handled by the higher realms*?

It is quite permissible to wield power to defend and protect yourself. Especially if you believe that malevolent humans, spirits or other enemies are trying to wrongfully douse the light, you may act to bind and disarm their attempts. Keep this activity private. Your intention to neutralize harm should be just that and not include an intention to extract revenge with punitive force. You may well need to act as a warrior to stop enemies from harming you and wreaking havoc in the world, but the true hero won't feel inclined to exact a pound of flesh and teach unconscious people a lesson by using torture.

Divine Providence determines the conditions and limitations of personal power. Understand that spiritual power is loaned to you, and it may be returned to its Source if you misuse it. If you exercise power in the spirit of manipulation, you will decay, delay, or prevent your full awakening. If you employ power in the spirit of control and domination, to greedily receive riches, or to demonstrate being ultra special, you threaten your progress.

If you are enlightened or vastly progressed and crystallization is accomplished, then power and gifts will remain more or less intact to be exercised at will, giving you evidence of having learned to responsibly manage them. Lastly, be prudent with the manner in which you manage authority itself, because you are being held accountable for its expression. *The greater the power bestowed to you, the greater your responsibility is in handling it.*

FIFTEEN

The Mission of the Mystical Heart

The vessel of your heart captures a mist decanted
by the cloud of unknowing. Even as the mist bubbles
past the vessel's rim it seeks to replenish,
for its unadulterated dew will never evanesce.

What is the Mystical Heart?

The mystical heart is the sacred heart, a cavernous inner portal through which the Self is exalted and the subtle and physical bodies are transfigured by divine love. The portal's innermost center point houses the seat of the awake Self, the Witness, the Atman.

In the Upanishads, the sacred heart is referred to as *Hrit Padma* (Heart Lotus), the secret inner kingdom of God. Also called the etheric heart, it is depicted as the esoteric eight petal lotus beneath the Anahata (heart chakra). In Christian mysticism, it is called the *Sacred Heart of Jesus*, shown aflame and encased in thorns. In the Vedas, the sacred heart is said to be located to the right of the physical heart, three finger widths below it.

The Heart-Point of Reality—the "point in the heart" of which the Sufis and Kabbalists speak—can be seen as a super-compressed particle stationed deep within the mystical heart into which the forces of creation are drawn tightly together, as if the entire cosmic ocean of God were bound into a single drop of consciousness. In Sanskrit, a particle is called *bindu*, meaning a dot, a drop, a point, an undifferentiated mass of pure potential—the stuff that the universe and all that it will ultimately hold are made of. When the point is activated, a big bang of explosive energy is released, blowing open an egress through which the white fire of Divine Consciousness flows to ignite the Self with the intelligence of love and the beatitude of glory. Tremendous

179

bliss and rapture follow, serving to unbind the knot that secures differentiated consciousness—the mind's sense that it is independent from Reality—and the knot's loosening opens the way to confirm your inseparability from The Beloved. It is by virtue of the force of divine love acting on your heart that Supreme Consciousness spontaneously perfects itself through your personal being. Thus, the sacred heart is the agent, medium and conduit for the intelligence of divine love and wisdom transmitting the soul's divine flame.

Newly unbound by the impact of Spirit, the temple of the sacred heart is quickened with vibratory frequencies of light which echo tremors that are felt on the right side of the chest at the level of the heart, the whole heart and within the heart's right chamber. The heart's cavern walls sync to vibrate, emitting a hum, the OM, triggering transcendent states of bliss and rapture that facilitate awakening, Gnosis and spiritual knowledge. One may feel an accompanying tremor in the sacred heart itself and have an inner vision of a flame of light centered within it.

Once the knot of differentiation is disassembled by The Beloved, the Self can push further upwards to attain Oneness with the All Pervading Reality. Thus, the knots in the sacred heart that prevent an upward flow of energized consciousness unravel, allowing consciousness to travel unimpeded through the subtle body system to the crown chakra, where one encounters the Divine Mind. Once united with The Divine in both heart and mind, the Self remains reposed in absolute completeness. Advanced practices of Tantric yoga, for instance, facilitate this process.

What is Divine Love?

Divine love is God's immense gift, the result of The Beloved's heart in action, the One Love that is conveyed, carried and dispensed by Shakti, Divine Mother, Holy Spirit and Ruach D'Kaddishin. Its divine name in Greek is *Theos Agape Estin*, meaning "God is love." *Agape* expresses the love for God that humans carry and the love that God feels for them. Just as God cannot be separated from its Spirit, Spirit is inseparable from love. As the mystic descends into the secret grotto of the mystical heart chamber to invoke divine love, a mist springs forth, offering an elixir of life-sustaining dew. The emission flows like a stream rushing out of Eden, issuing from a lush valley to collect in a pool. Here, the soul is baptized by The Holy Spirit, immersing the Self's sacred heart in divine love.

There is a continuous cascade of love being dispensed from the Heart of The Beloved into the secret cavern. Once accessed, this cave is destined to become a wellspring drawing from the harbor of divine consciousness, and the nature of this estuary is that it can never evanesce, be exhausted, tapped dry, spent down, or entirely depleted. Thus, you are built to be replenished time and time again, to be continually refreshed in Spirit's promise to drench you with an endless font of living water. Thus, the quicksilver fluid of rapture is ever able to quench your inexhaustible thirst.

Divine love seeks to forever bond you to its Source, *to teach you to love*, to remind you that your heart is never disunited from The Beloved's. The action of divine love empowers the mystical heart, radically transforms your emotional heart and irretrievably transfigures your being. The force intends to awaken you to your most beauteous state of realization—knowing that you cannot be mystically alive without also being tapped into the eternal stream of divine consciousness.

The Consequence of Divine Love

Once touched by the fire of divine love, you feel singled out, selected and known, forever identified by the finger of Shiva who impressed his indelible print on your pulse. When you taste divine love, its nourishment saturates and nourishes every square inch of your being. As it razes a path through your etheric heart, the quenching serves to incinerate the barriers that prevent you from experiencing bliss and passion. In being so richly loved, you are re-collected into the arms of The Beloved; you know for certain that you were never ignored or forgotten, and in kind, you remember that you were made to be an expression of God's love.

The rapturous quality of divine love is so intimate you feel as if you are being betrothed to God, your union consummating within the heart itself. Bliss strikes in a divine red kiss pressed to the breast like an emblem, signifying a marriage. The awakened Soul stirs queen bee Shekhinah, who deposits into the heart hive the copious honey of mercy to seduce the droning groom, luring The God Force toward its own creation so that the grace of bonding is conferred and reenacted. Enlightenment of the mystical heart is the ritual by which you and The Supreme are eternally wed, and the union serves as an inextricable welding of male/female consciousness. Thus, you are seeded, endowed with seminal nectar during the ecstasy of consummation.

In the blissful days after awakening, you are *in love with love itself.* Love rings out in a celebratory chime from the heart's bell signifying unification, and the resulting melody will never vacate the steeple, for its song is meant to be forever sung in the spire of the soul. Just the way performing the act of singing makes you a singer, then so by fulfilling the act of loving, you become a lover.

All because of love, you experience a deep appreciation for your existence. No matter how difficult your time on Earth has been, you see the value in your life. No matter how rough, jagged or inadequate the serrated edges of your world may have felt before enlightenment, they are buffed smooth and made flawless in your mind.

Awakened to a brand new *heart state*, you are entranced by the simple presence of nature and the workings of its creatures. You feel poignantly touched by the ladybug stretching its dotted, crimson wings over the glory's quivering blue petal, ingratiated by the periwinkle dragging its coiled shell over the polished stones, and revived by the snowdrops melting on your shoulder. You perceive the sound of your breath as being imbued with sacred currents; when you inhale, it seems the breeze feeds you its molecules as icy spheres of mercury, and as you exhale, steamed heat flees from your parted lips to gently disperse into the atmosphere. And as you experience these things, you know The Divine is watching itself and is being engaged by your watchfulness.

Divine love is the medicine of God, the mightiest of regenerative forces, a formula that seals the realization of faith and love. It is the one and only antidote. By becoming anointed with the medicinal oil of The Holy Spirit, charismatic gifts are bestowed to you, with each one offering a type of power.

Whatever mortal wound has been speared in your side, you may ask that Spirit mend you with love's holy remedy. This fertile treasure is the cure-all balsam, the panacea, the miracle ointment, the alchemical potion for every affliction known to mankind. Ever able to protect, sanctify and heal, love's medicament is made to be applied to every inner torment, each abrasion of misunderstanding and every disability of the mind. Thus, divine love is a balm that is so charged with never-ending power it will mitigate every shameful wound, cauterize every ugly cut and soothe every swollen bruise.

The Mission of the Human Heart

The human heart's mission is to embody, receive and transmit love in its loftiest, unconditioned, uncut purity so that you can reproduce its dynamic action from the core of your emotional being via loving intentions, thoughts and deeds toward others, self and The Divine. The purpose of the human heart is to exemplify love in order to emulate, reflect and offer the altruistic attributes of its divine Source.

The human heart's greatest task is to become deconditioned so that it becomes an elegant and refined medium to channel pure divine love. If there is one single thing to achieve while you are alive on Earth, then learning to love without conditions and extending your heart in compassion and loving-kindness will be enough. The truth is *it will be everything.*

The heart is not just a blood-pumping muscle—it is also a gland and sensory organ with the ability to produce peptides. Also, receptor sites are found within heart tissue, making it reactive to oxytocin, the hormone related to feelings of human bonding. When the mystical heart awakens, it's as if a floodgate in the heart ruptures, injecting love's electrifying current into your arteries to cascade through the body and enliven and empower every cell. Thus, due to the extraordinary chemistry of this love, a mixture of biochemicals, peptides and psychoactive compounds is released, causing bliss and rapture to mount to an overwhelming crescendo.

Interestingly, both the heart and the brain conduct electrical signals that generate independent electromagnetic fields but the heart field emits much more wave voltage than the brain's. Just as you can enhance the heart's mass by physical exercise, you can influence its field and increase its spiritual capacity by exercising volumes of compassion and unconditional love that in turn influence your mind. By exerting heart and radiating loving-kindness, you increase your capacity for emotional bonding and loving.

Just as you electrically charge the current of your personal heart field with the emotions you generate, you similarly power your own mind field with your intentions, thoughts and desires.

It makes sense that the heart field's electrical power overshadows the brain's energy because spiritually the heart modulates and refines the thinking mind itself, meaning *the sheer strength of unconditional love and all of its qualities are energetically designed to influence and override the mind.* Thus, as you learn to become love, you expand and perfect your heart state; you influence its energy field and its corresponding wavelength. *In turn, the resulting field not only affects you but everything and everyone in its sphere.* Thus, the mission of the awakened heart field is two-fold—*to radiate love and be altered by its stunning radiance.*

In knowing that the heart's sphere of authority extends to everything and everyone, to the universe and the multi-verse, it is part of our heart's mission to elevate and influence the sum of our thoughts, attitudes, behaviors and deeds so that the quality of energy that we contribute to the Universal Field of Consciousness is helpful and beneficial—that it advance and support human consciousness and not undermine its progress.

What is Unconditional Love?

Unconditional love is the complete signature of The Beloved's dispensation—the emission of perfection that flows from The Divine.

The human heart is equipped to echo this signature, to reverberate its traits. Being One Love, unconditional love is whole in essence, encompassing the additional qualities of mercy, acceptance, forgiveness, compassion, tolerance, loving-kindness, understanding, patience, devotion, generosity and more, all of which happen to be divine attributes.

Being so complete, One Love cannot be portioned or reduced. Unconditional love is thus *immutable*; it is like a flawless diamond that can't be cut or broken apart to single out aspects of the whole. Therefore, The Indivisible is not apt to be divided so much as it is *multiplied*. Thus, when you love someone unconditionally you multiply the principle of complete and unadulterated love by extracting its purity to replicate it. And when you multiply love's power, you will at the same time open and clear the many channels that lead to and away from your mystical heart, enabling it to be a perfect medium for divine love.

If you think to place conditions upon love and offer it how and when you think someone deserves it, you are dividing its gem, but One Love permits no such cleavage. It's much better for the soul to give away a whole diamond rather than try to section off a measly chip, for everyone's hand deserves to receive the Rock of Ages.

This means if deep down you intend to divide love rather than multiply it, you will offer but a fragment of its true power and you will miss an opportunity to decondition your heart.

Remember, *love is not so much a behavior but a state of being.* When you love unconditionally both your heart and the heart of the one you love are actually being transformed and transfigured, affected by the life changing essence of divine perfection.

Here are some tenets:

⊶ To earnestly decondition your heart, you must be willing to honestly bear witness to the conditions you hold within your mind that block your radiant ability to love.

⊶ It is by *reforming the impulse* to divide, limit and withhold, and by *erasing the intention* to harshly judge, criticize, punish, condemn, harm, shame and other such things, that creates a chance for you to deeply love. *As such impulses decrease, the heart naturally deconditions itself.* But one cannot control an impulse— one can only *notice* its drive.

⊶ You cannot bring light to any intention that is unconscious; thus, the key to uprooting unconsciousness held in your heart is to *bring awareness* to any attitudes, thoughts and intentions that cause you to withhold love.

To decondition the heart and open it to unconditional love, it helps you to become aware of your intentions behind withholding love. Each time you want to withhold love, just notice that you want to, that you are placing a condition upon it. Each time you want to behave more lovingly but the intention or thought beneath this action is misaligned to include anything else except plain love and its attributes, just notice. Each time you do something you consider to be a loving thing but it's done for the wrong reasons, just notice. Each time you love someone for the purpose of receiving something back in return, just notice. Then, push against your own resistance and take a risk to more fully give of yourself.

It is your loving presence that is the unadulterated, real you. By loving unconditionally, it shows you are committed to overcoming your fear of being hurt and rejected, and it implies that you are willing to risk being vulnerable enough to expose your heart. This kind of bravery to be authentic and open gives you the courage to let down your defenses and conquer your hesitation to extend your heart. You must explore the conditions that make you so concerned about taking the chance to love. You must believe you are strong enough to untangle the barbed wire that defends your guarded heart. When you disassemble your fences, you remove your self-imposed prison and develop the space for love to spontaneously expand within you. Only then will you be released from the impulse to resist the full force of being turned into love.

You will notice that the terms of your outer-world conflicts parallel ones you are holding within your heart. If you cannot forgive, resentment will stick the walls of your heart, and *a corresponding restriction will manifest in your material world.* You must believe it is worth it to let go of your resentment so that you can make room for love; only then can you create an unsurpassed chance to be unconditionally cared for by others in return.

Can any of us really offer unfiltered, unadulterated, unconditional love to one another? We can, at every turn of circumstance, try. And we can become aware of the terms when we cannot. Please understand that *being a loving and compassionate person is a means to awaken.* You might even ask, *by exerting sheer will power, can an unawakened person become divine love and bring on his enlightenment?*

Believe it or not, you can make progress to that end if you continually strive to use your head to apply heart. You will find that the beam of The Beloved will entrain to your heart, and indeed, the veils that prevent enlightenment will begin to thin, exposing the light within you.

During enlightenment The Beloved's action of loving you so thoroughly will teach you all you need to know about love. Because the quintessence of this love is so beyond the Richter scale of human emotional love, then one can only humbly attempt its fabrication, but in doing so, *by putting love and compassion into action*, it will be a triumph for the spirit. Each time you are able to express tiny multiples of unconditional loving-kindness, your heart and mind are being *re-conditioned*. Each time you tap into your capacity to love regardless of circumstance, you extract a semblance of the nectar of The Beloved, and you bring its pleasing drops down from above, where it falls upon your crown like a gentle rain that droppeth from heaven.

This is the message: As you become the lover and practice selfless giving from your heart, you will realize you have been duly changed because your impulse to withhold has finally been reversed—this is the mark of one who has dedicated his life to love.

When one day it no longer makes sense to restrict love, you will have gained tremendous progress—this is the emblem of the deconditioned, unfettered, unconcerned Soul. This is the badge of the lover. Pray for the arrival of this magnificent sign.

Love Yourself

To the exact degree you are able to love yourself, offering to your own heart the breadth and depth of the many attributes of unconditional love, is quite often the same degree you convey it to others. Imagine that your heart is a furnace and you are the one with your finger on the thermostat, selecting out the temperature. If you decide to give yourself only forty degrees of heat, you will be standing in a frigid home, furnishing to others who pay you a visit a very cold atmosphere. *The match is in precise proportion*, so bank the coals high and others will feel a steady burn. This is a very simple spiritual law; the more you increase the density of self-love, then by default, the more of its substance you become eligible to receive and transmit.

Whenever you sense an inner lack, you will unconsciously project that lack onto others. For example, if you are unable to love yourself because of your past mistakes and misguided choices, it shows you have placed conditions on the terms of your self-worth, and you will be prone to assign similar ones to others who make poor choices and big mistakes.

If you cannot begin to empathize with your own humanity in relation to your personal failures and then extend to your own heart self-compassion, then you will be tempted to parse out only meager amounts of this attribute to others when they fail or disappoint you.

If you feel you deserve little mercy for your past indiscretions, then you could be prone to be hardhearted when it comes to offering it to others who may do you wrong. If you have not forgiven yourself, then you are more likely to feel intolerant toward others when you feel they have done something that is seemingly unforgivable.

In all of these cases, your relationship with yourself will tend to be reflected onto your relationships with others and even the world at large. Therefore, you must be willing to leave your mistakes, misjudgments, failures, disappointments and indiscretions behind you and begin the process of self-understanding, self-forgiveness and acceptance.

Whenever you find there is less than 100% of an option to forgive yourself or others, *bring your awareness to your underlying tendency* to withhold love and place conditions. Upon each occasion that you become cognizant of passing a judgment to withhold forgiveness, it offers you a chance to identify that you are still harboring an intention to parse out love. It is then up to you to continue to work on yourself, to make an effort to set yourself free from the heavy and tiresome burden of this kind of restrictive and disruptive consciousness and see that love and forgiveness is the only thing that will liberate your heart.

And of course, there is one more consideration.

Many people can more easily or safely shower unconditional love and forgiveness on others, but they cannot offer these same gifts to themselves, showing that self-care comes in a sore second to giving to others. But understand that if you think you are so unlovable, the degree of love you put out to others will, by default, be colored by that sentiment.

When you starve yourself of self-love and self-forgiveness, don't be surprised if certain others unconsciously withhold their love and forgiveness from you, for they are only mirroring a degree of your inner process.

Love Is Enough

Trust in your capacity to remain loving. No matter the risks or circumstances, *love is always enough.* If you learn to live your life emulating the qualities of love, it will be a life unwasted. To extend compassionate love is the greatest act a human can commit —there is no accomplishment bigger than this, no matter how humane or helpful to society it appears. No amount of parenting children into successful, creative, productive citizens, no material sacrifice for the benefit of others, no heroic saving of people's lives, no monumental philanthropic, cultural or social achievements will minutely compare to accomplishing the daily act of loving.

Although love's power will cure you, your old patterns will threaten to repeatedly rise to the surface, requiring the reapplication of your clear awareness and discerning mind. You will see that when you extend love to actively heal yourself, you are in turn offering healing to others. This is the meaning of the phrase, *Healer, heal thyself*; as you conduct the energy of love through the medium of your own heart, you are also being healed by its energetic force. Heal yourself, and do not let this remedy go to waste!

Love is meant to exist *between things*; its intent is to bind, to interconnect sentient beings and creatures. Its impulse is to electrify and impassion, to purify and transmute every surface it touches. Love's fire is designed to dissolve anything which defies its power, incinerating that which obscures your understanding of God's love for you. Each time you seek to ignite love, you fire up a Force of God within you. Thus, love is meant to be internally contained, enkindled, released and shared, its flame of salvation spread to one and all.

If you are enlightened, you come to understand that you had been holding a secret in your heart that all along the stuff of God —the quality of pure unconditioned love—had always been carried within you, tucked as a tiny seed within your breast that was planned to take root. You discover you were born with the life-changing power of this love, and you find that all you ever needed was for it to grow and flower. Such love displayed within an open heart is intended to be the most beautiful expression of God's plan for your life.

SIXTEEN

Spiritual Means and Methods

There is the obtuse frog, haplessly jumping
from puddle to puddle, never making the creek.
Here is the golden fish that sharpens the swish of its fin
and steers to the one fluent stream. Meanwhile,
the frog croaks itself to sleep in shrinking pits of mud.

Do Spiritual Practice Methods Cause Enlightenment?

Yes and no. Methods certainly prepare your consciousness, mind and subtle body and contribute to your eventual enlightenment, but they do not necessarily *directly* cause it. There are several factors that create this causation. Although some think otherwise, the mystics whose sacred hearts have been attuned by The Beloved would say that you do not exalt yourself and elevate into Reality solely by your own volition. They would say The Supreme is the one that *by grace* lifts up the soul to allow this grand process to transpire. In this regard, you do not own full control of Spirit, so you cannot bestow divine grace upon yourself. *You see, enlightenment is not a gift you take—it is one you are given.* Even a guru will not so much bestow enlightenment to another person, but it is through his *God-given stature as a medium of Supreme light* that he may transmit *grace* in the form of spiritualized light, and it is *the consciousness of that grace* which enlightens.

Enlightenment initiates a *deconstructive process*, so it is fruitless for you to attempt to use your unawakened mind to construct anything that will cause the finite's destruction. Think about it—would your brain wish to temporarily destroy its own reasoning function? Of course not; in fact, it will resist its annihilation all the way up to the point of surrender. Thus, you cannot concoct a Reality that you can control, you cannot manipulate The Truth, and if you think you can do these things then this is a fantasy your base mind is creating. You can climb the ladder, but you cannot push your way past the last rung into formlessness because the blank and formless uppermost rung leans upon the sole shoulders of The Supreme who has the final say so about your ascent. Yes, there is a plan and framework for the ladder, but each higher step must *first be manifested via nothing other than your conscious awareness—your higher mind.* In approaching that which is formless, there is nothing for your thoughts to stand upon, for although high levels of awareness may be "known," the Ultimate Reality of Formlessness, which is above and beyond all knowing, cannot be.

Since your base mind cannot logically conceive of enlightenment, then you can neither invent nor manufacture it on a cognitive level. If you could appropriate enlightenment yourself, then you could theoretically control its effects and process, but you see, during unity, you will own no such volition. It is only after the process of unity winds down to separation do you have a sense of personal will.

Nevertheless, you can contribute to *creating the essential terms of inviting in grace* by practicing means and methods to refine the conscious mind. You can remove inner obstacles and bring your soul to the threshold of the heart so that The Divine can meet you at that junction. When the soul convenes with The Boundless One at the strait of Infinity, a permanent link is made to elevate it beyond the locks. Spirit then rushes in and ushers you through the aqueducts to transcendence and exaltation.

How then shall you bring yourself to the threshold and establish the inner terms for the conduction of grace?

Here are some suggestions:

☙ By walking the path and perpetuating your desire for communion with The Divine.

ℴ→ By repeating methods of inner recitation and inquiry that *create internal conditions* that reform your subtle body and systematically lessen the terms of duality that separate you from your divine nature. (As you solicit your non-differentiation, the natural Self and the kundalini/Shakti life force are encouraged to emerge.)

ℴ→ By practicing methods such as Tantra yoga, meditation, breathwork, concentration, contemplation, kirtan, purification, visualization, spiritual study and rituals, along with methods like mantra, overtone singing, chanting of seed syllables, reciting and singing The Names of God and more.

ℴ→ By receiving an outward grace that is conveyed to you by another enlightened human; thus, a trinity is formed connecting you, The Divine and the enlightened one, thereby multiplying the transforming, illuminating force.

ℴ→ By embracing peace and silence so that you become receptive and open to The Light.

ℴ→ By practicing the non-doing measure of *being* and by dedicating yourself to promoting conscious inner awareness. As your inner consciousness is reformed, the outer world shifts to become a mirror of that change—until finally inner and outer pictures coalesce to reflect your realization of The Absolute, unchanging light.

ℴ→ By reading and gaining wisdom of spiritual truths, for knowledge and understanding is a method unto itself.

ℴ→ By becoming love and offering compassion and loving-kindness.

Meditation methods have common threads, such as inviting in a sense of presence, developing the capacity for awareness, encouraging peace, stillness and equanimity, quieting the mind, reversing the outgoing flow of thoughts and senses, steering energized consciousness through the body's subtle pathways, promoting contemplation, generating intention and desire and evoking emotions that promote the production of biochemicals and compounds essential to peace, transcendence and inner growth.

Regardless of the method chosen, keep in mind that your *conscious awareness is the prime determinant of awakening*, so those methods that lead you to stay alert and aware will assist you on the path. Many methods stress repetition, apply the use of breath and sound, and train you to work with specific intentions. Methods that encourage stillness and awareness reframe the mind to become a medium for spiritual consciousness and contribute to an inner milieu conducive to awakening.

In addition to meditation, yoga asanas are beneficial because on a physical level, they help you maintain a healthy body, a flexible and straight spine and a sound nervous and glandular system to accommodate for the unobstructed movement of energized consciousness. Asanas may keep you physically fit, but the practice was originally designed as an ancient integrative spiritual discipline that opens many spiritual avenues leading to transcendence.

The question is, *are you likely to attain enlightenment if you have not devoted time and practice to methods?* I don't think there are tricks or shortcuts to self-actualization, yet "sudden" enlightenment (without the soul having been prepared by methods) is quite possible because "non-doers" are also excellent candidates for illumination. Remember, a mystic is often engaged in *doing* or *not doing; he is alternately active or passive in his activity, engaged in either seeking or finding.* As a note, the onset of enlightenment is sudden and abrupt, initiating in the blink of eye.

If you are a non-doer who has not dedicated himself to practices, but you have reached enlightenment nonetheless, it means that your life was destined for awakening! The classic mark of true enlightenment is its profound effects on the soul and the authentic expression of the spirit. Both enlightenment and awakening of the mystical heart create tremendous impacts and vast inner transformation. If you think you were enlightened without practicing any methods whatsoever, then wait and see if your inner state leads to future progress; if your experience dead-ends in little personal and spiritual growth, you will have your answer.

Although one might imagine that the primary focus of a method like meditation is to forcibly expunge the mind of thoughts, the prime goal is to cultivate inner states of receptive quietude *so that clarity and peace naturally arise as byproducts.* Vacancy leads to receptivity, which naturally leads to expansive awareness and perspicacity.

In terms of meditation, you cannot force yourself into silence, you cannot mandate stillness and you cannot demand peace. Over-trying to control the mind only conditions an ego desire to suppress thought. You cannot use a sledgehammer to pummel your thoughts into submission; it will not work. You can only notice what you notice. You can only evacuate the premises of your thoughts, clearing enough space to make way for the implantation of seeds of consciousness. Remember, you are not your thoughts, but rather you are your *higher mind.*

If you were a pianist and you wanted to learn to play a complex sonata, you would need to practice its composition with sheet music until you know it by heart. Methods help to expose the inner graph, the same one needed for the placement of chords and notes that produce transcendence. Methods do not form the musical staff; they help develop the system upon which octaves can be written and played. As you practice your technique to perfect the piece, before long you would find that playing becomes effortless, rather than forced. By simply repeating your practice, the composition will finally evolve into a masterpiece, made so by layering it with instruments of consciousness. In this way, the devoted musician *becomes the music he knows by heart.*

Depending on tradition and station, mystics may or may not continue to use methods their whole lifetimes. Some apply practices until they no longer seem necessary or helpful, but they may revisit them as a process requires attention. This is when The Way becomes graceful and unforced, devoted to non-doing and often centered on *being open* rather than attaining, for simply by reaching the level of "being," *one continually attains.*

The Challenge of Methods

The object of silent meditation is to use the mind's ability to "not think," to consciously exist in the witnessing mind-space *between and beyond* thoughts. However, it is the lower mind's job to think, and it wants to keep interrupting even short spans of silence. The salient point is that such a method is used to actually transcend the *unconscious activity* of the mind, so the initial inclination is to access *an inner state of alert awareness.*

Meditation methods attempt to dissolve hindrances that would prevent the Witness from arising, and certain measures contribute to *creating terms* for enlightenment. How then do methods work to enforce these terms?

1. They help to reframe consciousness so that barriers between you and Reality dissolve, and interestingly, it is the base mind that contributes to maintaining those barriers.

2. They help to turn the *mind* inward, meaning they subdue and then reverse and stabilize *the mind's natural outgoing tendency* to process thoughts of its objective view and project its experience onto the external, material world.

3. They help to turn the *senses* inward, meaning they *subdue the body's sensory system* and then reverse and stabilize the mind's inclination to process the external, material world through sensory experiences. With little to sense, both thought and sense correspondingly subdue.

Methods are akin to tree branches that echo the concept that the taproot of spiritual consciousness is buried and invisible beneath the soil of reason; as the root deepens it sends impulses to create fruit in the limbs *well above* the logical, cognitive mind. Once the fruit of your labor develops, the Witness of personal consciousness can arise, fly up like a hawk and perch high in the towering treetop, establishing clear vision and unimpeded perspective. The challenge is that too much strenuous practice with methods only creates the impulse for the mind to become even more solidified, more ego-driven and fixed on its desires, creating thick, gargantuan branches that will eventually topple the tree before the root is given a chance to deepen, setting you back in your development and creating a barricade to one day inviting in the lofty Observer.

Select Practices

It is called "practice" for a reason, for exercises are repeated time and time again over periods of months and years before one may gain appreciable results. This means that although methods have immediate effects on your mind, it can take years for those effects to create significant inner changes. As you build the inner temple with methods, you are continually stimulating a process by which you can acquire growth. Just as a pebble dropped into a still pond creates ripples that will later reach the opposite shore, spiritual consciousness stimulates an immediate process that is designed to unfold on the shoreline of your future.

If you stay loyal to your practice and push through resistance that tells you to give up, you will find your rigidity will soften. Whenever you gain progress due to methods, it means you have remained as the fish in the stream of consciousness, committed to perfecting its fin stroke, training its body and mind. Since time is needed to create inner change, the sooner you start your practice, the better. So please don't be the frog that is hopping about from path to path, dabbling in meditation once a week for a few months, complaining that nothing big seems to be happening yet.

Your nervous system is an infrastructure of The Path, with your heart, glands, central nervous system and corresponding subtle energy system being a framework. It requires a number of years for this system to be built and charged before it is activated and before you can master its function and capacity.

With methods like yoga you can notice subtle improvements after a few weeks of consistent practice. By meditating and applying measures geared to stillness, you will literally be constructing a neurological system that *carries the molecules of particular emotions that help build spiritual capacity*; this result enables the body to adapt by secreting hormones and releasing select enzymes, neurotransmitters, peptides, neuromodulators and the like that contribute to your process. By continually establishing a spiritual interior, you will cultivate and charge a precise *subtle network* of channels and chakras that receives energy and conducts energized consciousness.

Neurological receptors for all kinds of hormones and biochemical messengers are found within every organ and tissue in the body. On a basic level, when you apply your will to develop your soul, you influence the function and expression of your DNA and encode its higher algorithms; you fine-tune gateway receptor sites and synapses—the bridges between nerve endings that receive and release enzymes and chemical messengers. *These connections and receptors directly correlate to receiving and conveying the impulses of spiritualized consciousness, and they transmit biochemicals of transcendence that impact DNA.* For instance, it has been found that during psychedelic states, the pineal gland in the brain releases a compound called DMT (dimethyltryptamine). This kind of arrangement sets you up on a genetic and neuro-endocrine level to be a vessel of consciousness for expansion, exchange and sharing.

Methods require your continued investment to practice in order to make progress with them. Spiritual consciousness builds on itself over time—it divides, fractions and multiplies in precise amounts—it is *quantized* to do so. If you stop and start your practice, *you will lose precious momentum*. As you consistently continue to practice, you will gain momentum and theoretically reduce the time it will take you to awaken.

The Practice of Stillness

When you practice stillness you are being *receptive* to Spirit— *you are making yourself into an open vessel*. Whenever the mind is generating thoughts, energy goes outward, reversing receptivity. One point of receptivity is to embrace stillness so that it leads to awareness.

Contemplative mystics use meditation as a method to quiet the mind and turn their senses inward to receive revelation, gain knowledge, commune with God and stay ready for the approach of Spirit. Especially early on in your growth, it is important to focus your efforts on increasing inner serenity, for emotions related to tranquility *are prerequisite to building a nervous system capable of transporting molecules associated with transcendent states.*

Think of meditation as preparing a table, anticipating the arrival of The Guest. You attune to the moment by setting your presence there, and not only do you place a chair for yourself, you set before you a timeless expanse for The Guest, making room for your soul to be nourished by the rich manna of spaciousness.

Meditation creates intimacy with the present moment, and it is within this relationship that decent progress can be made. Meditative states promote relaxation and help you gain equanimity and it equips you to be still enough to actively listen for the call of Spirit. By committing to the deed of staying present, your mind's tendency to stray will purify. Without acquiring the capacity for stillness, little substantial progress is made.

To actively perceive Spirit, begin to foster and welcome quietness. A rambling, unfocused mind state prevents translation of messages and signs that come from the spiritual realms. If you are preoccupied with thoughts and making plans, you will block, miss or even misread Spirit's advancement. By promoting calmness, the constantly chattering mind becomes more relaxed and less loud and intrusive. When you are empty of distraction you become amenable to the fine rhythm of Spirit's intonation.

While the method of visualization can aid spiritual growth, so can meditation that is geared to receptive emptiness, where the mind does not reference or envision anything at all. Should your meditation focused on silence prove too challenging, meditation using the breath can prove to be very helpful in focusing the mind.

A noisy, distracted mind will dampen your awareness. One of the goals of certain types of Eastern meditation practice is to experience "no mind," meaning your brain's outward activity is temporarily quelled, the way a turbulent, roaring river is calmed to a pleasing trickle. You are so conditioned to pursue random thoughts, it is difficult for this process to reverse in order that incoming stillness be received, but it can be accomplished. Stillness creates room for your conscious presence to emerge.

Enlightenment rarely happens during moments of chaos. Although those who are quite practiced in meditation can access a state of serenity under any excitable circumstance, until you become more skillful at entering into stillness and remaining there for periods of time, you will find it easier to meditate in a quiet and tranquil atmosphere. Quiet natural settings and temples are perfect environments to commune with Spirit, but your uncluttered room is just as good a place to access Silence.

The Open Field Method of Meditation

If you are new to meditation, you can start this practice by sitting for five minutes at a time, and then work your way up to twenty minutes or even more time. To begin, settle into an upright position; by keeping the spine straight and erect, it will aid the movement of energy through the main chakras. To avoid falling asleep, it is best to sit, rather than lay down. Keep the chest open rather than caved in, the body and breath relaxed and the belly soft. You may sit in the lotus position—cross legged—or on a chair. Lay your open, relaxed hands on your lap, palms up, left hand on top of the right one (if you like, lightly touch both thumbs together). Pull the hands to rest against the belly beneath the navel or use them to make a different mudra (hand gesture).

Keep the eyes relaxed in their sockets, either open and softly fixed on an object or gently closed. If you keep your eyes open, you may close the lids slightly and gaze downward past the tip of your nose. To prevent your mind from darting about and to keep your senses from being overly stimulated, softly fix your gaze on an object, like a candle flame, a picture of your spiritual Master, or another point of spiritual reference. Relax the jaw and pull the head back enough so that your head is neither bowed nor lifted. You may keep the mouth closed or open, but if open, then allow a bit more air to come in through your mouth than the nose.

The following is an age-old foundation practice that attunes your awareness to promote stillness that encourages increased inner peace and clarity. It is a practice of *formlessness*, meaning you do not visualize or create options to think. Following the practice, I offer my understanding of its mystical parameters, giving the underlying purpose as it relates to consciousness.

Let's begin.

1. If you are engaged in thought, just notice your engagement. Release any upcoming thoughts so that the mind is temporarily wiped clean and made empty.

2. *Notice that a space arises in which there is no thought.* Place your awareness *in that space*, but do not generate thought.

3. Soon a thought will arise. Thoughts will want to continually erupt and emerge, for this activity is the normal nature of mind. Do not try to control or squash the thought. *Just notice that a thought is there.*

4. *Don't think the thought, but let it dissolve to be absorbed into nothingness.* After the thought dissolves, the open field automatically reemerges.

5. *Bring your awareness back to the field of space and place your consciousness there. Rest in that clear space for as long as the next thought arises*—this could be one second or several.

6. Predictably, another thought will arise. *Acknowledge the presence of that thought. Don't think the thought, but just notice it.*

7. Start over at step 5, and continue the practice for the length of the session. As you practice this simple method over a period of time, you will notice that the time span of emptiness between thoughts will lengthen, meaning you will be able to achieve states of non-thinking for longer intervals and *as a result, the field of receptivity grows wider and deeper.*

What have you accomplished? As the field expands, you are in turn expanding awareness. As thought dissolves into formlessness, *you create an open, receptive field of consciousness*, which allows you to sink deeper into your true nature. You cultivate a state of receptivity so that it may be filled with conscious awareness. Due to your awareness, the field is being *imbued with consciousness* but it is also being *created by conscious awareness*. Because you are actively bringing your presence into the field, you are in turn *animating the energy* within it. You are not alone in that field, for the All-Pervading force of Spirit also inhabits it. But here is the critical key—*the field itself is also independently affecting you.*

There is something more. *The mystic deliberately creates a space for his probability to exist.* Without an expanse being created opposite the boundary of the veils, then your potential to penetrate through the veils and stand in the expanse on the other side of them will not exist. Think about it. If there is no possible space to stand in, then the boundary is self-limiting; it is like a dividing wall, and with an impenetrable wall in place nothing beyond it can be created.

Here is the key: *You cannot tunnel through a veil without an expanse of space having first been created.* When you pierce the veil you create space, *but you do so by setting your intention to find that which resides in the field beyond the veil—presence, unity with God and divine love. Thus, your active conscious awareness establishes a personal atmosphere of receptivity.*

The Practice of Meditative Inquiry

This is a simple but profound method that promotes being-ness, stillness and peace, creates an automatic inclination to flex and release will and begins an action to deconstruct the illusion of duality that contributes to the veils that prevent you from seeing the Real Self. There is no need to visualize anything or worry about your breath.

1. Simply sit in meditation and each time a thought comes up, just notice its emergence. Create the empty field and do not think any thoughts that arise, but replace them with the question, *"Who is beyond thought?"*

2. Do not try to figure out the answer or think anymore about the question. Go back to your silent meditation.

3. After you repeat steps 1-2 a number of times, *begin to generate a genuine desire to receive the answer to your question.* As the desire is intensely felt, emotions will result, and as they emerge, fuel the emotions by amplifying their effects.

4. As you feel the effects of the emotions, realize that *you have become your intention of being answered, for the answer is found in the effect and its cause.*

5. Since the answer is found in the effect and its cause, *realize that you have just received the answer, and drop your desire to feel, sense, understand and know anything whatsoever.* Sit in your clear awareness of all of this.

What have you accomplished? *By inquiring into the perfect Reality that is already present within you*, you will seek the depth of your true nature and you will propagate consciousness that lays the foundation of faith. By inquiring to meet your Real self, you *knock on the veils*, an action The Creator answers by reciprocally allowing you some form of entry or penetration through them. In effect, when you conduct the method of inquiry, you as the seeker *turn yourself into the question*, asking for The Creator's response in the form of undifferentiated light.

It is well beyond the Self's capacity to understand the workings and purpose of the *undifferentiated Eternal Light, for the undifferentiated is so pure, its divine power is not meant to direct your mind to conceive anything.* This is why the enlightened ones, upon emerging from the state of divine love, make no immediate claims to know or understand the extreme nature of The Supreme or its actions, for it is during these states that the soul's capacity to understand is temporarily hidden. It is only due to Gnosis that realized ones may receive small fractions of the essence of such knowledge.

If you are unawakened, the "I" that thinks and conceptualizes your thoughts is the person you believe yourself to be. However, *the one who too fervently desires* is the same person you believe yourself to be. But neither of these options is the true case because the Real you is already present beyond thought, beyond desire and beyond your thinking mind.

The Practice of Becoming a Light Unto Yourself

This practice combines recitation (mantra chant) with visualization and intention, and it employs the objective mind, allowing you to work with thought forms. You may repeat the mantra silently, by whispering or vocally, but choose one method per sitting. Vocal chant speaks to the meridian system and physical body in a great number of ways, while silent mantra affects the chakras and subtle body. It is potent to repeat the mantra at least 108 times per sitting for forty days in a row.

The number 108 corresponds to the total number of subtle channels leading from the mystical heart to the rest of the subtle body, and by repeating the mantra 108 times it ensures that the entire subtle body system is saturated in its vibration. In Sanskrit mantra practice, another goal is to eventually reach a total of at least 125,000 repetitions in all. Mantra repetition helps you to focus the mind, while it mimics and induces the multiplication of energy, strengthens and increases the spiritual capacity of the chakras, incinerates karma, draws in the vital life force, loosens energy blockages, conducts Shakti, and *entrains the vibrations of the entire body with that of the mantra*. To keep count, you may use a rosary or mala beads. As you recite, rather than allow the words to become rote and automatic, *keep the meaning of the words in your mind, and stay focused on your intention of becoming a light unto yourself.*

The concept for the following recitation is inspired by the words of Jesus in the Gospel of John (8:12), "I am the light of the world." Variations of both the recitation and the accompanying visualization are known in the mystical world to be effective, age-old spiritual exercises. I will add the recitation's mystical keys based on my understanding.

Before you start the recitation, visualize that a beautiful blinking star is stationed five inches above the crown of your head. Intensify the starlight so that it glows as bright as the Sun.

Envision that the shining star is creating a flood of light which surrounds and penetrates through your whole body.

Focusing on the crown of your head, imagine that a single beam of white light emerges from the star and descends to pierce the top of your skull, where it enters the head and concentrates bright light in the pineal gland in the center of your brain. From there, expand the light in all directions so that it fills your brain and skull and also stimulates the pituitary gland at the brain's base.

Focus on the pineal gland and inhale generously. Exhale and send the pineal light to each and every cell in your body so that your entire form is filled with sparkling light.

Bring your attention to your physical heart and the mystical heart center, perhaps envisioning a flickering flame inside of each. See the physical and mystical hearts become filled to capacity with light before sparkling activated light-energy streams to your entire being.

Once you are filled with light, push it outwards beyond your skin about arms' length in all directions and then expand it to create a perimeter around you. You have turned into a light being, and you are shining a brilliant field of mind/heart light.

Generate emotions of peace and well-being as you acknowledge that you are filled with the enlivened light of Spirit. Inwardly perceive that the undifferentiated light of The Eternal is moving within and around you of its own accord, flowing from your etheric heart to your entire subtle body system and personal field.

Remaining seated in the mystical heart, generate an intention that you realize your true nature and then allow any resulting emotions to emerge. Notice if you perceive any tingling or other sensations, showing you that Spirit is indeed moving within you.

Now, conduct the following recitation, keeping the essence of the words' meaning in your mind as you remain illuminated:

I Am The Light.
The Light shines within me.
The Light streams throughout me.
I Am one with The Light.
I Am The Light of the world.

᠃ **I Am The Light** - "I" Am the sole consciousness, the one and only single eye that is Spirit. Because "I Am" The Light, I am inseparable from it. I Am The Alpha. I Am *being.* I Am the Eternal, unchanging consciousness. I Am *now.* I Am *Presence.* I Am that which I seek.

᠃ **The Light shines within me** - I *invoke* the wellspring, the tremor of Spirit. I perceive energetic currents and spirals of The Force as being active within my consciousness and body. I Will Be.

᠃ **The Light streams throughout me** - The undifferentiated, unending current flows in many directions, filling, replenishing and restoring me. I *evoke* the foaming font of the living waters and activate the tremor of Spirit within me, causing a surge. My consciousness is fired up with Divine Light. I perceive, join with and influence The Light's movement. I master The Light.

᠃ **I Am one with The Light** - My soul returns to its Source and achieves unity. My consciousness is absorbed within the Self. I am forever united with Supreme Consciousness. I am indistinguishable from that which is omnipresent. My soul light contributes to the Unified Field of Consciousness. From above, I am being made illuminated. I have been found by that which I seek.

᠃ **I Am The Light of the world** - I bear The Light. The activity of The Light *is me*; I energetically embody the Presence and action of God. The Alpha-Omega *is me.* The Omega *Am* I. I am made equal to The Light. I Am that which watches and perfects its Self. From below, I make of myself *an immortal flame* so that I may embody the Presence of The Eternal Light.

The Light acknowledges Itself. Presence witnesses Itself. I radiate that which I Am.

At the close of your meditation, send light to any part of you that needs physical, mental, emotional or spiritual healing. Next, share this healing light with individuals, the community, the world at large and even the cosmos by imagining that it is flowing from you to those entities you wish to help. *The action of sharing compounds the blessing of healing and multiplies the light energy you receive.*

The Practice of Resounding Divine Attributes

Divine attributes, also called the expressions, emanations, or sacred "Names" of God, are seen as forces of consciousness that embody and illustrate the nature, virtues, qualities, aspects and characteristics of The Supreme One. You could say that Names reflect the expressive face or illustrate The Word of God. Regarded as sacred codes and formulas, their power is beyond measure, and the vibratory force of one Name influences the rest.

The scriptures and mystical writings of every major religious tradition contain and repeat a wide variety of Names that address the complex and nuanced qualities that God represents. Understand that the totality of The Supreme One is indivisible, so divine traits reflect God's integrity in particular ways.

Attributes are communicated and sounded through human consciousness so that they may be personally attained. Once embodied, divine traits are simultaneously mirrored back to God and shone to others. Thus, attributes are communicable to postulants who then multiply and dispense their virtues to the world. You will find that you will be personally drawn to certain Names.

The attribute of unconditional love, regarded as a theological virtue, encompasses the qualities of mercy and compassion. Sounding the ancient Names specifically associated with God

"The Merciful and Compassionate One," such as *El Rachum* is regarded as being extremely powerful for recitation. Jewish tradition even recognizes thirteen ways of mercy by which God governs the world, including compassion, grace, forgiveness, pardon, tolerance and *Erech appayim*, meaning "slow to anger."

Although it appears that an attribute like mercy or compassion can be divided, its essence cannot—it is simply able to be highlighted and multiplied; hence, several ways of using Names to petition a focused need came into being which draw selective energies to the aspirant.

At its most basic level, reciting The Names brings to the mind and heart such things as clarity, focus, power, openness, inspiration and devotion. By reciting The Names you are really uttering a prayer, glorifying and worshiping The Almighty One.

There are many ways to work with The Names and their letters. Applying The Names is considered a spiritual science, and mystics have used them for millennia in prayer, worship and study for many different purposes, such as to advance consciousness, seed a protective and potent network of light within and around the physical body, commune with The Beloved, open the links between the inner and outer realms, reach transcendent states, heal and purify the body, tune the nervous and subtle body systems, to manifest, absorb, or dissolve energy, and other goals. The practice rhythmically synchronizes breath, sound and mind, and as the rhythm deepens and slows, meditation deepens. As the deepening process advances, inner expansion naturally takes place.

As you sing and recite Names, so shall you draw unto yourself cardinal light that encodes a vibratory power within you. When a mystic "acquires" an attribute, he is then recognized as *being close in proximity* to an aspect of The Divine, so that as you are exalted the veils thin to bring you nearer and akin to God. In this respect, you become a relative of God, so this is how you are so recognizable in the eyes of The Supreme.

With each elevation of your station, and as the attribute becomes configured into your consciousness and subtle body, you are correspondingly being embossed in God code, stamped with a sacred sign. Each sign is like an insignia drawn by The Beloved's hand, a blessed emblem etched by way of spiritual fire.

The emblem signifies that *you vibrate a harmonic, a frequency similar to the corresponding divine attribute you acquired.* In this regard, once embedded with particular frequencies the elevated Self is able to homeopathically resonate to its holy similar. These vibrations identify you by their sound and light codes, announcing their particulars to the world, such as *I am love, I am compassion, I am mercy, I am forgiveness, I am understanding, tolerance, loving-kindness, acceptance, devotion,* etc. As you reverberate to God, you are identified as God stuff, for The Names become written on your consciousness. *So it shall be written and so it shall be done.*

In devotional practice, The Names are envisioned and repetitively written, sung, chanted and recited silently, aloud or in a whisper. Similar to mantra work, with silent repetition, one's *inner light* and *subtle body system* is powerfully stimulated.

When Names are verbalized the *physical body* is influenced while an appeal is made *to outer realms of manifestation.* Recitation is enhanced by applying concentrated, focused intention and aligning the body, mind and spirit to the meaning and purpose of The Name.

Since your consciousness already sounds the notes of the original God Spark, you have been made to mystically vibrate to attributes of The Divine. Since The Divine is incomparable, it has no exact similar, but you can pray that your soul reflect and thereby duplicate a close semblance of The Divine's light. By sounding a Name, you are invoking a blessing and its corresponding energy. This devotional practice selects out, invokes and echoes the omnipresent emanations of The Creator and helps move the devotee beyond duality, manifesting within him a synthesis of sound and light.

When you acquire the attributes of The Names, their forces are woven into the multidimensional tapestry of your soul by The Weaver. Thus, Spirit anchors its immanence within you, reminding you that *Presence is power.*

Attributes are worn in *raiment*—in a personal garment of light, one that by virtue of its existence reveals that your shroud of unconsciousness has been removed. The garment is observed with the naked eye as a shimmering mantle surrounding the mystic *due to his ignited inner flame,* and from its threads, orbs and beams may be seen shining in the atmosphere. Thus, by sounding The Names, codes will ring and sparkle from your fiber.

Those who awaken through the power of The Names are eligible to be invested with *The Coat of Many Colors*, The Divine Gown of Light that is encoded with layers of *multiplying* attributes. You shine the colorful rainbow lights to display the majestic essence of your original nature, the elemental embodiment of light itself. Such a display shows that your body, soul and mind have been spiritually transformed. Appearing as an assembled array of multicolored lights, the rainbow is a sign of the covenant, an agreement that states you and The Creator are bound by a sacred contract. Visually, the rainbow appears in broad daylight in its full spectrum, rising off the mystic's hands or radiating from the mystic's body like a prism beaming a unified field of colors.

Here are some tenets for sounding and reciting The Names:

☙ Bring a prayerful and reverent attitude to the practice. Create stillness, and concentrate on the sacred essence of The Name you wish to utter so that you may invite in its inviolable quality. Let the recitation seamlessly flow from within you, and be sure to tune into the space of silence that exists between each start and ending.

❧ As you recite, devote your full attention to The Creator, rather than fall back on automatic, rote recitation. Each time you resound The Name, you repeat your return to Origin. Combine intention, feeling, thought and sound, understanding that your consciousness is being encoded with energy.

❧ To take vocalization to a multidimensional level, use your voice to tone (create ringing harmonics) vowels and sound diphthongs within The Names. As you sound harmonics, additional notes and tones are produced, some of which are audibly heard while others remain inaudible.

Each frequency, heard and unheard, elicits its complement, creating modulations—additional harmonic notes that manifest on a scale beneath and above the original note sounded. You may also experiment with droning, humming and buzzing, or create sibilant, consonant and other sounds, but remember that The Names are rich *with vowels* that permit perfect access to harmonics.

SEVENTEEN

The Awakening of Humanity

When a single person awakens, it is a sign
that the heart of humanity is being stirred.
When one advanced soul attains enlightenment,
the pulse of us all is quickened in a fervent and passionate pace.

Is Mankind Truly Waking Up?

Yes. The spiritual/material balance of the world's collective fulcrum has heavily shifted to the material side of unconsciousness, approaching proportions that place the Earth and its sentient beings in peril. In addition, it seems mankind is being dragged to the edge of reason and logic by the hands of a few people in positions of wealth and power—those who, instead of working to prevent harm and alleviate suffering at home and abroad, are instead invested in keeping individuals asleep and driving unconscionable political and corporate agendas that inflict collateral damage on massive scales, exposing humanity and the planet's ecosystems to irreversible loss and calamity. It is clear that only a huge injection of spiritual light can correct the obvious wrongs done to planet Earth and its inhabitants. Thus, in order to quell such an insidious proliferation of unconsciousness and fulfill an intention to protect the planet and help its guests thrive, a gigantic influx of consciousness is required to spur a collective awakening.

There is another reason. For thousands of years, it has been recorded in the cosmology and prophesies of ancient civilizations that humanity will undergo a rebirth of consciousness, followed by the disintegration of prior ways of being. Rebirth is now upon us. There is a convergence of fate underway as the destiny of a divinely-planned collective transformation intersects the ravages of man-made unconsciousness. The challenge is a battle, for we

214

must recalibrate the weight of the fulcrum and counterbalance it to the side of The Absolute. A call-to-arms has been issued to all lantern bearers and spiritual warriors to not only help wake up the masses but support those who speak out against injustice and aggression and aid those that resist the status quo and refuse to be complicit to corruption, domination, dishonesty and self-serving materialism.

As we choose to awaken our souls at this time in history, we are joining the fight to shift the world order from being an exclusive hierarchy run by elite factions that enforce systems that reward and feed only a privileged few in favor of a holistic system that is designed to encourage parity, safety, and cooperation, as well as emotional, spiritual and physical well-being for all. We must seize the day and be brave enough to accept the responsibility to establish a different future, one in which governments and corporations see the value in sustaining the Earth and its creatures, great and small, or else the Earth itself, in consummate wisdom, will eventually take matters into its own hands and cleanse the source of irrationality from its face.

Because unconsciousness is multiplying at such an alarming rate, Spirit is intervening by accelerating individual consciousness in an attempt to elevate mankind above unwise and short-sighted actions. Therefore, consciousness is speeding up for all of us, but this is especially true for certain people that have decided to use their gifts to advance humanity, protect the planet, and help us avoid crisis.

One of the symptoms of spiritual expansion is experiencing timelessness—the sense that minutes and hours have merged into one continuous thread. Timelessness signals acceleration, and we must use this quickening to reach the tipping point and correct the wrongs done in the name of "progress."

As individuals awaken and reach enlightenment, the condition of humanity is uplifted. Since each one of us is a part of the whole, what one person is able to accomplish is a stellar advancement, a victory for us all. Thus, it is mandatory that every individual do his or her part to stay conscious. It is not enough for us to awaken our individual souls if we cannot exercise our wakefulness to help one another. We cannot pretend to be ignorant of the crimes that are being wantonly inflicted against humanity and planet Earth. There is no excuse that warrants turning a blind eye to blatant acts of neglect, abuse and aggression, for remaining sightless and silent constitutes complicity.

We, as citizens of Earth, must make haste and join together now in our wakefulness to expose truths and right injustices so that we may change the present course of history. We must bring the Earth and its occupants back from the brink of ruination that was intentionally created by the sleeping ones out of self-serving greed and political agendas, and in doing so, we will fire up the lighthouse of the soul and set its beam in watchful motion. We as awakened ones must decide to expand our horizons beyond the comfort of our own backyards and take steps to end global geological, atmospheric and oceanic damage. We must refuse to support corporate and political violence, aggression and oppression. We must obliterate human trafficking, slavery and crimes against humanity. We must serve as activists to educate and mobilize the masses toward a common goal of freedom, peace and harmony across the globe.

In regard to the urgency of waking up, we are living in unprecedented times, where electronic access to the ancient teachings of Masters and illumined Souls is readily available. Once kept secret, these teachings have become declassified, so there is no reason for people to remain spiritually asleep when the vaults have finally been opened. There is a reason why the vaults of advance teachings have been unsealed, and that is to educate and awaken increased numbers of souls.

Since new mystics are made based on the contributions of former ones, modern mystics will need to contribute their own translations and unique perspectives of Reality, which will in turn advance present day civilization. Hence, the mystic is entirely needed, as he is the one who elects to stand vigil with glowing lantern in hand, maintaining watch and illuminating the world from his elevated station.

There are many avenues to advancement. Since teachings are now spelled out in published works, progress can be made with independent study. Besides reading, engaging in presence and committing to spiritual practice, some people will need the assistance of a teacher who embodies being-ness.

Your teacher does more than instruct you; just by being in the vicinity of an advanced Soul, a transmission of consciousness occurs to speed your progress, whether or not you are conscious of that action. Besides being in your teacher's presence, you can also join a spiritual group so that you may share and reflect on your process and so that the field of consciousness created by the group contributes to your growth. The group can then expand its mission and send out healing and hope to the community, nation and world.

EIGHTEEN

The Blueprint of the Soul

Soul is pre-seeded with a promise to awaken.
Thus, you are made for transcendence,
created to realize ecstasy, bliss and passion.
You were born to enter the dimensions of the sacred heart
and one day dissolve into formlessness.

The Perfect Design

Everything that transpires to awaken you happens not by whimsy, accident or dumb luck but according to a sacred plan—*the blueprint of the soul*—the original, consecrated pattern of consciousness. Think of the blueprint as being the design of the soul created and coded by The Architect.

You are never far away from The Limitless One because you carry its seminal God seed within your spirit. Since a shard of consciousness from The Architect is embedded within you, it is found in every aspect of your physical and subtle bodies. This means you are designed to accommodate a mixture, a synthesis of consciousness, meaning your personal soul consciousness *blends and mingles with The Divine's.*

The blueprint is instilled with the origin of your primordial essence—The Infinite Light, Spirit, cosmic consciousness—*and it is alive*. Spirit and soul are thus already equipped to work together to vitalize your plan wherever you are in your growth.

The blueprint is faultless in its potential. Because it is infused with the God spark, your soul does not inherit a broken or defective blueprint, so nothing about the plan is too weak or damaged for you to awaken. Regardless of your past history or the cause and extent of your suffering, the blueprint itself remains intact. Even if horrendous trauma is inflicted on your body or mind, your original plan remains constant and unwavering.

Therefore, your essence is indestructible, immortal. While your body may be a material creation of Narayana, your soul is no such creature, meaning your soul is eternal, having no end, no beginning.

When you are born, you come outfitted with tremendous capabilities and potential. Thus, the blueprint of the soul is equipped to evolve—it is *pre-planned to allow for expansion and elevation.*

Standard in your blueprint is the hibernating soul that harbors a memory of The Divine. Beyond the basic plan there are options available to add on structures of consciousness similar to a foundation, walls and doorways that help you to awaken. There is also room in the plan for several additions, like corridors and stairs and private passageways that lead to secret inner realms. If you are asleep, none of these options has been built yet because you are still living the basic plan. To add to this, as you age and do little to awaken, the soul accumulates barriers such as illusions of the mind, delusions of the ego and conditions of the heart; it is as if your interior consciousness becomes enclosed by a dense fortress that prevents wakefulness.

Here is the good news. *You are already equipped to start building the life of the soul.* You can be transformed from a rustic one-room cabin into a magnificent temple tiled with marble floors, fitted with stained glass windows and landscaped in gardens and dazzling reflecting pools. Why settle for a rickety shack when you can one day become the Sistine Chapel, the Taj Mahal, or the Great Pyramid?

How will you accomplish this task of building? To begin, you must *desire to dismantle the fortress.* You must also lay a new foundation, erect different stairways, doors and hallways and rewire the whole place. Before you are fully transformed to a temple, you must receive from The Architect building permits. There are even construction rules to be aware of and abide by, because spiritual laws dictate how a blueprint is enhanced. Article

Number 1 of the building code states: *If there is a fortress or too much unconsciousness present, no holy temple will be built.*

How does expansion happen?

Personal consciousness is equipped to act as an interrelated, correlated, joined force, so it is able *to influence*, and *be influenced by*, cause and effect. This means that higher consciousness forces are in constant interplay with your soul and are responding to many factors within you, especially the manner in which you apply your human will to promulgate six factors: *thoughts, attitudes, deeds, behaviors, words and intentions.* Think of these six factors as rolling together in frequency to emit waves and particles of light. Responding to the valiance and totality of these waves and particles, Spirit calibrates a response, a precise calculation to deliver a *complementing force*—one that acts to *construct, sustain, coalesce, or dissolve energy* so that you are offered a perfect mixture of consciousness which you may use for growth.

The calibration itself is predetermined; in other words, its operations are pre-mapped to act and respond like functions of sacred geometry, calculus, fractals, division and multiplicity. Thus, if internally you are displaying the correct spiritual formula, you are being seen as one who is working to draw near in approximation to the solution, and based on your actions *automatic calibrations are conducted* so that adjustments take place to provide an inner solution.

Understand something. *You are the enigma—the mysterious sacred equation—and God is The Mathematician.* You are the alchemist, seeking to formulate attributes, and God is the solver of the enigmatic formula that turns you into gold. It is not as if The Mathematician *reacts* to resolve anything within you, for the solution to every problem has already been calculated in advance. You are the one who arrays his body and soul for each calibration of the plan. Thus, during the state of union, it is as if your internal formula has been equated—*made relative* to the fundamental equations of Creation, God, and the cosmos itself.

The Membrane of the Heart

The heart center is a focal point of energy and divine consciousness, for without tending to feelings like kindness, love and devotion, your awakening would be incomplete. The Architect designed the soul *out of an act of love*; thus, you were created *from* love, *out of* love. You were built *to* love. You were made to *be* loved, and no amount of accomplishing a state of emptiness can overshadow the completeness that divine love accomplishes.

Imagine that your soul is a compact point of energy surrounded by a fine membrane of insulation—a capsule that is infiltrated with intricate layers. The Kabbalah hints at these layers, suggesting they are screens that filter consciousness and also strain, by varying degrees, the soul's light against the brightness of The Architect's. If the point in the heart is the portal that encases the embryo of the soul, it is due to the condition of this membrane that your mystical heart is nourished and born. A soft and permeable membrane is akin to a fertile womb that nurtures the soul with the oxygenated blood of breathable Supernal Light.

Although you were born with a porous membrane that is fairly privy to Supernal Light, due to your unconsciousness and transgressions made in life, the membrane accumulates a hardened outer shell, sealing off its supply of nourishing manna and erasing the memory of The Architect. The concretized shell stops light from reaching the membrane, causing the mystical heart to contract and hibernate. This stony, brick-like barrier also walls off your emotions, making you less apt to give and receive love and mercy. It is up to you to destroy the wall, to be willing to crack open the dense shell, to re-expose the soul's inner capsule to the light that will awaken the mystical heart from its long hibernation.

To start, consciously *revolve your attention around matters of the heart* to develop a capacity to rest inside of it and become a heart-centered person. *Invest in arousing desire for The Beloved*, calling upon its power to flood you with the sweet sustenance of devotion. Soon, *the membrane itself will crave the manna of milky light* and the shell will start to crumble. Spiritual desire will begin to spontaneously emerge of its own accord. Base desires will abate and you will be drawn to spiritual pursuits. Such pursuits suggest that *God is the One that places such elevated desire within your soul's breast, while at the same time the bricks turn brittle and dissolve*. As you witness such operations of Spirit working within you, they are signs that your mystical heart is being resurrected and that its corpuscles are being pulsed with divine, living light.

The Fortress of the Mind

Barriers are structures placed between you and Reality that prevent your awakening. As symbols of duality, they are the result of the concretized consciousness of separateness. The fortress of the mind is a mental barrier that prevents you from realizing the Higher Self's power; it is a wall that surrounds and imprisons you, one that obscures divine wisdom and stops you from building faith.

The fortress is in effect the same brick wall that conceals the membrane of the heart and prevents the awakening of divine love. Individual bricks are primarily formed by intentions, attitudes, emotions, behaviors, deeds and thoughts that are counterproductive to awakening; the fortress is strengthened and enhanced, made stronger and higher, by those which are *unconscious* and *unconscionable*. For example, each time you willfully choose to commit an insensible act, another brick in the wall of the fortress is inserted. When you are being mean to another person or creature, bricks are added. If you choose to harm yourself or others, you place another brick in the wall. Every time you choose to participate in self-destructive tendencies, the fortress grows thicker. When you willingly inflict damage upon the Earth and its creatures, the wall is fortified.

When the wall grows to be too much of a defensive fortress, the mystical heart remains asleep and the mind stays unenlightened. *You see, you are the one adding bricks. You are the one laying mortar, walling off your own awakening. You are the one building the barrier's strength, both personal and collective. Even if you are doing your best to remain a conscious person, your fear is a veil. Ignorance is a veil. Wrongful thoughts are a veil.*

Secondarily, additional boundaries are present that are a byproduct of three-dimensional time/space that under normal, non-translucent conditions, *are designed to stay intact until the point of broad awakening.* In other words, the normal thinking mind was made to act and react to three-dimensional reality. The only way to see beyond the 3-D world is to peer into Reality itself.

If the fortress is not disassembled you will continue in your slumber, perpetuating the basic plan, lifetime after lifetime. The blueprint of the soul is enhanced by the cause of your *wakefulness*, while wanton unconsciousness delays and decays the plan's expansion. If your awakening is important to you, begin the work of removing the wall, brick by brick. This is done with openhearted, valiant awareness—this is accomplished by bringing your full presence and your courageous and open heart to each and every moment of life.

Continually search your mind and heart to bring attention to your thoughts, attitudes, deeds, behaviors, intentions and emotions, and attempt to uncover anything that points to limitation or promotes unconsciousness.

As you display your willingness to dismantle the boundary between yourself and Reality, your heart will put pressure on the fortress and Spirit will dissolve it to reveal who you really are—pure Presence, pure love.

The Changeable Blueprint

If soul is asleep, you can apply your free will to awaken it, for *human will has been given to you to use for this purpose.* Because Spirit permeates the blueprint, none of your efforts to awaken will go unnoticed by The Architect. Remember, everything you *do or do not do* is being seen as an act of *willfulness or willingness.*

Since no intention can be hidden and nothing about you remains outside the realm of God's understanding, every imploration and petition you make on behalf of your soul is being heard and acted upon. In addition, The Architect anticipates your every want and need, for God does not so much react outside of you as continue to supply consciousness based on your reactions and actions as well.

Every stage of advancement is built on that which precedes and follows it, meaning as you acquire the universal essence of that which is stationed above you, you will integrate its force and draw down its *potential* into the macrocosm of your own presence. All the various avenues of growth that you pursue converge and become *one path through you as the individual;* thus, *you transcend in order to funnel down the light to be ultimately grounded into the experience of your being* and so that you *embody the holy.* As you begin in God, you end in God. But there is no end or beginning—there is simply an exchange, a transaction taking place to realize wholeness. Just as the natural world flashes an intrinsic impulse to continually recreate itself, your own ability to reinvent yourself is innate, made so by the original wish of The Creator.

Here are some keys:

☞ Growth builds on growth. Once you consistently hold up

your end of the plan to dismantle your own barriers, Spirit complies and *soul will correspondingly begin to expand*. As soul awakens, that activity causes pressure to build within your interior consciousness; increased pressure causes a corresponding requirement that the blueprint be expanded to affect both your inner and the outer worlds.

→ It is The Architect that grants permission to expand and make improvements to the blueprint. You need that building permit signed, sealed and delivered so that portals leading to awakening will be allowed to be accessed, framed, opened, or sealed. To acquire the permit, one must first *give* in order to *receive. Thus, you pay your attention. You pay your devotion, worship, honor, glory and adoration—you pay your presence—to The Architect.* Everything else you give in terms of right action, methods of service to the world, positive effort and intention, deep desire and commitment is being accounted for by The Architect and is being taken in exchange as currency.

→ It is The Architect who decides to create doors, to etch keyholes, to smelt and bestow the keys to the kingdoms, to open the passageways leading to the inner temple. It is The Architect who amends the plan.

→ Your fullest state—that of *being* in inseparable unity with The Divine while invoking grace to *become* The Beloved's emissary—results from making manifest the elaborate dimensions of the cavern of the mystical heart. Paradoxically, in your emptiest state, the cave widens so far beyond its confines that its dimensions become *un-manifested.* During this state, The Supreme places enormous space between *being and becoming so that every parameter collapses,* and you will see there is nothing standing between the Self and God. You will enter into formlessness —your inviolable, intangible, dimensionless, illimitable, ceaseless and immortal state of Origin. Thus, in Reality, all plans and forms collapse as the Soul returns to God to recognize its Self, to cleave to its boundless Source of power.

NINETEEN

The Mystic's Ultimate Vision

*Just as a droplet chills on a window pane to constellate a flake of snow,
reverence will surface, and you will see with consummate eyes
the clear cut sequence of God written in every slant and void.
Are you the sky blue flake, the open space between and beyond
its angles, or the glass upon which the crystal emerges?*

If you become a mystic, you will endure as the mirror that reflects the light of divine fire. Your very presence will enhance and increase the amount of light in the world, and you will thereby be an eternal flame, obviating its Source.

Just as you will be lifted so celestially high at the moments of your ascension, then so you will be carried back down to the mundane world. What goes up must come down, and you must descend from the crest of the great zenith to ground the extraordinary into your everyday waking life.

Your mind is meant to stabilize in this integrative stage because it is part of the plan that you reencounter the mundane world with a spiritualized mind. You see, it is within the shale of the simple that the extraordinary is mined, discovered like a vein of precious platinum daggering through ordinary ground. And when you find it, it means The Divine is drawing your undivided attention to witness the shining patina of your Soul.

By the time you reach this stage you will have been formally entrusted with the keys to the castle doors, *and you shall dwell in the temple of the mystic, forever and ever.* Now you can simply embrace *being*, having acquired the mastery to call down from above the animated force of Spirit so that you can co-create with The Boundless One.

In this stage, your allegiance with The Creator is secured. You find yourself not outside of The Eternal's influence, but instead you know that your life depends on it. Spirit thus seats faith and trust in God's personalized covenant within the sanctum of the Soul.

Within this stage the Self gains so much sustenance from The Truth that only the love of God will suffice for its deepest nourishment. It is at this point *your personal will is stationed in relation to the will of The Creator*, and you freely submit to God's unmatched sovereignty. Humility is formed and perfected. You concede that God acts in unanticipated, unfathomable ways and see that the unknown is a means through which an opposite—the known—arises of its own accord.

Purity of heart results from your continual wish that Spirit fill your heart's golden cup with the ambrosial fluid of love and mercy. Sweetness of mind is found by bringing the bejeweled chalice to your lips, by savoring the syrupy brew being replenished by the flourishing Well of Eternity. Increasingly, you feel the friendship of The Creator and enjoy times of inner peace, satisfaction and joy. You discover the prizes of gratefulness, appreciation and patience embedded in the many trials of life. Forgiveness and compassion emerge and shine from the holding places of your heart having burnished every tarnished recess with polishing flames.

Once you return to normal life, expect to reencounter its typical challenges. Being human, you will still feel challenges and emotional ups and downs, but now you have the help of your awakened mind and clear-seeing Witness. *Witness is the result of utter presence*—it is not built from reaction. Its ability to observe does not sway with the riptides of emotion, buckle under the weight of difficulty, feel better when things are going well, or get jaded when circumstances spoil. Thus, Witness never waivers in its changeless presence. It is the one undaunted force to which your being-ness has given life. You see, your Witness is the precious gift of Spirit—it is your Wisdom Mind, the mystic's pilot light, elucidating its crystal-clear clarity.

Having been set ablaze on the mountain's summit, the lantern of your mind forever encases The Everlasting Brightness. Its effulgence serves to illuminate the path so that others do not stumble in their climb up the face of the mighty rock, but instead find The Clear Way. And amidst the darkened skies of human misconception, you will forever uphold your cherished flame so that others can witness your watchfulness and see The Light for themselves. And so you shall descend from the highest crest to cast upon the world your radiant countenance, and you shall shine forth a lustrous gleam of compassion, wisdom and grace.

Because you have been so blessed, you feel a sense of responsibility to others and you are compelled to extend your gifts to the world. Although the supply of light that inhabits you is never-ending, you can only carry so much of its voltage. Thus, when you give your gift to others the voltage can't help but intensify and multiply, perpetuating the Eternal flame within you, spreading light to the world, catching soul after soul on fire.

TWENTY

The Light of Infinity

Your life is being cast through the looking glass of Creation.
Dust off the mirror! In whose image is your vessel being made
when you see your reflection haloed by photons of light?

What is Infinite Light?

Infinite Light is the endless light of the All-Pervasive Presence. It is the formless, eternal, primordial essence of The Supreme. It is the Diamond Light, the clear light, The Limitless Light that represents The Creator's Divine and Crowning Glory. It is The Agent of God, The Dimensionless Point of Unification and The One Light above creation. It is the Source and Origin of all energy, the instigator of all motion, the Cause from which all things proceed and to which all things return.

Those who have eyes to see will observe an emission of The Infinite Light, for it displays as a *non-glowing* spiritual fire. It can be detected in broad daylight with the naked eye, appearing as *clear light* or the "shadow" of white light. The glinting White Light is the mystic's *kinetic fever*, the animated flame that swirls within his spirit. The flame's tip extends from the mystic's being like a spire, a superior point to which he aspires to reach and be reached.

The Sign of Infinity ~ ∞

Consciousness is linked to flow from the soul to Infinity, perpetually drawing the soul back to its Source. Consider the sign of infinity—the symbol whose end always leads back to its beginning. It is a design that represents one's eventual return to center, source and origin, a figure of rhythm, flux, flow, motion and momentum, representing orbits, twists and turns, eternal continuum and unity. In mathematics, it represents a factor that is infinitely large.

Imagine that the left side of the sign represents "being" and the right "becoming." The left loop embodies the presence of the soul, and the right one symbolizes the ceaseless, creative force of Spirit's emission. Rather than being energetic opposites, the loops represent reciprocating, interdependent aspects of the other's energy, the way *light does not exist without the equal of its scintillating vibration.*

If the sign were unbent, if its knot were severed and the torque relaxed, it would unfold into a wheel. Add dimension and you have a donut-shaped ring torus. Should the ring's center space collapse upon itself, the torus would evolve to a sphere, like a single, all-seeing eye.

There is a perpetual rolling of consciousness being exchanged between the soul and Eternity. The rolling motion further influences energy that infiltrates and then radiates from the entire symbol to manifest a grand field of unified light.

Bring your attention to the cross point—the Axis Mundi—the crux of the sign that holds its link. This neutral still point, the zero point, resides in the very core of the cross. The crux creates a kind of gateway through which the perfection of the soul and healing of the mind/body is facilitated.

The central link is the inception point of the soul, wherein the ray of the awakened Self perpetuates its persistent will to return to its Origin, to reconcile and reunite itself with the cause of its being and the source of all light from which it is born. It is within the precise center of the crux, within *the seat of the mystical heart,* that a massive energetic exchange of consciousness takes place—a supreme action that zeroes out its sum, absolves duality, removes the separation between object and subject and dissolves the notion of "me" and "it." And when you are absolved, you are being excluded of everything that is outside of Reality.

In the moments when such an equalization of consciousness fully manifests, symmetry results—*you become Reality and Reality becomes you.* The entanglements of the mind and heart unravel, and your being becomes a transparent mirror, a skyless sky in which the ceaselessly spiraling Light of Infinity flashes its splendorous unimpeded light. In this state, the Self is engaged in *being pure consciousness*, while at the *same exact moment* the Eternal Presence regards its consciousness-presence as being *coexistent with its radiant energetic action.*

Turn the infinity sign upright, and it can be seen as a ladder upon which the soul may ascend and descend. Prior to awakening, you must continuously climb upwards toward the celestial realm only to disconnect from it and return to the terrestrial one, traveling in a loop until the activity of absolution removes this requirement. It is then that the central rung—the gateway of enlightenment—maintains its open status so that you may rest in being-ness within the receptivity of mind. And finally you rest, not seeking, not desiring a thing. You join in the flow of the divine circling dance being led by the ceaseless cadence of Spirit's unremitting grace, delivering you again and again through the Heart-point of Reality.

Your Infinite Promise

Your infinite promise—your immortal presence—spontaneously emerges when you have entered your mystical heart. Like a massive Turning of the Wheel, love and light will whirl through your core and turn you into love itself.

Because you are built for enlightenment, your unlimited potential is already waiting to unfold and crystallize. *This mammoth realization is preconceived because the original blueprint of the soul made it so.*

To reach your promise, *you must choose to be chosen.* You must be willing to toss away the looking glass, to shatter your image in the mirror, to *abandon everything you think you are and assume the world to be* and kneel to The Mystery.

If only you would take a risk, *leap across the Abyss* into The Mysterium and allow the self you think you are to be voided by The Infinite. Only then will you begin to experience your boundless presence.

When you take the leap to know your Self, you will be launched into the atmosphere of the Eternal Stillness of Being. Every seal will be loosed, the knot of infinity will unfold and every last restraint will be released. You will be free at last. You will rest within the gaze of the All-Seeing Eye and assume your station with The Ancient of Ancients.

You will gaze upon The Infinite Light with wonderment and it will animate, rising into curving yods from the tracks of your veins, ascending in front of your eyes as if the fiery radiance of the midday sun were lifting off the heat of your flesh! The Divine Perfection will reflect itself as a field of living light lifting up from your body, and you will be amazed by God's grace hovering above your skin, waving in an undulating haze of soft, clear sparks.

And you will know that your spirit has been raised above, for it will have been made resurrected from below. And you will know that you are The Light. And the Self will shine *The Infinite Splendor, The Light of God's Name, The Eternal Flame, the Diamond Light, The Radiance, the Light of Lights, The Eternal Presence, the Light of Transcendence and Ascension!*

You will bring light out of the void of darkness. You will dispense light against the shadow. You will erect the speculum lighthouse of Spirit, and its beam will streak forth from its brilliant iris, infiltrating the night, its iridescent gaze throwing its crystalline signature to the skies. You will become the perfect spectrum for the Prism Light born from the cloud of the covenant. You will be the meaning of the words, "Let there be light."

The indigo print of the Soul will emerge as a mist from within your third eye, and a pinpoint of fire will pierce through its core. And all the lights, the seen and unseen, the revealed and concealed, will be yours. You will be given the authority to *assemble the lights—to activate their luminosity.* You *will* shed light, and your spirit *will* be able to radiate clarity, and you *will* gleam that light or keep it secret in non-glowing radiance.

And the Self will display the inextinguishable flame, The White Light of Infinity. And by your presence, you will glorify The Numinous Presence of God. And the Soul will know the potential of its formless being. And then all of your strife will finally come to an end, and you will rest on the breast of The Beloved.

By virtue of the fulfillment of your highest potential, there will be nothing left to prove, nothing else to manifest. You will live your life in this world as an awakened one, your presence sheathed as Spirit itself. Forever held in the Everlasting Arms, you will be emancipated, made boundless, and you will endure as a colossal and gleaming pillar standing parallel with All That Is.

Parting Wishes

You are this close to awakening. Within every moment, your eyes can be instantaneously opened. You are not really sleeping every second of the day, for each time you become aware of your desires and attachments, you are waking up. Every second that you stay present you are creating your own becoming.

Don't fall back to sleep. Just keep present. If you'd only stay awake, the path delivers on its promise for passage. If you deeply awaken, it means that the order of your life was supposed to be transformed, that your transfiguration was planned. Thus, the destiny of your awakened life is waiting inside you.

Freedom is already here, standing right across the border of your mind. No matter how grave your heart's burdens, no matter how discouraged you are by the struggles of your mind, you will ride through every dark night if you only keep the wheel on the path. You are bound to reach the frothy shoreline, you are sure to part the unruly seas to engrave a singular way, and the turbulent waters will unscroll before you to reveal a royal carpet of gilded sand.

So call to your heart courage and unrelenting fortitude to slash the veils of ignorance. Demand of yourself a daring boldness to conquer with the sharpened blade of your mind every feral and unpredictable creature lurking at the gateways. And before long, you will surrender your sword in peace and humility before the precious throne of The Supreme.

Trust yourself enough to preserve the burgeoning flame inside your heart and stoke it with your warm, moist breath. Don't run from yourself—stay, and choose love. When the mysterious light approaches and comes near to you, *be not afraid*, for The Beloved is with you and will not forsake you.

When Spirit appears, don't turn your gaze from the light, the dust, the mist, the cloud, the Void, the Abyss or the burning bush on the mountain. Look upon it with open eyes. And The Breath of Spirit will stir you, and the darkness of your heart will be spun into whirling fire and by the grace of The Merciful One your Soul will be revived so that you will shine the Infinite Flame. You only have to call upon your exquisite presence. You only have to keep your arms open long enough to beckon love's lasting hold before you dissolve into God's revolving embrace.

And never again will you be a lone and aimless ember, drifting away and lost to a bleak and starless wilderness. For the stormy night will lift, and the Heart of Hearts will cherish you, and you will see above you the Supernal sun stationed in the endless sky, cradled in the opal arc of the moon, just where it has been all along, resting, silently burning and waiting to rise.

May you recognize the Self's Infinite Light of Being. May the Presence of God's light live within you. May your mystical heart's chalice brim with the glory of Spirit, and may its chambers overflow with the splendor of love and faith, forever and ever.

Acknowledgments

During the writing of this book, I did not anticipate the multiple ways that Spirit would continue to impart its unremitting grace, showing me signs, defining the book's path and unfolding keys of knowledge and wisdom that are included within its pages. In turn, I was offered further crystallization that moved me even deeper into The Boundless Mystery of the Infinite Light. For this, I am eternally grateful.

To my friends, colleagues and family, your inspiring presence in my life has been a treasure. Thank you for the jewels of your companionship, honesty and love, for reminding me to speak my truth and for offering your generous and spirited guidance.

To my mother Pearl Natalie Upton, who crossed into the Everlasting Arms of The Beloved just before this teaching was released, I want to honor her for embodying her lustrous name. I thank her from the bottom of my heart for her witness, her fierce and unrelenting belief in me, and for her love, sacrifice and support, without which this book may not have been born.

⚮

To learn more about Paula Dianne Upton, please visit
www.PaulaDianneUpton.com

If you enjoyed this book, it would be very much appreciated if you reviewed it on the internet site you purchased it from.

235

CPSIA information can be obtained
at www.ICGtesting.com
Printed in the USA
BVHW041922260219
541225BV00011B/73/P